What's the Best Trivia Book? Volume 2

Over 3,000 Questions in 10 Categories

David Fickes

Printed in the United States of America

First Printing: 2019

Introduction

By nature, I tend to collect trivia without trying. Until relatively recently, I had never sought out trivia; however, after creating a holiday trivia presentation for a community party and showing it at one of our fitness studio spinning classes, I found myself creating weekly trivia. The cycling clients enjoyed the diversion of answering questions while they exercised, so I continued.

What you find in most trivia is a lot of erroneous or outdated information or questions that are so simple or esoteric that they aren't interesting. It takes effort to create interesting questions at the right level of difficulty that a wide variety of people can enjoy and that are something you feel you should know or want to know.

I have tried to ensure that the information is as accurate as possible, and to retain its accuracy, I have also tried to avoid questions whose answers can quickly change with time. Since the simple answer is often not all you want to know, the answers also frequently include additional details to put them in context and provide further information.

There are over 3,000 questions in 10 wide-ranging categories – Animals, History, Miscellaneous, Movies, Science and Nature, Sports, Television, U.S. Geography, U.S. Presidents, and World Geography. To make it quick and easy to test yourself or others without initially seeing the answers, each category is divided into short quizzes with 10 questions followed by their answers.

This is book 7 of my *What's the Best Trivia?* series; I hope you enjoy it, and if you do, look for other books in the series covering a variety of trivia topics.

Contents

Animals

Quiz 1

1) What is the fleshy protuberance above a turkey's bill called?
2) What animal's fingerprints are virtually indistinguishable from human fingerprints even with careful analysis under a microscope?
3) What body part do frogs use to force food down their throats?
4) What is the only bird with two toes on each foot?
5) What name is given to a female mouse?
6) What country has the lone sub-species of horse that is still entirely wild, having never been domesticated by humans?
7) Male giraffes determine whether a female is fertile and ready to mate by getting the female to do what?
8) What is the largest rat free populated area in the world?
9) What country has the most reptile species?
10) What is the name for a male mule?

Quiz 1 Answers

1) Snood
2) Koala bear - They have the same loopy, whirling ridges as humans.
3) Eyes - Since they don't have muscles to chew their food, they use their eyes to force food down their throats. Their eyes sink down inside their skull to push the food down.
4) Ostrich
5) Doe
6) Mongolia - The endangered Przewalski's horse is native to the steppes of Mongolia; all other wild horses are feral horses that are descendants of domesticated horses.
7) Urinate - The male bumps the female until she urinates and then tastes the urine for hormones indicating she is in heat.
8) Canadian province of Alberta - The government has had very aggressive rat control measures since the 1950s, and only the brown rat can survive in the prairie region.
9) Australia - It has over 860 different reptile species including

lizards, crocodiles, turtles, and snakes. North America only has 280 species of reptile.

10) John

Quiz 2

1) What makes an animal viviparous?
2) What is the name for the short, erect tail of a hare, rabbit, or deer?
3) What is the primary reason a dog's nose is wet?
4) Ravens, crows, jays, and some songbirds lie in anthills and roll around letting the ants swarm on them, or they chew up the ants and rub them on their feathers; what is this behavior called?
5) Camels don't store water in their humps; where do they store it?
6) To what bird family does the roadrunner belong?
7) What animal has the most names?
8) What is the second largest bird in the world and is also considered the most dangerous bird?
9) Lemurs in Madagascar capture what animal to get a narcotic hit and ward off insects?
10) What country has the most horses?

Quiz 2 Answers

1) Viviparous animals are born as live young individuals; they do not lay eggs.
2) Scut
3) They secrete a mucus that aids their sense of smell.
4) Anting - It isn't understood why they do it.
5) Bloodstream - They can drink up to 20 gallons at a time; the hump is almost all fat and serves as an alternative energy source and to help regulate body temperature. By concentrating fat in the hump as opposed to being spread over their body, they are better able to handle hot climates.
6) Cuckoo
7) Cougar - It is called puma, mountain lion, panther, catamount, or one of another 40 English, 18 native South American, and 25 native North American names.
8) Cassowary - They are up to 6 feet tall and weigh up to 130 pounds

and have a 4-inch, dagger-like claw on each foot that can slice open a predator or threat with a single kick. They are native to the tropical forests of Papua New Guinea, Indonesia, and northeastern Australia.

9) Red millipedes - The lemurs bite the millipede gently and throw it back on the ground; when millipedes are picked up, they secrete a toxic combination of chemicals, including cyanide, as a defense mechanism. The lemurs rub the secretion all over their fur which functions as a natural pesticide and wards off malaria carrying mosquitoes. The secretion also acts as a narcotic, which causes the lemurs to salivate profusely and enter a state of intoxication.
10) United States

Quiz 3

1) Instead of the five tastes that humans can detect, whales and dolphins only perceive what single taste?
2) What mammal sweats milk?
3) What is a group of pandas called?
4) What is the fastest known running insect?
5) What animal does mohair come from?
6) Goldfish are members of what fish family?
7) The wolverine is the largest land member of what animal family?
8) What is the name for a group of locusts?
9) What color are flamingos naturally?
10) What is the longest snake?

Quiz 3 Answers

1) Salty
2) Platypus - They secrete milk from mammary glands like other animals, but they don't have nipples, so the milk oozes from the surface of their skin more like sweat. Because the delivery system is less hygienic, platypus milk contains antibacterial proteins to protect the babies.
3) Embarrassment
4) Australian tiger beetle - 5.6 mph
5) Angora goats
6) Carp

7) Weasel - Wolverines can be up to 70 pounds.
8) Plague
9) White - Their diet of brine shrimp and algae turns them pink.
10) Reticulated python - up to 30 feet long

Quiz 4

1) What is the most abundant wild bird species?
2) What freshwater lake has the most fish species in the world?
3) What kind of animal is a geoduck?
4) What is the only known immortal creature which can transform itself back to a juvenile state?
5) Cats don't seem to have an overall paw preference for right or left like humans do, but they do have a gender-based preference; what paw do male cats favor?
6) What is the most populous large (average of 10 pounds or more) mammal?
7) What is the loudest land animal?
8) What land animal can go the longest without drinking water?
9) What current multi-organ animal has existed the longest?
10) What is the largest species of bee in the world?

Quiz 4 Answers

1) Red-billed quelea – They are sparrow sized birds found in sub-Saharan Africa.
2) Lake Malawi - It is located between Malawi, Mozambique, and Tanzania and is the fourth largest freshwater lake by volume in the world. There are more than 1,000 species of cichlid fish alone.
3) Clam - It is a very large, edible saltwater clam native to the coastal waters of western Canada and the northwest United States.
4) Immortal jellyfish (Turritopsis dohrnii) - Once the adult jellyfish has reproduced, they transform themselves back into their juvenile state. Their tentacles retract, their bodies shrink, and they sink to the ocean floor and start their life cycle all over again. They can do it repeatedly making them essentially immortal unless they are eaten by another animal or struck by disease.
5) Left - Females are significantly more likely to be right paw dominant.

6) Humans
7) Howler monkey – up to 140 decibels and can be heard 3 miles away
8) Kangaroo rat - They can go their whole life of up to 10 years without drinking.
9) Jellyfish - They evolved 550 million years ago and have no brain or nervous system, and their body is 90% water.
10) Wallace's giant bee - It is native to Indonesia and was thought to be extinct for over a century until it was rediscovered in 1981. Females have a 2.5-inch wingspan and a body length of about 1.5 inches; the males are 0.9 inches long.

Quiz 5

1) A jellyfish's mouth also serves as what?
2) Dire wolves, as seen in *Game of Thrones*, existed up to about 10,000 years ago on what continents?
3) What is the technical name for the pouch of a kangaroo or other marsupial?
4) Not including insects and crustaceans, what are the only two animals that can see completely behind themselves without turning their heads?
5) What is Britain's largest native carnivore?
6) As part of its reproductive process, what animal will sting a cockroach twice, first in the thorax to partially immobilize it and then in the head to block its normal escape reflex?
7) What animal's name literally means "pig fish"?
8) The fennec is the smallest species of what animal?
9) Chameleons don't change color for camouflage purposes; instead, they change to communicate with other chameleons and for what other reason?
10) What is an ungulate?

Quiz 5 Answers

1) Anus
2) North and South America - They were about the same size as the largest modern gray wolves at about 150 pounds on average, but their teeth were larger with greater shearing ability, and they had the highest bite force of any known Canis species.

3) Marsupium
4) Rabbit and parrot
5) Badger
6) Jewel wasp - The wasp is too small to carry the cockroach, so it leads it back to its burrow by pulling on one of its antennae. Once in the burrow, the wasp lays an egg on the roach's abdomen and exits and fills in the burrow entrance with pebbles. With the effect of the wasp venom, the roach rests in the burrow. In about three days, the wasp's egg hatches, and the larva begins feeding on the roach for four to five days before chewing its way into the roach's abdomen. It continues to reside inside the roach, and over a period of eight days, it consumes the roach's internal organs in an order to maximize the time the roach is still alive. The larva enters a pupal stage and forms a cocoon inside the roach, and the fully-grown wasp eventually emerges from the roach's body completing the reproductive cycle.
7) Porpoise - from Latin
8) Fox - They are found mainly in the Sahara and elsewhere in North Africa, they only weigh two to three pounds but have six-inch ears.
9) Regulate their temperature - They change color by stretching and relaxing cells that contain crystals which affects how light is reflected.
10) Hoofed mammal

Quiz 6

1) Lake Nicaragua in Central America is one of the very few freshwater lakes in the world with what animal?
2) How does a giraffe clean its ears?
3) What are the tufts of hair in a cat's ear called?
4) A male donkey and a female horse produce what offspring?
5) What is coprophagy?
6) What was the largest known flying animal that ever lived?
7) What is the dung of an otter called?
8) What is the highest level of sociality called where animals like ants and termites have a single female or caste that produces the offspring, and nonreproductive individuals cooperate in caring for the young?
9) Macaroni, gentoo, and chinstrap are species of what animal?

10) What animal gives birth to the largest young?

Quiz 6 Answers

1) Sharks - Bull sharks can survive in both fresh and saltwater and make their way back and forth from the Caribbean Sea to Lake Nicaragua via a 120-mile route though the San Juan river.
2) Its tongue
3) Ear furnishings - They help keep out dirt, direct sounds, and insulate the ears.
4) Mule
5) Eating your own poop - Rats and most rodents have simple digestive systems and eat their own poop to recover additional nutrients.
6) Quetzalcoatlus - It was a pterodactyloid pterosaur from the Late Cretaceous period of North America and had a wingspan up to 36 feet and may have weighed as much as 500 pounds.
7) Spraint
8) Eusocial
9) Penguins
10) Blue whale – Calves are about 23 feet long and weigh 5,000 to 6,000 pounds.

Quiz 7

1) What are baby porcupines called?
2) What animal kills the most people in world?
3) What do scientists believe is the most abundant vertebrate (animal with backbone) species?
4) What prehistoric animal from about 150 million years ago is widely considered a transitional fossil between birds and reptiles and the first bird?
5) What is the name for animals that are the opposite of albinos and are all black?
6) China owns all the giant pandas in the world except for two pandas in what country?
7) What is the name for a baby beaver?
8) The aardvark is the first animal alphabetically; what's the second?

9) If you include speed on land or in the air or water, what is the fastest known mammal?
10) A leveret is the young of what animal?

Quiz 7 Answers

1) Porcupettes
2) Mosquitoes - They are by far the deadliest animal in the world killing over 700,000 people worldwide annually primarily from malaria. Snakes are the second most deadly animal killing about 50,000 people; dogs are third at about 25,000 people annually mainly through rabies. Crocodiles are the biggest killer of the large animals at about 1,000 people worldwide; the hippopotamus is the world's deadliest large land mammal, killing an estimated 500 people per year.
3) Bristlemouth - They are small deep-sea fish that are only about three inches long and usually live at depths exceeding 1,000 feet. They are believed to number in the quadrillions or more.
4) Archaeopteryx - It was about the size of a common raven and weighed about two pounds.
5) Melanistic - An excess of melanin makes their skin, hair, or fur very dark or black.
6) Mexico - Any panda in a foreign zoo is on loan from China with the agreement that China owns the panda and any offspring, and that any offspring must be returned to China before they are four years old. The only exceptions are two pandas China gave to Mexico prior to implementing the current policy.
7) Kit
8) Aardwolf - It is native to eastern and southern Africa; it is a member of the hyena family and looks like a small striped hyena. It feeds on insects, primarily termites.
9) Mexican free-tailed bat – It can achieve speeds of 100 mph in normal flight.
10) Hare

Quiz 8

1) Rats don't sweat; what part of their body do they use to regulate their temperature?
2) What dinosaur's name literally means "roof lizard" in Greek?

3) What are turkeys called in the country of Turkey?
4) What are the three main parts of an insect's body?
5) What do polled cattle not have?
6) What is the most poached (illegally hunted) animal in the world?
7) What horse breed has a greater bone density than other horses, a shorter back with one fewer lumbar vertebrae, and one fewer pair of ribs?
8) Reindeer eyes change color from gold in the summer to what color in winter?
9) What animal has the highest brain to body weight ratio?
10) What endangered New Zealand parrot is the heaviest parrot and the only flightless parrot?

Quiz 8 Answers

1) Tail - They constrict or expand blood vessels in their tails.
2) Stegosaurus
3) Hindi - meaning from India
4) Head, thorax, and abdomen
5) Horns
6) Pangolin - It is a small mammal covered in large overlapping scales that eats ants and termites and is generally found in Asia and sub-Saharan Africa. It is poached for its scales which are used in traditional medicine and for its meat.
7) Arabian
8) Blue - During bright summer light, their eyes reflect most light and look gold; during winter, the tissue behind their retina becomes less reflective, and their eyes appear blue. This increases their light sensitivity and vision in the low winter light.
9) Ant - Some species have 14-15% of their mass in their brain; humans are at about 2.5%.
10) Kakapo - It weighs up to nine pounds.

Quiz 9

1) What animal's milk won't curdle?
2) What is a baby spider called?
3) What is the only insect that has both a king and a queen?

4) What is the national animal of the U.S.?
5) Why can't giraffes cough?
6) What is the largest mollusk in the world?
7) What mammal only poops once a week and can lose one-third of its body weight from pooping?
8) Vulpine relates to what kind of animal?
9) What small shark, reaching only about two feet in length, is named for its unusual feeding method where it gouges out round plugs of flesh from larger animals?
10) Opossums don't play dead; if frightened, what do they do?

Quiz 9 Answers

1) Camel - The structure of the protein in camel milk differs from cows, goats, sheep, and other animals; due to its composition, camel milk does not curdle naturally.
2) Spiderling
3) Termite - The king helps found the colony with the queen and will mate with the queen during his life. There may be more than one pair of kings and queens in the termite mound.
4) Bison
5) Their necks are too long which means their lungs are too far away from their epiglottis, and coughing is a combination movement of the lungs and epiglottis.
6) Giant clam - They can reach 4 feet in length and weigh more than 500 pounds. They live in the warm waters of the South Pacific and Indian Oceans and can live more than 100 years.
7) Sloth - They do it on the ground, making them an easy target for predators, and it all comes out in one push. They dig a small hole to go in and cover it up when they are done and head back into the trees.
8) Foxes
9) Cookiecutter shark
10) They go into shock which induces a comatose state that can last from 40 minutes to 4 hours.

Quiz 10

1) What is largest known flying insect to ever exist?

2) Cats, rabbits, and goats all share what breed name?
3) What is the only animal with four forward-facing knees?
4) What is the only bird with a bill longer than its body?
5) What mammal has the longest pregnancy?
6) What was Didus Ineptus better known as?
7) As a defense mechanism when threatened, what sea creature can eviscerate themselves and shoot out their internal organs?
8) Are zebras black with white stripes or white with black stripes?
9) What is the largest species of monkey?
10) What animal is featured on the state flag of California?

Quiz 10 Answers

1) Meganeura - It existed more than 300 million years ago during the Carboniferous Period and was a dragonfly-like insect with a wingspan of about 2.5 feet. It was a carnivore and fed on other insects and small amphibians.
2) Angora
3) Elephant - All other four-legged animals have at least one pair of legs with knees that face backwards.
4) Sword-billed hummingbird
5) Elephant - up to 22 months
6) Dodo bird
7) Sea cucumbers - They are echinoderms which also include marine animals like starfish and sea urchins. Depending on the species, they can shoot the organs out their head or butt, but they can regrow the organs.
8) Black with white stripes - Zebra embryos are completely black; the white stripes appear during the last embryonic stage.
9) Mandrill - They are found mostly in tropical rainforests in southern Cameroon, Gabon, Equatorial Guinea, and the Congo and can be up to 120 pounds.
10) Bear - the once common but now extinct California grizzly bear

Quiz 11

1) What country has the most wild elephants?
2) What animals are in the order Chiroptera?

3) What is the fastest known flying insect?
4) What is the second largest rodent in the world?
5) What animal has the longest tongue?
6) Ophidian refers to what type of animal?
7) As a mosquito sucks your blood, what else do they do to maintain their fluid and salt balance?
8) A male donkey is called a jack; what is a female donkey called?
9) What is the largest amphibian in the world?
10) What is the largest snake ever known to have ever existed?

Quiz 11 Answers

1) Botswana
2) Bats
3) Horsefly - 90 mph
4) North American beaver - up to 110 pounds
5) Blue whale - about 18 feet long
6) Snake
7) They pee on you. Mosquitoes need to get rid of excess fluid and salts as they suck blood.
8) Jenny
9) Chinese giant salamander - They can grow to lengths of almost six feet.
10) Titanoboa - It lived about 60 million years ago and was up to 42 feet long and weighed up to 2,500 pounds.

Quiz 12

1) What animal has more neck vertebrae than any other warm-blooded animal?
2) What animal has the largest size difference between the sexes of any land vertebrate?
3) What color is hippo milk?
4) What species kills its leader when they become too old or unproductive by clustering around them in a tight ball until they overheat and die?
5) What is a young eel called?

6) What is the largest tree dwelling animal?
7) What is the first animal whose evidence is legally admissible in some U.S. courts?
8) What country has the world's longest earthworms?
9) What is the national animal of Canada?
10) Why do dogs typically stare at you when they poop?

Quiz 12 Answers

1) Swan - 24 vertebrae
2) Anaconda - Females are on average 4.7 times larger than males.
3) Bright pink - Hippos secrete two unique acids, hipposudoric acid and norhipposudoric acid, that function as a natural sunscreen and antimicrobial agent. The acids are red and orange in color, and when mixed with a hippo mother's milk, they turn it bright pink.
4) Bees - In a process known as "cuddle death" or "balling," the worker bees dispose of the queen by clustering around her in a tight ball until she overheats and dies.
5) Elver
6) Orangutan - They are 48-54 inches tall and weigh up to 200 pounds and spend nearly all their time in the forest canopy.
7) Bloodhound
8) South Africa - They can grow as large as 22 feet with the average length being about 6 feet.
9) Beaver
10) They know they are vulnerable at that time, and they are looking to you, a member of their pack, for protection.

Quiz 13

1) What is the name for a group of leopards?
2) Horses have a single toe like other equines such as zebras and donkeys, but their ancient ancestors that lived 55 million years ago were dog like in size and had how many total toes?
3) What is the largest species of flatfish?
4) When male pandas urinate, they perform an unusual move to get their pee higher up the tree allowing their scent to be carried further and increasing their mating chances; what do they do?

5) Male goats urinate on their own heads for what reason?
6) What crustacean has 10 eyes spread all over their body including the top of their shell, on their tail, and near their mouth?
7) Lobsters have nozzles right under their eyes which they use to communicate with each other; what is released from the nozzles?
8) What insect lives the longest?
9) The gender of most turtles, alligators, and crocodiles is determined after fertilization by what?
10) Some expensive perfumes still contain poop from what animal?

Quiz 13 Answers

1) Leap
2) 14 toes - four toes on their front feet and three on their back.
3) Halibut - up to 500 pounds
4) They do a handstand.
5) To smell more attractive to females
6) Horseshoe crab
7) Urine
8) Termite queen - They have been known to live for at least 50 years, and some scientists believe they may live to 100.
9) The temperature of the eggs decides whether the offspring will be male or female. This is called temperature-dependent sex determination.
10) Sperm whale - Ambergris, a waxy substance produced in the intestines of sperm whales, has been incorporated in perfumes for a long time as a binding agent to help the fragrances linger on the skin and intensify the scent of the perfume. It has now been mostly replaced by synthetic alternatives.

Quiz 14

1) What is the primary food for a koala?
2) What is South Africa's national animal?
3) How many tusks does a warthog have?
4) What is the smallest mammal native to North America?
5) Outside of micro-organisms, what animal has existed the longest?

6) While there are more than 60 species of eagles worldwide, how many species live in North America?
7) By mass, what is the smallest known mammal?
8) Male horses typically have 40 teeth; how many do females have?
9) As part of its mating, what species has two individuals competing to see which one can inject sperm into the other with the winner becoming the father and the loser becoming the mother?
10) Humans have six muscles in each ear; how many muscles do cats have in each ear?

Quiz 14 Answers

1) Eucalyptus leaves
2) Springbok - a type of antelope
3) Four
4) American pygmy shrew - Its body is about two inches long including tail, and it weighs about 0.07 to 0.16 ounces.
5) Sponge - Fossils dating back 760 million years have been found.
6) Two - bald eagle and golden eagle
7) Etruscan shrew - On average, they weigh about 0.06 ounces. It also has the fastest heartbeat of any mammal at 1,500 beats per minute.
8) 36 - Males usually have four canine teeth which are located between the front incisors and the cheek teeth; females don't usually have canine teeth.
9) Flatworms - They are hermaphroditic having both male and female reproductive organs.
10) 32 - They can move each ear independently and can swivel and rotate their ears 180 degrees.

Quiz 15

1) What is the smallest animal that represents a year in the Chinese zodiac?
2) Where is the only population of wild monkeys in Europe?
3) What animal has the densest fur?
4) What is the only animal in the world with cube shaped poop?
5) Crocodiles don't sweat; what body part do they use to keep cool?
6) What is the name for a group of giraffes?

7) What large reptile only has two species in the world, one that is native to the U.S. and one that is native to China?
8) If a giraffe has seven neck vertebrae, how many does a mouse have?
9) What is the larva of a fly called?
10) What is the world's loudest insect?

Quiz 15 Answers

1) Rat
2) Gibraltar (on Spain's southern coast) - Barbary macaque
3) Sea otter - They have up to 1 million hairs per square inch on the densest parts of their bodies.
4) Wombat - It appears to be due to the irregular shape and elasticity of their intestines.
5) Mouth - They open it like panting.
6) Tower
7) Alligator
8) Seven - With a couple of exceptions (sloth and manatee), all mammals regardless of size or neck have seven neck vertebrae.
9) Maggot
10) Cicada - They can reach about 120 decibels which is equivalent to sitting in the front row of a loud rock concert.

Quiz 16

1) What is the first animal ever discovered that is also part plant?
2) Including tentacles, how many arms does a squid have?
3) What animal's name means "river horse" in Greek?
4) What is the tallest bird in North America?
5) What is an eagle's nest called?
6) What is the name for a baby opossum?
7) What other animals besides humans have chins?
8) What is the name for a group of hummingbirds?
9) What is the name for a group of mosquitoes?
10) A spider's muscles pull its legs inward, but they can't push them out again; what does it do to push them out again?

Quiz 16 Answers

1) Green sea slug (Elysia Chlorotica) – They live off the east coast of the United States and take chloroplasts into their skin which turns them emerald green and makes them capable of photosynthesis. They can go without eating for nine months or more, photosynthesizing as they bask in the sun.
2) 10 - two tentacles and eight arms
3) Hippopotamus
4) Whooping crane - over five feet tall
5) Eyrie
6) Joey
7) None - Humans are the only animal with a chin; no one knows why.
8) Charm
9) Scourge
10) It pumps a watery liquid into its legs.

Quiz 17

1) What is the only animal with two kneecaps on each knee?
2) What is the name for a group of porcupines?
3) Why is it illegal in Switzerland to own just one guinea pig?
4) What is the name for a group of rhinoceroses?
5) What are the patterns starlings create when they flock together in the sky in swooping coordinated movements called?
6) What animal has the largest sperm?
7) What is the only animal born with horns?
8) Compared to humans, cats have six to eight times more of what cells in their eye which gives them their superior night vision?
9) What insect's large compound eyes each have about 30,000 individual lenses?
10) What animal's name literally translates as "earth pig"?

Quiz 17 Answers

1) Ostrich

2) Prickle
3) Because they are social animals, and it is considered animal cruelty to deny them companionship.
4) Crash
5) Murmurations
6) Fruit flies - Their sperm is coiled up and unspools to about 2.3 inches which is 20 times the length of their body and about 1,000 times bigger than human sperm.
7) Giraffe - Both male and female giraffes are born with two horn-like structures on their heads called ossicones which consist of hard cartilage.
8) Rod cells
9) Dragonfly
10) Aardvark

Quiz 18

1) A male horse and a female donkey produce what offspring?
2) What is the largest marsupial?
3) Lobsters don't have blood like vertebrate animals; the liquid in their body is colorless and is called what?
4) What is the name for a male alligator?
5) What is a diadromous fish?
6) Arkansas, Florida, Mississippi, Tennessee, and Texas all share what official state bird?
7) The creature most people identify as a daddy-longlegs spider is not a spider at all; what is it?
8) What is the only known venomous primate?
9) Queen Alexandra's birdwing is the largest what?
10) A cat is feline; what animal is murine?

Quiz 18 Answers

1) Hinny
2) Red kangaroo - It is up to 5.3 feet from its head to rump, and its tail can be up to 3.6 feet long, and it weighs about 200 pounds.
3) Hemolymph - It turns blue when exposed to air; this is due to

oxygen reacting with the copper in the fluid.

4) Bull
5) Species that spends part of their lives in freshwater and part in saltwater
6) Mockingbird
7) Long-legged harvestmen - It is an arachnid but not a spider. Harvestmen have one body section instead of the two spiders have, two eyes instead of eight, a segmented body instead of unsegmented in spiders, no silk, no venom, and a totally different respiratory system than spiders among other differences.
8) Slow loris - They are nocturnal and live in southeast Asia. If they lick a gland under their arms and combine it with their saliva, they have a toxic bite.
9) Butterfly - Females can have a wingspan over 10 inches; they are native to Papua New Guinea.
10) Mouse or rat

Quiz 19

1) Cats and some dogs have a fold of skin forming an open pouch at the outer base of their ear; what is it called?
2) How many eyes does a honeybee have?
3) What term is given to creatures such as earthworms which are both male and female?
4) What insect did Napoleon use as his official emblem?
5) What is the only cat species that can't retract its claws?
6) What two birds can swim but not fly?
7) What is the more common name for an animal's vibrissae?
8) If an animal is edentulous, what is it lacking?
9) What animal is related to common earthworms but spends its entire life in glaciers and requires below freezing temperatures to survive?
10) What type of insect is most commonly eaten by humans?

Quiz 19 Answers

1) Cutaneous marginal pouch or informally known as Henry's pocket - The reason it exists isn't clear.

2) Five – They have two large compound eyes, one on either side of their head, and three smaller eyes at the top of their head.
3) Hermaphrodite
4) Honeybee
5) Cheetah
6) Penguin and flightless cormorant
7) Whiskers
8) Teeth
9) Ice worms - They are found across the northern United States and Canada in Alaska, Washington, Oregon and British Columbia and come to the surface of glaciers to feed on snow algae. At temperatures even five degrees above freezing, their internal membranes start to fall apart, and they essentially liquefy and die.
10) Beetles

Quiz 20

1) A shark's teeth aren't embedded in its jaw; what are they attached to?
2) What is unique about a palmiped animal?
3) What is the largest frog?
4) The term ursine relates to what kind of animals?
5) What animal can snap their specialized claw shut producing a cavitation bubble that releases a sound as loud as 218 decibels, louder than a rocket launch?
6) What is the part of a horse between the fetlock and the hoof called?
7) What are the only two sea creatures with ivory tusks?
8) What is the heaviest member of the weasel family?
9) What is a group of ravens called?
10) About 80% of all plant and animal species found on what very large island are endemic (not found elsewhere)?

Quiz 20 Answers

1) Skin covering the jaw - A shark can have over 30,000 teeth in its lifetime. New teeth are continually being grown in a groove in the shark's mouth, and the skin moves the teeth forward into new positions. If they didn't have the ability to quickly replace their

teeth, they wouldn't have been able to develop such a strong bite which causes them to lose so many teeth.

2) Web-footed
3) Goliath frog - It can be more than a foot long and weigh more than seven pounds; it lives in Cameroon and Equatorial Guinea.
4) Bears
5) Snapping shrimp - When the cavitation bubble collapses, it can reach temperatures of 4,700 degrees Celsius which is almost as hot as the surface of the Sun which is 5,500 degrees Celsius.
6) Pastern
7) Narwhal and walrus
8) Sea otter - up to 100 pounds
9) Unkindness or conspiracy.
10) Madagascar

Quiz 21

1) What is the largest member of the dolphin family?
2) What is the only living animal that has the same common and scientific name?
3) Insects don't flap their wings like birds do; how do they move their wings?
4) Where did the Lhasa Apso dog breed originate?
5) What animal is the source of the Middle East Respiratory Syndrome (MERS) virus and is also likely the source of the common cold which spread to humans?
6) In some circumstances, what female insect fakes death to avoid mating?
7) Due to the color inside its mouth, what is another name for the water moccasin?
8) To minimize the risk of drowning, how are dolphins born?
9) During their lifetime, what animal likely spends the most time standing?
10) What dog breed gets its name from the Russian word for swift?

Quiz 21 Answers

1) Killer whale - They are dolphins and not whales. The similarities

with dolphins include teeth, streamlined bodies, rounded head, beak, echolocation, living in pods, and group hunting.

2) Boa constrictor
3) They contract their muscles and force their whole body to vibrate causing the wings which are attached to its exoskeleton to vibrate.
4) Tibet - They were originally kept exclusively by nobility and holy men of Tibet and lived in the monastery and palace of the Dalai Lama and the surrounding monasteries.
5) Camel
6) Dragonfly - The process is called sexual death feigning; a female dragonfly will drop to the ground as if dead to avoid an overly aggressive male. Scientists found that it worked about 60% of the time.
7) Cottonmouth - The inside of its mouth is white.
8) Tail first
9) Elephant - In the wild, they live up to 70 years and only sleep about two hours a day, and they often sleep standing up, only lying down every few nights.
10) Borzoi

Quiz 22

1) Bee sting venom contains what acid?
2) What is the smallest species of apes?
3) What type of feeding is ophiophagy?
4) If an animal is oviparous, what does it do?
5) When a horse curls their upper lip and raises their head in the air, what are they trying to do?
6) Why can't owls move or roll their eyes?
7) What is the largest species of antelope?
8) What do frogs have in their mouths that toads don't?
9) What is the heaviest web-footed bird?
10) What is a group of hippos called?

Quiz 22 Answers

1) Formic acid

2) Gibbon - up to 3 feet tall when standing upright and 12-20 pounds
3) Eating snakes - There are ophiophagous mammals, birds, lizards, and even other snakes.
4) Lay eggs - There is no embryonic development inside the mother.
5) Get a better smell - The behavior is called the flehmen response and is used to transfer inhaled scent molecules into the vomeronasal organ (VNO), a specialized chemosensory structure found in many mammals.
6) Their eyes aren't round; they are elongated tubes and held in place by a bony structure in the skull.
7) Giant eland - They can be almost 6 feet at the shoulder and weigh up to 2,200 pounds.
8) Teeth
9) Emperor penguin - up to 100 pounds
10) Bloat

Quiz 23

1) What animal causes 10%-20% of all power outages in the United States?
2) What is the name for a female mule?
3) Relative to its body size, what mammal has the largest eyes?
4) What is a baby owl called?
5) What is the part of an animal's skin that it can't reach to scratch itself, usually the area between the shoulder blades, called?
6) The poodle didn't originate in France; where did it originate?
7) What is the specific name for a female pig less than six months old?
8) What is the name for a young female cow that has not had a calf?
9) The term caprine relates to what kind of animals?
10) What is the only domestic animal not mentioned in the Bible?

Quiz 23 Answers

1) Squirrel - Squirrel outages tend to be more localized and more quickly fixed than those caused by storms.
2) Molly

3) Tarsier - It is a small primate found on various islands in Southeast Asia, including the Philippines. It is known for its extremely large eyes; even though it is about the size of a squirrel, each eye has a diameter of about 0.6 inches, as large as its brain.
4) Owlet
5) Acnestis
6) Germany - It comes from the German "pudel" which means to "to splash about."
7) Gilt
8) Heifer
9) Goats
10) Cat

Quiz 24

1) Without even flapping their wings, what bird can travel 500-600 miles in a single day and maintain speeds higher than 79 mph for more than 8 hours?
2) Puppies have 28 teeth; how many teeth do adult dogs have?
3) Several species of what kind of animal can breathe through their anus?
4) What mites eat, crawl, and reproduce on human faces and are more likely to exist the older you get?
5) What is the name for a male woodchuck?
6) What is the main visual difference between a monkey and an ape?
7) The hominid or great ape family includes humans, gorillas, chimpanzees, and what?
8) What is the heaviest North American flying bird?
9) Alcatraz Island derives its name from the Spanish for what bird?
10) Since 1994, all dogs are banned in Antarctica; why?

Quiz 24 Answers

1) Wandering albatross - They can do it through a cycle called dynamic soaring which has four major components: a windward climb, a turn from windward to leeward at the flight's peak, a leeward descent, and a curve from leeward to windward at the flight's base.

2) 42
3) Turtle - The Fitzroy River turtle, a species that can only be found in the Fitzroy River in Australia, can breathe through its anus; they are constantly pumping water in and out of their anus collecting as much as 70% of all the oxygen they need to survive. Consequently, they can stay underwater for up to three weeks at a time. They are not the only turtle species that can breathe through its anus, but they are able to use the function to a greater extent.
4) Demodex mites - They are sausage shaped with eight legs clustered in their front third; the largest are about one-third of a millimeter long. They spend most of their time buried head down in your hair follicles; they're most commonly found in the eyelids, nose, cheeks, forehead, and chin.
5) He-chuck
6) Monkeys have tails.
7) Orangutans
8) Trumpeter swan - up to 38 pounds
9) Pelican
10) Stop them from introducing diseases to native seals

Quiz 25

1) What is an obligate carnivore?
2) In animals, what is urohidrosis?
3) How many species of cats live and hunt in groups?
4) What is the technical term for a cat's hairball and applies to a mass of indigestible material found in the gastrointestinal tract of other animals including humans?
5) Starfish don't have blood; what makes up most of their circulatory system?
6) What are the young of bats called?
7) What bird has the world's longest feathers?
8) What animal's name means "nose horn"?
9) What dinosaur named after a South American country is possibly the largest and heaviest land animal that ever lived?
10) What is the smallest species of monkey in the world?

Quiz 25 Answers

1) Animal that must eat meat as a biological necessity - such as cats
2) The habit of some birds of defecating onto their legs and feet to cool themselves. For birds, solid and liquid wastes are expelled together, so it is a liquid mixture of feces and urine. Flamingos, several species of storks, and some vultures exhibit this behavior.
3) One - lion
4) Bezoar
5) Sea water
6) Pups
7) Onagadori chicken of Japan - Its tail feathers can measure over 33 feet.
8) Rhinoceros
9) Argentinosaurus - It was discovered in Argentina in 1987; they were up to 115 feet long and probably weighed 70-85 tons. They existed during the Cretaceous period, about 92-100 million years ago.
10) Pygmy marmoset - It is native to the Amazon rainforest; an adult weighs five ounces and measures six inches from head to tail.

History

Quiz 1

1) What year did "In God We Trust" become the official U.S. national motto?
2) What pandemic beginning in 541 AD is believed to be the first significant occurrence of the bubonic plague?
3) In medieval times, a moment was a unit of time equal to what?
4) What general led the Mexican forces at the Battle of the Alamo?
5) What year did Great Britain formally acknowledge American independence?
6) Who was on the first postage stamp ever issued in the world?
7) Where was the peace treaty that ended WWI signed?
8) The Peloponnesian War from 431–404 BC was fought between Athens and who?
9) What year did the U.S. effectively go off the gold standard?
10) Hannibal's crossing of the Alps in 218 BC was one of the major events of what war?

Quiz 1 Answers

1) 1956
2) Justinian Plague - It is estimated to have killed 25-50 million people over the following two centuries of recurrence.
3) 1/40th of an hour - An hour was defined as 1/12th of the time between sunrise and sunset, so the length of an hour depended on the time of year. Therefore, the length of a moment wasn't fixed either, but on average, it corresponded to 90 seconds.
4) Santa Anna
5) 1783 - The Treaty of Paris officially brought the war to a close.
6) Queen Victoria - 1840
7) Versailles
8) Sparta
9) 1933 - Franklin D. Roosevelt took the U.S. off the gold standard during the Great Depression.

10) Second Punic War - It was the second of three Punic Wars between Carthage and Rome.

Quiz 2

1) What African country gained its independence from the United Kingdom in 1962?
2) What does "E Pluribus Unum," the motto on the U.S. great seal, mean?
3) What war greatly increased the number of American women wearing bras?
4) Who are the only mother and daughter to both win Nobel Prizes?
5) Since the British Centurion tank was introduced in 1945, all British tanks and most armored fighting vehicles come equipped with a boiling vessel for what purpose?
6) What year were TV dinners first sold?
7) What ancient dome is still the largest unreinforced, concrete dome in the world?
8) Why was New Amsterdam renamed New York in 1664?
9) What historical event involved ships named the Beaver, Dartmouth, and the Eleanor?
10) What year did the last guillotining in France occur?

Quiz 2 Answers

1) Uganda
2) Out of many, one
3) WWI - Before that time, corsets were still the norm, but corset frames were mostly made of metal which was needed for the war effort. In 1917, the U.S. War Industries Board asked American women to stop buying them accelerating the move to bras.
4) Marie Curie (1903 Physics and 1911 Chemistry) and her daughter Irene Juliot-Curie (1935 Chemistry)
5) Make tea
6) 1954 - Swanson had 260 tons of leftover frozen turkeys from Thanksgiving sitting in refrigerated railroad cars. Inspired by the food trays on airlines, they created a meal of turkey with cornbread dressing, gravy, peas, and sweet potatoes.
7) Roman Pantheon dome - It is 142 feet in diameter and was built in

125 AD.

8) Change from Dutch to English rule - Dutch Governor Peter Stuyvesant surrendered New Amsterdam to an English naval squadron under Colonel Richard Nicolls.
9) Boston Tea Party (1773) - The tea belonged to the East India Tea Company, but the ships themselves were American.
10) 1977

Quiz 3

1) What two airlines each had two planes hijacked in the 9/11 terrorist attacks on America?
2) Lasting about 38 minutes, what was the shortest war in history fought on August 27, 1896?
3) The *Demologos* was the first steam powered what?
4) Who invented the first mercury thermometer?
5) Who was the first pharaoh of a unified Egypt and was also supposedly killed by a hippopotamus?
6) What date was the Declaration of Independence signed?
7) In what year did the first African American serve as a U.S. state governor?
8) Who was the first female head of state in the Western Hemisphere?
9) Who was the first African American secretary of state?
10) Thirteenth century Pope Gregory IX believed that what animal was an instrument of Satan and condemned them to death across Europe?

Quiz 3 Answers

1) American Airlines and United Airlines
2) Anglo-Zanzibar War - It was a military conflict fought between the United Kingdom and the Zanzibar Sultanate.
3) Warship - It was built to defend New York Harbor from the Royal Navy during the War of 1812 and was launched in 1815.
4) Gabriel Fahrenheit - 1714
5) Menes – about 3000 BC
6) August 2, 1776 - It was adopted on July 4, 1776 but wasn't signed until August.

7) 1872 - P.B.S. Pinchback became the first African American state governor. He had been a Louisiana state senator and was serving as lieutenant governor when Governor Henry Clay Warmoth had to step down temporarily while he battled impeachment charges for election tampering. Pinchback served as governor for 36 days; there wouldn't be another African American governor in the U.S. until 1990.
8) Isabel Peron - Argentina (1974)
9) General Colin Powell - 2000
10) Black cats

Quiz 4

1) What country did Panama gain its independence from in 1903?
2) What year was the first man-made object landed on the Moon?
3) What is the better-known name of Charles I who was king of the Franks and Lombards, and emperor of the Romans and united the majority of western and central Europe during the early Middle Ages?
4) What was the first state to adopt the gas chamber as an execution method in 1921?
5) In what war did submarines make their first appearance?
6) Who was the first Windsor to rule the United Kingdom?
7) The oldest surviving photograph in existence was taken in what year?
8) Who is Mount Rushmore named after?
9) Who originally said, "Houston, we've had a problem here"?
10) Who led a band of abolitionists that seized the federal arsenal at Harpers Ferry, Virginia in October 1859?

Quiz 4 Answers

1) Colombia
2) 1959 - Soviet Union's *Luna* 2
3) Charlemagne
4) Nevada
5) American Revolutionary War - The *Turtle*, a submersible built by American David Bushnell in 1775, was used in an attempted attack on the British ship *Eagle* on September 6, 1776.

6) George V – He reigned from 1910–1936.
7) 1826 - French photography pioneer Joseph Nicéphore Niépce took a picture of the view from the window of an estate in Burgundy, France; it was taken with an eight-hour exposure and was made on a pewter plate using asphalt.
8) Charles Edward Rushmore - He was a New York attorney who visited the Black Hills area in 1884 on business. He asked a guide what the name of the mountain was, and the guide said they would name it now. The name somehow stuck.
9) Jack Swigert - The quote is sometimes incorrectly attributed to James Lovell who repeated "Houston, we've had a problem" after Swigert, and it is not "Houston, we have a problem" as depicted in the movie.
10) John Brown

Quiz 5

1) What did Pope Gregory XIII introduce in 1582?
2) In what century was the practice of using BC and AD for years established?
3) Why was the Pentagon designed with twice the number of bathrooms needed for its anticipated staffing?
4) Who was the first wife of King Henry VIII?
5) What year did the space shuttle *Challenger* explode killing all seven crew members?
6) What was the largest contiguous land area empire in world history?
7) What conqueror may have been responsible for as many as 40 million deaths and may have reduced the entire world population by up to 11%?
8) What state elected the first African American governor?
9) What was Queen Victoria's first name?
10) Who was the first chancellor of the 20th century unified Germany?

Quiz 5 Answers

1) Gregorian calendar - our current calendar
2) 6th century
3) Segregation considerations - President Franklin Roosevelt issued an executive order banning segregation in federal buildings before

the building was open, so it opened as a desegregated facility and was for a time the only desegregated building in Virginia since state laws required segregation.

4) Catherine of Aragon - She was queen from 1509-1533 until the marriage was declared invalid.
5) 1986
6) Mongol Empire - It spanned 9.27 million square miles in one mass at its peak in 1270.
7) Genghis Khan
8) Virginia - L. Douglas Wilder in 1990
9) Alexandrina
10) Helmut Kohl - Chancellor of Germany from 1982 to 1998

Quiz 6

1) Who was the first U.S. Supreme Court chief justice?
2) Who invented a rudimentary water thermometer in 1593 which allowed temperature variations to be measured for the first time?
3) What year did the Falklands War between Argentina and the United Kingdom occur?
4) Killing or attempting to kill a U.S. president wasn't a federal offense until what year?
5) What was the name of John Glenn's first Earth orbital spacecraft in 1962?
6) What year did the first American woman receive a medical degree?
7) What was the largest denomination currency ever printed in the U.S.?
8) Iosif Vissarionovich Dzhugashvili became famous under what name?
9) What did Alfred Nobel invent to make his money and establish the Nobel Prizes?
10) What was the first U.S. state to legalize assisted suicide?

Quiz 6 Answers

1) John Jay - 1789
2) Galileo Galilei
3) 1982

4) 1965 - two years after John F. Kennedy's death
5) *Friendship 7*
6) 1849 - Elizabeth Blackwell was the first woman to earn a medical degree in America; she graduated first in her class at New York's Geneva College.
7) $100,000 bill - It featured a picture of Woodrow Wilson and was only printed for three weeks in December 1934 and January 1935. It was only used for official transactions between Federal Reserve Banks.
8) Joseph Stalin
9) Dynamite
10) Oregon - 1994

Quiz 7

1) What year was the first woman elected governor of a state?
2) What Wild West legend was born Henry McCarty in 1859?
3) What year did Egypt gain its independence from the British?
4) Who met at Ujiji, a town on the shore of Lake Tanganyika in western Tanzania, in 1871?
5) Who was the most photographed American of the 19th century?
6) What pioneering American female journalist was widely known for her 1889-1890 record-breaking trip around the world in 72 days?
7) Practiced between the 5th and 16th centuries, what was a poetic exchange of insults called?
8) Who was the first woman to appear on U.S. paper currency?
9) Istanbul was previously called Constantinople; what was it called before Constantinople?
10) What year did the Soviet Union break up into independent republics?

Quiz 7 Answers

1) 1925 - Nellie Tayloe Ross, governor of Wyoming
2) Billy the Kid
3) 1922
4) Henry Stanley and David Livingstone

5) Frederick Douglass - He wanted to ensure a more accurate depiction of black Americans and sat for upwards of 160 portraits.
6) Elizabeth Cochran Seaman better known by her pen name Nellie Bly (1864–1922)
7) Flyting - The exchange of insults could get quite rude including accusations of cowardice or sexual perversion.
8) Pocahontas - She appeared on the back of the $20 bill in 1865.
9) Byzantium
10) 1991

Quiz 8

1) What century was the first hot air balloon?
2) Forks were introduced in Italy in what century?
3) Hitler, Stalin, and Mussolini were all nominated for what prize?
4) From what country did Angola gain its independence in 1975?
5) Who was the father of Alexander the Great?
6) Based on his medical records, Adolf Hitler had a huge problem with what common condition and took 28 different drugs to try to control it?
7) Who was the first person who wasn't a head of state depicted on a postage stamp anywhere in the world?
8) Haile Selassie ruled what country?
9) What state was the setting of the Battle of the Little Bighorn?
10) What woman is widely regarded as the greatest pirate ever with control of more than 1,500 ships and 80,000 sailors at her peak?

Quiz 8 Answers

1) 18th century - 1783
2) 11th century - They were originally seen as an offense to God since they were considered artificial hands and therefore sacrilegious.
3) Nobel Peace Prize
4) Portugal
5) Philip II of Macedon - He was king of Macedon from 359 BC until his assassination in 336 BC.
6) Flatulence - Some of the anti-gas pills he used contained a base of

strychnine which caused further stomach and liver issues.

7) Benjamin Franklin - 1847 U.S. stamp
8) Ethiopia - emperor from 1930 to 1974
9) Montana
10) Ching Shih (1775-1844) - She was a Chinese prostitute and had one of the biggest naval armies in the history of the world. She robbed and taxed towns and plundered ships along the coast of the South China Sea.

Quiz 9

1) Who are the only two people to win two Nobel Prizes in two different categories?
2) Ratified in 1781, the Articles of Confederation were the original constitution of the United States which were replaced by the U.S. Constitution in 1789; they included an open invitation for what country to join the United States without any consent from the other states?
3) What was the first recorded Chinese dynasty?
4) What country effectively banned Christmas from 1647-1660?
5) What iconic New York city landmark was under construction the year of Custer's defeat at the Battle of Little Bighorn in 1876?
6) What city was home to the first official skyscraper in 1884?
7) What year did the Panama Canal open?
8) What year was the Three Mile Island partial nuclear meltdown in Pennsylvania?
9) What was the name the American pilot shot down in a U-2 spy plane over Russia in 1960?
10) Who replaced Nikita Khrushchev as leader of the Soviet Union?

Quiz 9 Answers

1) Marie Curie (1903 Physics and 1911 Chemistry) and Linus Pauling (1954 Chemistry and 1962 Peace)
2) Canada
3) Xia Dynasty (2070–1600 BC)
4) England - Puritans believed that people needed strict rules to be religious and that any kind of merrymaking was sinful.

5) Brooklyn Bridge
6) Chicago - The Home Insurance Building in downtown Chicago was 10 stories and 136 feet tall; it was demolished in 1931.
7) 1914
8) 1979
9) Francis Garry Powers
10) Leonid Brezhnev - He led the Soviet Union from 1964 until his death in 1982.

Quiz 10

1) What oil tanker was the cause of a massive oil spill in Alaska in 1989?
2) In Boston in January 1919, a 50-foot-tall holding tank burst and sent a 15-foot tall wave through the streets; it crushed houses and swallowed everything in its path killing 21 people and injuring 150; what was in the tank?
3) What was George Armstrong Custer's rank when he was killed at Little Bighorn in 1876?
4) What was the name of the first space shuttle to go into space?
5) The word deadline originated in what war?
6) What two foods were the most popular staples of the ancient Egyptian diet and were consumed by most everyone every day?
7) When Disneyland opened in 1955, Tomorrowland was designed to look like what year?
8) The Middle Ages is traditionally thought to have started with the fall of what empire?
9) In what century did Pope Urban II call for the initiation of the Crusades?
10) Ancient Rome had 24 hours in a day, but what was different about their hours?

Quiz 10 Answers

1) *Exxon Valdez*
2) Molasses
3) Lieutenant Colonel
4) *Columbia* - April 1981

5) American Civil War - In Civil War prison camps, it was the line that prisoners couldn't go beyond, or they would be shot.
6) Bread and beer - Laborers would have a morning meal of bread, beer, and often onions, and a heartier dinner with boiled vegetables, meat and more bread and beer.
7) 1986
8) Roman Empire - The Middle Ages started in 476 and lasted about 1,000 years.
9) 11th century - 1095
10) The hours varied in length based on the time of year. They ensured that there were 12 hours of daylight and 12 hours of darkness adjusting the length of the hours accordingly.

Quiz 11

1) Who was the last emperor of France?
2) What mobster offered a $10,000 reward for information leading to the capture of the Lindbergh baby kidnapper and that he and his men would search for the perpetrators if he was released from prison?
3) What civilization was the first to divide the day into 24 hours?
4) What year did the French Revolution begin?
5) Punctuation as we largely know it today did not exist until what century?
6) In ancient Greece, any citizen could be voted out and expelled for 10 years which was called ostrakismos and led to what English word?
7) Rounded to the nearest 100 years, how long before Christopher Columbus did Leif Erikson arrive in North America?
8) Who was Russia's longest ruling female leader?
9) Sandwiches didn't appear in American cookbooks until what century?
10) What was the name of the pandemic that killed 50-100 million people starting in 1918?

Quiz 11 Answers

1) Napoleon III (Charles-Louis Napoléon Bonaparte) - He ruled from 1852-1870 and was the nephew of Napoleon Bonaparte (Napoleon I).

2) Al Capone
3) Egyptian - Ancient Egyptians used a base 12 system instead of our base 10 system; they counted the knuckles of each finger using their thumbs as pointers. They had 12 hours of light and 12 hours of darkness, so the length of the hours varied by time of the year. Fixed length hours were proposed by the Greeks in the 2nd century BC, but they did not become common until mechanical clocks first appeared in Europe during the 14th century.
4) 1789
5) 15th century
6) Ostracism
7) 500 years - Erikson arrived in Newfoundland in about 1000 AD.
8) Catherine the Great - She ruled from 1762-1796.
9) 19th century
10) Spanish flu - It infected an estimated 500 million people worldwide, about one-third of the world's population.

Quiz 12

1) What current candy was part of U.S. soldier rations in WWII?
2) In what century did Martin Luther initiate the Reformation?
3) In what century was the Taj Mahal completed?
4) What country had the first elected female head of state in the Western Hemisphere?
5) What year did Christmas become a U.S. federal holiday?
6) Since 1869, over a million people have been buried on what island that serves as the burial place for unclaimed bodies for New York City?
7) What year was the first human killed by a robot?
8) What year was the modern paper clip designed?
9) Who is the only woman to have married the kings of both France and England?
10) What two countries are part of the world's oldest alliance that is still in effect?

Quiz 12 Answers

1) Tootsie Rolls - They were durable in all weather conditions and

were good for quick energy.

2) 16th century - 1517
3) 17th century - 1643
4) Nicaragua - Violeta Chamorro in 1990
5) 1870
6) Hart Island - The island is at the western end of Long Island Sound and is 1 mile long by 1⁄3 mile wide.
7) 1979 - On January 25, 1979, Robert Williams died when he was hit in the head by a mechanical arm at a Ford casting plant.
8) 1899
9) Eleanor of Aquitaine - She married Louis VII of France and Henry II of England.
10) England and Portugal - Anglo-Portuguese Alliance from 1373

Quiz 13

1) What was the first country in Europe to give women the right to vote?
2) Who was the first leader of the People's Republic of China?
3) What year was the first Ford Model T produced?
4) How old was the youngest signer of the Declaration of Independence?
5) What year did the Korean War start?
6) In April 1933, Eleanor Roosevelt snuck out of a White House event and went on an airplane joyride with what well known person?
7) Who was the first democratically elected president of Russia?
8) What year was the first text message sent?
9) What century was the earliest woodblock printed paper book?
10) What is the ancient practice of trying to protect yourself against poisoning by taking non-lethal doses of poison to build immunity called?

Quiz 13 Answers

1) Finland - 1906
2) Mao Zedong
3) 1908

4) 26 - Edward Rutledge was a lawyer from South Carolina.
5) 1950
6) Amelia Earhart
7) Boris Yeltsin - 1991
8) 1992 - It was sent by a Vodafone engineer working on developing SMS.
9) 9th century - the Chinese book Diamond Sutra was created in 868, almost 600 years before the Gutenberg Bible was the first book printed on a mechanical press.
10) Mithridatism - From the end of the 1st century AD, Roman emperors adopted the daily habit of taking a small amount of every known poison to gain immunity. It can be effective against some types of poisons, but depending on the poison, it can lead to a lethal accumulation in the body over time.

Quiz 14

1) What famous philosopher said, "Children today are tyrants. They contradict their parents, gobble their food, and tyrannize their teachers"?
2) Who was the last Tudor monarch of England?
3) Who was the first person to cross the Antarctic Circle?
4) Who was Israel's first prime minister?
5) What king was offered plans for the first bacteriological weapon?
6) Functional buttons with buttonholes for fastening or closing clothes first appeared in what century?
7) After his defeat at Waterloo, Napoleon spent the last six years of his life under British supervision on what island?
8) At what Ohio university were four students shot dead in 1970?
9) Who was the first woman to appear on a U.S. postage stamp?
10) What conqueror once had a feast with his army while seated on top of Russian army generals and nobility?

Quiz 14 Answers

1) Socrates (470-399 BC)
2) Elizabeth I - She was the daughter of Henry VIII and ruled from 1558-1603.

3) Captain James Cook - 1773
4) David Ben-Gurion - 1948
5) King Louis XIV - He ruled France from 1643-1715 and was offered plans for the first bacteriological weapon by an Italian chemist; he refused instantly and paid the scientist to keep the discovery a secret.
6) 13th century
7) St. Helena - It is in the South Atlantic 1,162 miles off the west coast of Africa.
8) Kent State
9) Martha Washington - 1902
10) Genghis Khan - In Russia in 1223, the Mongolian army had just won the Battle of the Kalka River; the Russian army surrendered, and the Mongols decided to have a feast to celebrate. The Russian army generals and nobility were forced to lie on the ground, and a heavy wooden gate was thrown on top of them. Chairs and tables were set on top of the gate, and the Mongols sat down for a feast on top of the still living bodies of their enemies.

Quiz 15

1) What date was the atomic bomb dropped on Hiroshima?
2) In what century did Marco Polo begin his travels to Asia?
3) Who was the last British monarch to ascend to the throne as a teenager?
4) Who was the first woman to appear on the front of U.S. paper currency?
5) After the fall of the Roman Empire, the technology to make what building material was lost for 1,000 years?
6) Recent research suggests that rats are not likely to blame for transmitting the Black Death bubonic plague that wiped out one-third of Europe's population. What animal likely transmitted the lice and fleas that spread the disease?
7) Who was the first African American U.S. Supreme Court justice?
8) Who did the Greeks defeat at the Battle of Marathon in 490 BC?
9) Where did the Pilgrims first land in America?
10) Who was leader of the Greek forces during the Trojan War?

Quiz 15 Answers

1) August 06, 1945
2) 13th century - 1271
3) Queen Victoria - She was 18 when she became queen in 1837.
4) Martha Washington - She appeared on the $1 silver certificate in 1886.
5) Concrete - Roman concrete is still more durable than the concrete we make today, and it gets stronger over time. Their concrete was created with volcanic ash, lime and seawater mixed with more volcanic rock as aggregate which created a rock-like concrete we haven't been able to duplicate.
6) Humans - The transmission was more likely due to human fleas and lice.
7) Thurgood Marshall - 1967
8) Persians - It was during the first Persian invasion of Greece.
9) Provincetown, Massachusetts - The Pilgrims didn't first land at Plymouth Rock; they landed in what is now Provincetown, Massachusetts and signed the Mayflower Compact there. They arrived at Plymouth Rock five weeks later.
10) Agamemnon

Quiz 16

1) Sideburns are named after what American Civil War general?
2) What year was the People's Republic of China established?
3) In what state were the only U.S. mainland combat deaths in WWII?
4) During what century did Denmark rule England?
5) Who was shot and killed in New Delhi, India on October 31, 1984?
6) Who was the first president to appear on a U.S. postage stamp?
7) In 2000, what was the last U.S. state to overturn its law against interracial marriage?
8) What island was invaded by the U.S. in 1983?
9) What country had the first openly gay or lesbian prime minister?
10) What year was the word robot first used?

Quiz 16 Answers

1) Ambrose Burnside - He was known for having an unusual facial hairstyle with a moustache connected to thick sideburns with a clean-shaven chin.
2) 1949
3) Oregon - On the May 5, 1945, a Japanese balloon bomb exploded and killed a woman and five children in Oregon. The balloon bombs had a 33-foot diameter balloon with 35 pounds of explosives and were designed to rise to 30,000 feet and ride the jet stream east, making it from Japan to the U.S. in about three days. An altimeter would trigger a reaction that would jettison the bombs; Japan released about 9,000 of the bombs. A Sunday school teacher and five students happened upon an unexploded balloon bomb on the ground; it exploded while they were investigating it.
4) 11th century - The Danish House of Knýtlinga ruled the Kingdom of England from 1013 to 1014 and from 1016 to 1042.
5) Indira Gandhi - She was India's first female prime minister and was the daughter of Jawaharlal Nehru, the first prime minister of India. She served as prime minister from 1966-1977 and again from 1980 until her assassination in 1984.
6) George Washington - 1847
7) Alabama
8) Grenada
9) Iceland - Jóhanna Sigurðardóttir was prime minister from 2009-2013.
10) 1920 - It was first used in a 1920 play called *Rossum's Universal Robots* by Czech writer Karel Čapek; it comes from the Slavic word "rabota" meaning slave labor.

Quiz 17

1) What year did the first true ATM debut?
2) Who was the first American to win a Nobel Prize?
3) Who was the British prime minister when WWII broke out?
4) Who personally saved the U.S. from financial collapse during the War of 1812 by placing most of his personal assets at the disposal of the government and underwriting about 95% of the war loans?
5) What year was the first nonstop transatlantic flight?

6) Who was emperor of Japan during World War II?
7) What year was the Boston Marathon bombing which killed three people?
8) Meaning apple orchard in Spanish, what is the name of the concentration camp in California where thousands of Japanese Americans were imprisoned during WWII?
9) What is the only Southeast Asian country never colonized by Europeans?
10) Who is the longest reigning monarch ever?

Quiz 17 Answers

1) 1967 at Barclay's Bank in London - They wouldn't become commonplace until at least 1990.
2) Theodore Roosevelt - 1906 Peace Prize
3) Neville Chamberlain
4) Stephen Girard - He was one of the wealthiest men in American history.
5) 1919 - John Alcock and Arthur Whitten Brown made the flight eight years before Charles Lindbergh who made the first solo flight.
6) Hirohito - He was emperor from 1926 until his death in 1989 and is the longest reigning monarch in Japanese history.
7) 2013
8) Manzanar
9) Thailand
10) King Sobhuza II of Swaziland - 82 years 253 days (1899-1982)

Quiz 18

1) What type of gun did John Wilkes Booth use to assassinate Abraham Lincoln?
2) The U.S. secret service was created specifically to battle what type of crime?
3) What year was the first woman elected to the U.S. Congress?
4) Who was the first female Speaker of the U.S. House of Representatives?
5) What were the two cities at the ends of the Pony Express?
6) What Soviet leader plotted to kill actor John Wayne and sent two

men to pose as FBI agents to assassinate him?

7) What country was first to introduce emergency three-digit phone numbers?
8) What did English Queen Mary II die of at age 32?
9) "Make Your Wet Dreams Come True" was a U.S. presidential campaign slogan for what candidate?
10) What was the first nation to officially recognize the independence of the United States?

Quiz 18 Answers

1) Derringer pistol
2) Counterfeiting - Shortly after the Civil War, one-third to one-half of all U.S. currency was counterfeit. This was a major threat to the economy, and the Secret Service was founded in 1865 specifically to reduce counterfeiting.
3) 1916 - It was four years before women were given the right to vote.
4) Nancy Pelosi - 2007
5) St. Joseph, Missouri and Sacramento, California – The Pony Express could transport a letter over 1,800 miles in 10 days but only ran for 18 months from April 1860 to October 1861.
6) Joseph Stalin - He was a big film fan and considered Wayne a threat to the Soviet Union because of his strong anti-communist beliefs.
7) United Kingdom - They were first introduced in London in 1937 after a fire killed five people, and the person calling for the fire brigade was kept waiting by the operator. The original number was 999.
8) Smallpox
9) Al Smith - In 1928, former New York governor Al Smith ran for president against Herbert Hoover; a major debate was over whether the prohibition alcohol ban should continue. Drys were people who supported prohibition, and Wets were against it. Smith was against prohibition and thus the slogan.
10) Morocco - 1777

Quiz 19

1) Who was murdered at Canterbury Cathedral on December 29, 1170?

2) What are the only three crimes mentioned in the U.S. Constitution?
3) Who was the oldest signer of the Declaration of Independence?
4) In what century was the Aztec Empire at its height as the Spanish arrived?
5) What year was the Great Fire of London which burned for five days and destroyed almost 90% of London's homes?
6) Who was the wife of French King Louis XVI?
7) What were the surnames of Bonnie and Clyde?
8) What year did the U.S. have its first female cabinet member?
9) What year was the first pedestrian killed by a car?
10) In what year were the first free multiracial elections held in South Africa?

Quiz 19 Answers

1) Thomas Beckett - He was Archbishop of Canterbury and was killed by followers of King Henry II.
2) Treason, piracy, counterfeiting
3) Benjamin Franklin - 70
4) 16th century - 1519
5) 1666
6) Marie Antoinette
7) Clyde Barrow and Bonnie Parker
8) 1933 - Frances Perkins was Secretary of Labor under Franklin D. Roosevelt.
9) 1896 - Bridget Driscoll was struck by a demonstration car which was traveling at four miles per hour.
10) 1994

Quiz 20

1) Who was the first American woman to win the Nobel Peace Prize?
2) What year was the first color photograph taken?
3) Who did Adolf Hitler succeed as Germany's head of state?
4) As attorney general of the U.S., what government organization did Charles Bonaparte, French Emperor Napoleon's great-nephew, found in 1908?

5) What was the first man-made object to achieve sub-orbital space flight?
6) By land area, what was the largest empire in world history?
7) In what century was Pompeii buried by Mount Vesuvius?
8) In Victorian times, photography subjects were encouraged to say what instead of "cheese"?
9) What was the name of the Italian cruise ship hijacked by Palestinian terrorists in October 1985?
10) What was the first U.S. state to give women the right to vote?

Quiz 20 Answers

1) Jane Addams - 1931
2) 1861 - While Kodak didn't introduce color film to the masses until 1935, the first color photograph was taken in 1861. Thomas Sutton and James Clerk Maxwell created a picture of a Scottish tartan ribbon of red, white, and green. They created the photo by taking three separate photos using three different filters (red, green, and blue violet) and superimposing them together. This is the basic three-color method that is used in all color imaging today.
3) Paul von Hindenburg - Hitler assumed leadership in 1934 on Hindenburg's death.
4) FBI - He created the Bureau of Investigation which was renamed the Federal Bureau of Investigation in 1935.
5) German V2 rocket - June 1944
6) British Empire - In 1922, it ruled over about 24% of the world's land.
7) 1st century - 79 AD
8) Prunes - Among other reasons, Victorians thought it was classless to show a big toothy smile.
9) *Achille Lauro*
10) Wyoming - 1890

Quiz 21

1) What century was the first Viking raid on England?
2) What was the first U.S. state to legalize same-sex marriage?
3) Which of the seven wonders of the ancient world was demolished by an earthquake in 226 BC?

4) What are the names of the two supercontinents that the landmass of Pangaea broke up into about 200 million years ago?
5) What automobile manufacturer invented the three-point seat belt used today?
6) The word salary derives from the Latin "salarium" which referred to a soldier's allowance to buy what?
7) What leader once ordered his army to eat every tenth man?
8) Who was the first explorer to reach the Cape of Good Hope?
9) The French village of Domremy was the birthplace of what famous figure of the 15th century?
10) Why is a ship's speed measured in knots?

Quiz 21 Answers

1) 8th century - 793 AD
2) Massachusetts - 2004
3) Colossus of Rhodes
4) Laurasia (northern side) and Gondwana (southern side) - These two supercontinents later broke up to form our current continents.
5) Volvo - They gave away the 1962 patent for free to save lives.
6) Salt - In ancient Rome, soldiers were sometimes paid in salt or given an allowance to purchase it.
7) Genghis Khan - In 1214, Khan was battling the Jin empire in China and laid siege to the city of Chingdu, capital of the Jin empire. The siege went on for a long time, and supplies were short for the Mongols; they were also ravaged by plague. Khan ordered that every tenth man should be sacrificed to feed the others. Khan later personally abandoned the siege leaving it to one of his generals, and Chungdu eventually fell in 1215
8) Bartolomeu Dias - 1488
9) Joan of Arc (1412-1431)
10) Actual knots were used to measure speed. By the late 16th century, sailors measured a ship's speed by throwing out a piece of wood attached to a length of rope with knots tied at regular intervals. They allowed the rope to go out as the ship moved forward, and after a set length of time, they pulled the rope back in counting the knots that had gone out and calculated the speed. A knot eventually came to mean one nautical mile per hour.

Quiz 22

1) The word computer was first referenced in what century?
2) Duncan Hines (1880–1959) was a real person; what was he known for?
3) What year did Princess Diana die?
4) In what century did Nostradamus live?
5) Who led the Greek forces against the vastly larger Persian army in the Battle of Thermopylae in 480 BC?
6) What year did Joseph Gayetty commercialize toilet paper much as we know it today?
7) Who was the last Roman Catholic king of England?
8) What was the name of the royal house that ruled Russia from 1613 to 1917?
9) What year did the dollar become the U.S. standard currency?
10) What famous poet was San Francisco's first African American female streetcar conductor?

Quiz 22 Answers

1) 17th century - It originally meant a person who did arithmetic calculations. It didn't take on its meaning of being a machine until the late 1800s or an electronic device until the mid-1900s.
2) He was an American pioneer of restaurant ratings for travelers.
3) 1997
4) 16th century - He lived from 1503 to 1566.
5) King Leonidas of Sparta
6) 1857 - Toilet paper traces its origins back to at least 6th century China when it was first referenced in writings. However, most people didn't experience it until at least 1857 when American inventor Joseph Gayetty commercialized the product much as we know it today.
7) James II - He ruled from 1685-1688.
8) Romanov
9) 1792
10) Maya Angelou

Quiz 23

1) What is the oldest English-speaking university in the world?
2) What year did women receive the right to vote in the United States?
3) When the Gregorian calendar replaced the Julian calendar, how many days had to be skipped to get the calendar back on track with the position of the Sun?
4) What year did the United States first adopt the 911 emergency phone number?
5) What year were East and West Germany unified?
6) In ancient Greece, certain women wore sandals that left the words "follow me" imprinted on the ground as they walked; who were they?
7) Who was the last king of the Aztecs?
8) Originally, the term third world country did not mean a developing country; it was coined during the Cold War in 1952 by a French demographer and referred to what?
9) What year was the microwave oven patented?
10) In what century were the last chariot races held in Circus Maximus in Rome which could seat 250,000 spectators?

Quiz 23 Answers

1) Oxford - It existed about 350 years before the start of the Inca and Aztec empires. There was teaching at Oxford as early as 1076 making it the third oldest university in continuous operation in the world and the oldest English-speaking university.
2) 1920
3) 10 days - October 4, 1582 was followed by October 15, 1582.
4) 1968 - The first call was made in Haleyville, Alabama.
5) 1990
6) Prostitutes - In ancient Greece, prostitution was common, accepted, and regulated.
7) Montezuma II (1466-1520)
8) Countries that weren't aligned with either the United States or Soviet Union.
9) 1945 - Raytheon Engineer Percy Spencer first discovered the heating powers of microwaves when he accidentally melted a candy

bar in his pocket.

10) 6th century

Quiz 24

1) What is the only crime defined in the U.S. Constitution?
2) What famous world leader wrote a romance novel called *Clisson et Eugénie* about the doomed romance of a soldier and his lover?
3) Which king of England was executed in 1649 during the English Civil War?
4) Who was the first English monarch to live in Buckingham Palace?
5) In 1958, a B-47 carrying an atomic bomb larger than the one dropped on Nagasaki accidentally dropped it on what state?
6) Where was the Magna Carta signed in 1215?
7) What was the name of the secret German government program from 1935 to 1945 that encouraged racially fit women to bear children for the Third Reich?
8) What famous world leader said, "How can anyone govern a nation that has two hundred and forty-six different kinds of cheese"?
9) What Russian czar was born Pyotr Alekseyevich in 1672?
10) What century did the Incan Empire start?

Quiz 24 Answers

1) Treason - Article III, Section 3
2) Napoleon Bonaparte - It was based on Bonaparte's own relationship with Eugenie Desiree Clary.
3) Charles I
4) Queen Victoria - 1837
5) South Carolina - The core of the bomb was still on the plane, so there wasn't a nuclear explosion, but the 6,000 pounds of conventional high explosives detonated. The bomb fell on a garden in a rural area and created a 35-foot-deep by 75-foot-wide crater and destroyed the nearby house and outbuildings. Fortunately, no one was killed, and there were only minor injuries.
6) Runnymede - It is a meadow alongside the River Thames 20 miles west of central London.
7) Lebensborn - Women in the program were required to hand their children over to the SS to be raised. The program originally started

in Germany but spread to other occupied European countries during WWII. There were an estimated 20,000 Lebensborn children born; the most famous is ABBA singer Anni-Frid Lyngstad who was born of a Norwegian mother and a German sergeant.

8) Charles de Gaulle
9) Peter the Great (1672-1725)
10) 15th century - 1438

Quiz 25

1) Who was India's first prime minister?
2) What English king made boiling to death a form of capital punishment?
3) In what year did Johannes Gutenberg's movable-type printing press produce the first Bible?
4) On which island was Napoleon Bonaparte born?
5) The Black Death bubonic plague that wiped out one-third of Europe's population occurred in what century?
6) What year was Jell-O invented?
7) To the nearest year, how many years was Texas an independent country?
8) What year did the *Hindenburg* explode in New Jersey?
9) What is the earliest surviving system of laws?
10) What year was the first digital still camera created?

Quiz 25 Answers

1) Jawaharlal Nehru - 1947
2) Henry VIII (1491-1547)
3) 1455
4) Corsica
5) 14th century - It peaked in 1347-1351
6) 1897 - In LeRoy, New York, Pearl Wait added fruit syrup to gelatin which had been invented in the 1600s.
7) 10 years - The Republic of Texas was a sovereign state from March 2, 1836, to February 19, 1846.
8) 1937

9) The Code of Hammurabi - Hammurabi was a ruler of ancient Babylon from 1792-1750 BC.
10) 1975 – It was created by Kodak and weighed eight pounds and took 0.01-megapixel black-and-white photos that took 23 seconds to render onto a cassette tape that displayed the image on a television set.

Quiz 26

1) What explorer brought the first pigs to what is now the United States?
2) Who was the first *Time* magazine Woman of the Year in 1936?
3) Who was the first person to sight the Antarctic continent?
4) What country was divided by the 38th parallel after WWII?
5) Why was the Pentagon, the headquarters for the U.S. Department of Defense, designed in the shape of a pentagon?
6) Measured by its share of the world's population, what is the largest empire in history?
7) In what country did Mahatma Gandhi first employ nonviolent civil disobedience to fight for Indian civil rights?
8) What year was the first known selfie taken?
9) What was the last war that Liechtenstein ever participated in?
10) Pirates wore eye patches for what reason other than to cover up a missing or injured eye?

Quiz 26 Answers

1) Hernando de Soto - He brought 13 pigs to Tampa Bay, Florida in 1539.
2) Wallis Simpson - Her marriage to British King Edward VIII forced his abdication.
3) Fabian Gottlieb von Bellingshausen - 1820
4) Korea
5) It was originally designed to fit on a piece of land that was bordered on five sides by roads. It was decided that the original site was too close to Arlington Cemetery, so it was moved to its current location. Since the design was already complete, it was slightly modified but kept its pentagon shape even though it wasn't essential any longer.

6) Persian Empire - It accounted for approximately 44% of the world's population in 480 BC. In contrast, the British Empire accounted for about 23% of the world's population at its peak.
7) South Africa - Gandhi initially fought for the right of the resident Indian community in South Africa. He went to South Africa to work at age 23 and spent 21 years there before returning to India in 1915.
8) 1839 - While the first usage of the word selfie didn't occur until 2002, the world's first known selfie was taken in 1839. Robert Cornelius took the first selfie inside his family's store in Philadelphia; he had to remove the camera's lens cap, run into frame, and hold his pose for a full minute.
9) Austro-Prussian War - In 1866, Liechtenstein sent out an army of 80 men for the Austro-Prussian War; they came back with 81 men. They had no casualties and picked up an extra soldier along the way.
10) To see in the dark - They were constantly going above and below deck, and it takes the human eye up to 25 minutes to adapt to seeing in the dark. By wearing a patch, they kept one eye dark adjusted, so they could see in the dark immediately by just moving the eye patch either for normal duties or for fighting.

Quiz 27

1) Who was the first African American Miss America?
2) Who was the British prime minister when Japan surrendered in WWII?
3) What year was the first video uploaded to YouTube?
4) What agricultural byproduct was commonly used for toilet paper by early Americans?
5) No one who has walked on the Moon was born after what year?
6) What amendment to the U.S. Constitution allows the federal government to collect an income tax from all Americans?
7) What was the date of VE Day?
8) What year was the Chernobyl nuclear disaster in the Soviet Union?
9) Prior to changing their name to Windsor in 1917, what was the family name of the British royal family?
10) For what war did the first American woman receive a U.S. military pension?

Quiz 27 Answers

1) Vanessa Williams - 1983
2) Clement Attlee - He was prime minister from July 26, 1945 to October 26, 1951; he was preceded and succeeded by Winston Churchill.
3) 2005 - On April 23, 2005, the first video ever uploaded to YouTube was *Meet Me at the Zoo*; it was 19 seconds of a boy explaining that elephants have long tusks.
4) Corn cobs - Dried corncobs were plentiful, efficient, and quite soft and flexible.
5) 1935 - Charles Duke, the tenth person to walk on the Moon, was born the latest, October 3, 1935.
6) 16th Amendment – ratified in 1913
7) May 08, 1945
8) 1986
9) Saxe-Coburg and Gotha - Due to anti-German sentiment during WWI, the British royal family chose to change their name in 1917 to Windsor, so the family is named after the castle and not the other way around.
10) American Revolutionary War - Margaret Corbin was the first woman recognized as a soldier in the American Revolutionary War and was also the first woman to receive a U.S. military pension.

Miscellaneous

Quiz 1

1) What is a string of typographical symbols (for example, %@$&*!) used in place of an obscenity called?
2) Owyhee is the original English spelling of what?
3) Karl Marx was once a foreign correspondent for what U.S. newspaper?
4) Beethoven's third symphony is nicknamed what?
5) In Gustav Holst's *The Planets*, what planet represents old age?
6) What country created the Smurfs?
7) What year was the first video game console created?
8) Who wrote "To err is human; to forgive, divine"?
9) What is the only music group where every member has written more than one number one single?
10) What was classical composer Mussorgsky's first name?

Quiz 1 Answers

1) Grawlix
2) Hawaii
3) *New York Daily Tribune*
4) Eroica
5) Saturn
6) Belgium
7) 1972 – It was the Magnavox Odyssey and was five years before the first Atari and 13 years before the first Nintendo; it had no sound or color.
8) Alexander Pope
9) Queen - All four members have been inducted into the Songwriters Hall of Fame.
10) Modest

Quiz 2

1) What is the fleshy end of your nose that splits your nostrils called?
2) Who was the only apostle of Jesus to die a natural death?
3) What does the Bible say Adam and Eve ate to get expelled from the Garden of Eden?
4) In music, what does the term da capo mean?
5) What plant is linen made from?
6) Humans are naturally drawn towards characteristics including a rounded belly, big head, big eyes, loose limbs, etc. Puppies, kittens, and other animals including human babies trigger this. What is this set of physical characteristics called?
7) As a description of a person, what is an ultracrepidarian?
8) Based on number of weeks at number one on Billboard's Hot 100, who was the top artist of the 2000s?
9) Nudiustertian is a time reference; what does it mean?
10) What year was wheeled luggage first sold?

Quiz 2 Answers

1) Columella nasi
2) Saint John
3) Forbidden fruit - It never says it was an apple.
4) From the beginning - It is a composer or publisher's directive to repeat the previous piece of music.
5) Flax
6) Kinderschema
7) Person who expresses opinions on matters outside the scope of their knowledge or expertise.
8) Usher
9) Day before yesterday
10) 1970 - Macy's department stores in the U.S.

Quiz 3

1) What is the little paper tail sticking out of a Hershey's Kiss called?
2) In English, what is the shortest three syllable word?

3) If you started with \$0.01 and had a 100% daily return on your money, how long would it take to become a millionaire?
4) What martial arts action movie star is also a popstar in Asia?
5) "If you really want to hear about it, the first thing you'll probably want to know is where I was born, and what my lousy childhood was like, and how my parents were occupied and all before they had me, and all that David Copperfield kind of crap, but I don't feel like going into it, if you want to know the truth," is the opening line to what novel?
6) What is the unfilled space between a bottle top and the liquid inside called?
7) Dunce caps were originally a sign of what?
8) If something is quotidian, how often does it occur?
9) What composer and musician died in 1750 and fathered twenty children, nine of whom survived him, by two wives?
10) What is the name of the lion in C.S. Lewis' *The Lion, the Witch and the Wardrobe*?

Quiz 3 Answers

1) Niggly wiggly
2) W - The letters of the alphabet are generally also considered words since they are nouns referring to the letter.
3) 27 days
4) Jackie Chan - He is a classically trained singer and has produced over 20 different albums including over 100 songs in five languages and won the Best Foreign Singer Award in Japan in 1984.
5) *The Catcher in the Rye* – J.D. Salinger
6) Ulage
7) Intelligence - Thirteenth century philosopher John Duns Scotus created the idea of the pointy hat as a reverse funnel to spread knowledge into the brain; the hats became popular and a symbol of high intelligence. In the 1500s, Scotus' ideas fell out of favor, and the pointy hat eventually came to mean the opposite as we know it today.
8) Daily
9) Johann Sebastian Bach
10) Aslan

Quiz 4

1) What is the largest private home ever built in the U.S.?
2) What was the name of the airplane Buddy Holly died in?
3) What is it called when there is a situation in chess and other games where a player must move, but all the moves are bad or put them at a disadvantage?
4) The modern hula hoop idea came from bamboo hoops used by children for exercise and later sold in stores in what country?
5) In the Middle Ages, men who wanted a boy sometimes had what removed to try to ensure having a baby boy?
6) What common clothing item comes from the Persian for "leg garment"?
7) What singer is known as the "Empress of the Blues"?
8) In the Humpty Dumpty nursery rhyme, there is no indication that he is an egg; what did early illustrations portray him as?
9) The Motel 6 and Super 8 motel chains both got their names from what?
10) What is the most popular birth month in the U.S.?

Quiz 4 Answers

1) Biltmore Estate in Asheville, North Carolina - It was built for George Washington Vanderbilt II and was completed in 1895; it has 175,856 square feet.
2) *American Pie* - Don McLean later used it as the title for his number one song in 1972.
3) Zugzwang
4) Australia - The founders of Wham-O noticed the popularity of the Australian product and began making plastic hoops.
5) Their left testicle - People believed that the right testicle made boy sperm, and the left made girl sperm.
6) Pajamas
7) Bessie Smith
8) Young boy
9) Their original room rates - Motel 6 charged $6 per night when it started in 1962, and Super 8 charged $8.88 per night when it started in 1974.

10) September - The time between September 9 and September 20 contains a majority of the 10 most popular birthdates. September is popular due to holiday time conceptions nine months earlier.

Quiz 5

1) The palm of your hand can be described as glabrous; what does glabrous mean?
2) What is pantheism?
3) In the 15th century, King Louis XI of France ordered Abbot de Beigne to create a musical instrument using the voices of what animal?
4) In British peerage, what is the highest rank?
5) What was the name of the only son of William Shakespeare?
6) What is the tall, pleated chef's hat called?
7) What is the difference between coffins and caskets?
8) What is the name for traditional Sardinian sheep milk cheese that contains live maggots?
9) The author of *Moll Flanders* wrote what more famous work?
10) What does the distress signal SOS stand for?

Quiz 5 Answers

1) Smooth and without hair
2) Belief that the universe is God
3) Pigs - He built a keyboard which jabbed a spike into the rumps of pigs to produce a squeal.
4) Duke
5) Hamnet
6) Toque - The 100 folds in the toque are said to represent 100 ways to cook an egg.
7) Coffins are typically tapered and six-sided; caskets are rectangular.
8) Casu marzu - The maggots are put into the cheese to promote more fermentation and break down the cheese's fats. The cheese has a very soft texture, and the maggots appear as translucent white worms. Aficionados consider it unsafe to eat the cheese if the maggots in the cheese have died, so only cheese with living maggots is usually eaten.

9) *Robinson Crusoe* - Daniel Defoe
10) Nothing - It doesn't stand for "save our ship" or anything else; it was selected as a distress signal because it is easy to transmit - three dots, three dashes, three dots.

Quiz 6

1) Mozart wrote a six-piece canon titled *Leck mich im Arsch* which translates as what?
2) Why is a second called a second?
3) What does the Spanish snack or appetizer tapas literally mean?
4) What is the largest company in the world based on revenue?
5) The name arctic is from the Greek word "arktos" meaning bear which is a reference to what?
6) The Bank of Italy, founded in San Francisco, California in 1904, grew to become what current bank?
7) What is the name of the device they use to measure your foot at a shoe store?
8) What are the only two English words with three consecutive double letters?
9) In what century did Michelangelo paint the Sistine Chapel?
10) What is a susurration?

Quiz 6 Answers

1) *Kiss My Ass*
2) It was the second division of the hour; the original term was "second minute."
3) Covers or lids
4) Walmart
5) Great and Little Bear constellations of the Northern Hemisphere
6) Bank of America
7) Brannock Device
8) Bookkeeper and bookkeeping
9) 16th century - started in 1509
10) A whisper or murmur

Quiz 7

1) According to Billboard, what was the best-selling and most-played song in the U.S. during the 1970s?
2) What celebrity inspired the name for the cartoon dog Scooby-Doo?
3) What real life person is Captain Morgan rum named after?
4) Why do pen caps have a hole in them?
5) What Jane Austen novel was originally titled *First Impressions.*
6) What does the brand name WD-40 stand for?
7) What country originated the croissant?
8) Based on concerns that there were obscene lyrics inserted, the FBI investigated what 1963 song?
9) Based on number of weeks at number one on Billboard's Hot 100, who was the top artist of the 1970s?
10) In Frank Herbert's *Dune*, what is the name of the drug commonly referred to as "the spice" that is central to the story?

Quiz 7 Answers

1) "You Light Up My Life" - Debby Boone
2) Frank Sinatra - Fred Silverman suggested naming him Scooby-Doo based on the refrain "Scooby-dooby-doo" from Sinatra's song "Strangers in the Night."
3) Sir Henry Morgan - He was a 17th century Welsh privateer. A privateer is essentially a pirate who is sanctioned by the government; he was hired by the British to protect their interests in the Caribbean from the Spanish.
4) Prevent suffocation in case they are swallowed
5) *Pride and Prejudice*
6) Water displacement, 40th formula - The chemist who developed it was trying to create a product to prevent corrosion which is done by displacing water.
7) Austria - It started in Vienna as early as the 13th century as a denser crescent shaped pastry called a kipferl and didn't show up in France in its current form until the early 1800s.
8) "Louie Louie" - They abandoned the investigation after three months in 1964 unable to discern what the lyrics really were.
9) Bee Gees

10) Melange

Quiz 8

1) If something is natiform, what does it resemble?
2) In music, what is meant by the term pianissimo?
3) What century were Chaucer's *Canterbury Tales* written?
4) Hawaiian pizza was invented in what country?
5) What is the line between two numbers in a fraction called?
6) What novel ends with "It is a far better thing I do, than I have ever done; it is a far, far better rest that I go to than I have ever known"?
7) What 19th century French painter was known for his pictures of ballet dancers?
8) Who said, "Tis better to have loved and lost than never to have loved at all"?
9) What are the small strips of wood, plastic, or metal between individual panes of glass called?
10) When Colgate started the mass production of its toothpaste in 1873, what was it originally sold in?

Quiz 8 Answers

1) A butt
2) Very softly
3) 14th century - 1387 to 1400
4) Canada - It was first created in 1962 in Ontario, Canada.
5) Vinculum
6) *A Tale of Two Cities*
7) Edgar Degas
8) Alfred Lord Tennyson
9) Muntins
10) Jars - They didn't put it in tubes until the 1890s.

Quiz 9

1) Cynophobia is fear of what?
2) What was the first country to ban corporal or physical punishment

in all forms?

3) What is Eugene O'Neill's autobiographical play?
4) What is unique about the word unprosperousness?
5) Who would use a plessor?
6) What is arachibutyrophobia?
7) What is careless handwriting, or a crude or illegible scrawl called?
8) To the nearest percent, how much larger is a British (imperial) pint compared to an American pint?
9) What is the first name of Agatha Christie's character Miss Marple?
10) What is the longest running play in history?

Quiz 9 Answers

1) Dogs - Cyno means dog in Greek.
2) Sweden - Since 1979, corporal or physical punishment in all forms is banned including parental spanking.
3) *Long Day's Journey into Night*
4) Longest English word where each letter occurs at least twice - 16 letters
5) Doctor – It is the small hammer with a rubber head used to test reflexes.
6) Fear of peanut butter sticking to the roof of your mouth
7) Griffonage
8) 20% larger
9) Jane
10) *The Mousetrap* - It is an Agatha Christie murder mystery play and has been running in London's West End since 1952 - over 27,000 performances.

Quiz 10

1) Lexico was the original name for what popular board game?
2) Who has been on the cover of *Time* magazine more times than any other person?
3) What was the first soft drink sold in all aluminum cans?
4) What was Buddy Holly's real first name?
5) What is the sound from the rustling of silk or similar cloth called?

6) What is the oldest surviving musical instrument?
7) In "The Twelve Days of Christmas," my true love sent to me 10 what?
8) When bubble wrap was invented, it was originally intended to be used for what?
9) What does Crayola (as in the crayon) mean?
10) What was Elvis Presley's first song to hit number one on Billboard's Hot 100?

Quiz 10 Answers

1) Scrabble
2) Richard Nixon - 55 appearances
3) RC Cola or Diet-Rite Cola - 1964
4) Charles
5) Scroop
6) Flute - Flutes as old as 43,000 years have been found.
7) Lords a leaping
8) Wallpaper
9) Oily chalk - It combines the French word "craie" meaning chalk with "ola" shortened from the French word "oléagineux" meaning oily.
10) "Heartbreak Hotel" - 1956

Quiz 11

1) What was the first book Mark Twain published?
2) On a building, what is an interfenestration?
3) In what century was Cervantes's *Don Quixote* first published?
4) September's name comes from the Latin "septem" meaning seven, so why is it the ninth month of the year?
5) In human behavior, what is dysania?
6) What is the most popular school name in the U.S.?
7) Most Japanese schools don't employ janitors or custodians; who cleans the schools?
8) In *Peter and the Wolf*, what instrument represents the duck?
9) What is the name of the Russian triangular guitar?

10) Who wrote the short story "Rip Van Winkle"?

Quiz 11 Answers

1) The *Celebrated Jumping Frog of Calaveras County* - 1867
2) Space between two windows
3) 17th century - 1605
4) It was the seventh month in the old Roman calendar where the year started with March; its name was carried over to the Julian and current Gregorian calendars where it is the ninth month.
5) State of finding it hard to get out of bed in the morning
6) Lincoln Elementary School
7) Students - They believe that requiring students to clean the school teaches respect, responsibility, and promotes equality.
8) Oboe
9) Balalaika
10) Washington Irving

Quiz 12

1) What is it called when you mishear or misinterpret a phrase in a way that gives it a new meaning such as when you mishear the lyrics of a song and insert words that sound similar and make sense?
2) How many languages are written right to left?
3) Who was the Roman goddess of wisdom?
4) What is the name for a word with two opposite meanings such as clip which can mean to fasten or detach?
5) The device that would evolve into the chainsaw was developed for what purpose?
6) If you have a buccula, what do you have?
7) Mr. and Mrs. are abbreviations for what?
8) What was the first pizza chain in the U.S.?
9) Charles Stratton became famous as what circus act under P.T. Barnum?
10) In Greek mythology, who was the youngest son of Cronos and Rhea?

Quiz 12 Answers

1) Mondegreen
2) 12 - Arabic, Aramaic, Azeri, Divehi, Fula, Hebrew, Kurdish, N'ko, Persian, Rohingya, Syriac, Urdu
3) Minerva
4) Contronym
5) Childbirth aid - Around 1780, two doctors were trying to create something to help remove bone and cartilage from the birth canal to widen it during problematic childbirths. At the time, this method was preferred to caesarians and was done with a saw and knife. The early chainsaw developed for this purpose looked like a regular knife with a small chain around it operated by a hand crank.
6) Double chin
7) Master and mistress
8) Pizza Hut - 1958
9) General Tom Thumb
10) Zeus

Quiz 13

1) What is a letter or combination of letters in a word that are not pronounced (for example, the "gh" combination in the word night) called?
2) Who was the first woman other than the queen to appear on British currency?
3) What is the Statue of Liberty made of?
4) What is the feeling you get when you experience something you're already very familiar with, but it feels completely new to you like it is your first time called?
5) Written out in English, what is the first number that contains the letter a?
6) Who is likely the bestselling author in history?
7) In France, most toilet paper sold for home use is what color?
8) What is the only U.S. state that doesn't have an open bottle law prohibiting drivers or passengers from drinking while driving?
9) The S.O.S Soap Pad is a household cleaning product made from steel wool saturated with soap; what does S.O.S stand for in this

case?

10) Based on number of weeks at number one on Billboard's Hot 100, who was the top artist of the 1990s?

Quiz 13 Answers

1) Aphthong
2) Florence Nightingale - in circulation from 1975-1994
3) Copper - About 62,000 pounds of copper were used to create it, and it looked like a new penny when it was first created.
4) Jamais vu - It is the opposite of déjà vu.
5) One thousand
6) Agatha Christie - 2 to 4 billion copies
7) Pink
8) Mississippi - If the driver maintains a blood alcohol content below the 0.08 legal limit; it is legal to drink and drive.
9) Save our saucepans - The inventor's wife came up with the name; the period after the last "S" is left off so the name wasn't identical to the distress signal and could be trademarked.
10) Mariah Carey

Quiz 14

1) In what country was pepperoni created?
2) In the novel *The Wonderful Wizard of Oz*, what is the name of the Good Witch of the South?
3) What is arithmomania?
4) In the Peanuts comic strip, what is the name of Snoopy's sister?
5) What common word comes from Greek meaning "drawing with light"?
6) Who was the Greek equivalent of the Roman god Jupiter?
7) What author created more than 1,700 of our common English words, more than any other person?
8) Which two Shakespeare plays are written entirely in verse?
9) A butt is an actual measurement unit for wine; a buttload of wine is how many U.S. gallons?
10) What is the burnt part of a candlewick called?

Quiz 14 Answers

1) United States
2) Glinda
3) Compulsion to count things - In traditional vampire lore, it is one of the weaknesses of vampires and can be used to defend against them by putting grains of rice or sand out which they will be compelled to count.
4) Belle
5) Photography
6) Zeus - king of the gods
7) William Shakespeare - He did it by changing nouns into verbs, changing verbs into adjectives, connecting words never used together, adding prefixes and suffixes, and creating original words; he also created many common phrases. Some examples of his creations include fancy-free, lie low, foregone conclusion, a sorry sight, for goodness sake, good riddance, dishearten, eventful, new-fangled, hot-blooded, rant, laughable, a wild goose chase.
8) *Richard II and King John*
9) 126 gallons
10) Snaste

Quiz 15

1) Based on number of weeks at number one on Billboard's Hot 100, who was the top artist of the 1960s?
2) According to Billboard, what was the best-selling and most-played song in the U.S. during the 1990s?
3) What is the word for the day after tomorrow?
4) Who is the largest private employer in the world?
5) What is the longest word in the English language with only one vowel?
6) Who was on the cover of the first *People* magazine in 1974?
7) What is unique about the word "eunoia"?
8) According to Billboard, what was the best-selling and most-played song in the U.S. during the 1960s?
9) What famous European writer was captured by Turkish pirates and held as a slave for five years in Algiers?

10) What two books in the Bible list the Ten Commandments?

Quiz 15 Answers

1) Beatles
2) "How Do I Live" - LeAnn Rimes
3) Overmorrow
4) Walmart
5) Strengths – nine letters
6) Mia Farrow
7) It is the shortest English word that contains all five vowels. It means goodwill towards an audience, either perceived or real.
8) "The Twist" - Chubby Checker
9) Miguel de Cervantes - author of *Don Quixote*
10) Exodus and Deuteronomy

Quiz 16

1) What was the first rock and roll song to hit number one on Billboard's pop charts?
2) What is the primary difference between our current Gregorian calendar and the prior Julian calendar?
3) What is the piece of cardboard that goes around your hot cup of coffee called?
4) What is the name of the leader of the pigs in George Orwell's *Animal Farm*?
5) What is the feeling of having already dreamed something that you are now experiencing called?
6) How did the 3 Musketeers candy bar get its name?
7) What is an autological word?
8) The world's largest condom manufacturer is headquartered in what country?
9) Daniel Quilp, an ill-tempered dwarf, is one of the main antagonists in what Dickens novel?
10) In Shakespeare's *Romeo and Juliet*, who is Romeo's love before he meets Juliet?

Quiz 16 Answers

1) "Rock Around the Clock" - 1955
2) Years that are evenly divisible by 100 are not leap years unless they are also evenly divisible by 400. This corrects for the inaccuracy in the length of the year in the Julian calendar.
3) Zarf
4) Napoleon
5) Deja reve
6) It originally came in a package with three pieces with different nougat flavors - vanilla, chocolate, and strawberry.
7) A word that describes itself. Some examples include word, noun, polysyllabic, unhyphenated, suffixed.
8) Malaysia - Karex is the largest manufacturer in the world.
9) *The Old Curiosity Shop*
10) Rosaline

Quiz 17

1) Portland cement gets its name from what country?
2) What is the shape of a Pringles chip called?
3) What novel opens with the line "The Mole had been working very hard all the morning, spring-cleaning his little home"?
4) Why are sewer manhole covers always round instead of square or rectangular?
5) If you wrote out every number in English (one, two, three, etc.), you wouldn't use the letter b until what number?
6) In Sanskrit, what well known geographic feature means "house of snow"?
7) A university has a campus; what does campus literally mean?
8) In what century was Milton's *Paradise Lost* published?
9) Based on number of weeks at number one on Billboard's Hot 100, who was the top artist of the 2010s?
10) What do the words uncopyrightable and dermatoglyphics have in common?

Quiz 17 Answers

1) England - It was created in the mid-19th century and is named because of its similarity to Portland stone, which was quarried on the Isle of Portland off the coast of England.
2) Hyperbolic paraboloid - It allows easier stacking and reduces broken chips.
3) *The Wind in the Willows* - 1908
4) A round cover can't fall through the opening. The cover rests on a lip that is smaller than the cover; no matter its dimensions, a square or rectangular cover could always fall through.
5) One billion
6) Himalayas
7) Field - from Latin
8) 17th century - 1667
9) Drake
10) Longest English words with no repeated letters

Quiz 18

1) In the original story of *Pinocchio*, he gets mad at the talking cricket when he gets some advice he doesn't like and does what?
2) Casanova graduated from college at the age of 17 with a degree in what?
3) What mythic character rode horses called Llamrei and Hengroen?
4) In food, what is the cornicione?
5) What musical term means to play a piece of music lively and fast?
6) What is the singular form of spaghetti?
7) If you complete courses in archery, pistol shooting, sailing, and fencing at MIT, you can be recognized as a certified what?
8) Written out in English, what is the first number alphabetically no matter how high you go?
9) What was first food product tested in a microwave oven?
10) What city was Superman born in?

Quiz 18 Answers

1) He kills the cricket. The talking cricket returns later as a ghost to

give Pinocchio additional advice.

2) Law - He started college at age 12.
3) King Arthur
4) Outer part of a pizza crust
5) Allegro
6) Spaghetto
7) Pirate
8) Eight
9) Popcorn
10) Kryptonopolis

Quiz 19

1) Percivale, Lionell, Gareth, Bleoberis, Lucan, Palomedes, Lamorak, and Pelleas were members of what mythic group?
2) What is the loop on a belt that keeps the end in place after it has passed through the buckle called?
3) French filmmaker Albert Lamorisse (1922-1970) is best known for creating award winning short films such as *The Red Balloon* (1956) which won the grand prize at Cannes and an Oscar, but he also invented what well known board game?
4) In the U.S., who is the second largest purchaser of explosive devices behind the U.S. Department of Defense?
5) In the Chinese zodiac, what animal comes last alphabetically?
6) What is unique about the words bulb, angel, and month?
7) What is a word, art form, or other symbolic representation whose elements retain meaning when viewed or interpreted from a different direction, perspective, or orientation (for example, the word swims reads the same when it is rotated 180 degrees) called?
8) Based on number of weeks at number one on Billboard's Hot 100, who was the top artist of the 1980s?
9) Who is the largest employer in the world?
10) In the Anglo-Saxon epic poem, who kills Grendel?

Quiz 19 Answers

1) Knights of the Round Table

2) Keeper
3) Risk - 1957
4) Walt Disney Company
5) Tiger
6) They have no rhyming words in the English language.
7) Ambigram
8) Michael Jackson
9) United States Department of Defense
10) Beowulf

Quiz 20

1) According to the nursery rhyme, how many blackbirds were baked in a pie?
2) According to Billboard, what was the best-selling and most-played song in the U.S. during the 2000s?
3) What country has the most post offices?
4) The term "pixel" is short for what?
5) Floccinaucinihilipilification is one of the longer words in the English language; what does it mean?
6) What is the name of Rudolph the Red-Nosed Reindeer's girlfriend?
7) What is the name of the mascot depicted as a portly older man with a moustache, suit, bowtie and top hat in the game Monopoly?
8) What does alma mater literally mean?
9) According to Billboard, what was the best-selling and most-played song in the U.S. during the 1980s?
10) Which of her characters did Agatha Christie call "a detestable, bombastic, tiresome, egocentric little creep"?

Quiz 20 Answers

1) 24 - four and twenty
2) "We Belong Together" - Mariah Carey
3) India
4) Picture element
5) The action of estimating something as worthless.

6) Clarice
7) Rich Uncle Pennybags - He was inspired by tycoon J.P. Morgan.
8) Generous mother - from Latin
9) "Physical" - Olivia Newton John
10) Hercule Poirot

Quiz 21

1) What female voice comes between contralto and soprano?
2) Who wrote *Peter Pan*?
3) What is the only work of art Michelangelo ever signed?
4) Who said, "That which does not kill us makes us stronger"?
5) On *Sesame Street*, what is the name of Big Bird's teddy bear?
6) David kills Goliath in what book of the Bible?
7) Who wrote "The Gift of the Magi" and is known for his surprise endings?
8) What is the ringing or tinkling sound a bell makes called?
9) With just the current pope, how many popes per square mile are there in Vatican City?
10) What was the Beatles first U.S. number one hit?

Quiz 21 Answers

1) Mezzo-soprano
2) James Matthew Barrie
3) *The Pieta*
4) Friedrich Nietzsche
5) Radar - It is a tribute Gary Burghoff who played Walter "Radar" O'Reilly on *M*A*S*H*.
6) Samuel
7) O. Henry or William Sydney Porter
8) Tintinnabulation
9) 5.9
10) "I Want to Hold Your Hand"

Quiz 22

1) Junk email is called spam because of what comedy group?
2) What is the only king in standard card deck of cards that doesn't have a mustache?
3) Before being dropped, what symbol that is still used today was the 27th letter of the English alphabet?
4) In early Greece and Rome, why was it essentially impossible to understand a text on a first reading?
5) How many of the Beatles could read or write music?
6) What is the metal part of a pencil that holds the eraser called?
7) What does hors d'oeuvre literally mean in French?
8) What did the toy company Mattel originally sell?
9) Which of Shakespeare's plays is responsible for starlings being introduced to North America?
10) What is the more common name for serigraphy?

Quiz 22 Answers

1) Monty Python - The 1970 *Monty Python's Flying Circus* sketch where a waitress is reading out the menu with an endless variety of Spam options and a chorus of Vikings begins singing "Spam, Spam, Spam, Spam" resulted in spam being used generically for something that drowns out or overrides everything else like junk email does.
2) King of hearts
3) Ampersand (&) - It wasn't called an ampersand at that time and was referred to as "and."
4) There was no punctuation or spacing and no distinction between uppercase and lowercase letters; text was just a run on string of letters.
5) None - When they needed to write music for others to play, arrangers at sheet music publishing companies would do it.
6) Ferrule
7) Outside the work – It is not part of the normal meal courses.
8) Picture frames and later dollhouse furniture
9) *Henry IV, Part 1* - The starling is only mentioned in Shakespeare's plays in *Henry IV, Part 1* and was purposefully introduced to North

America in 1890 by Eugene Schieffelin who wanted to import every bird mentioned in Shakespeare's works. He released starlings in New York's Central Park.

10) Silk screen printing

Quiz 23

1) One floor above the U.S. Supreme Court is an area named "The Highest Court in the Land"; what is it?
2) What is unique about the words facetiously, abstemiously, and arseniously?
3) What are the little bumps on the surface of a table tennis paddle called?
4) In Sweden, blood donors get what each time their blood is used?
5) Cellophane was invented in 1908 for what purpose?
6) What food gets its name from the French word for melted?
7) In what country was Nutella invented?
8) What is the groove in the upper lip that runs from the top of the lip to the nose called?
9) Why are pencils typically yellow?
10) What food dish gets its name from the French meaning "stirred food"?

Quiz 23 Answers

1) Basketball court - It was once a spare room to house journals. In the 1940s, it was converted into a workout area for courthouse workers, and backboards and baskets were installed later to create a smaller than regulation basketball court.
2) They each contain all six vowels (including y) in alphabetical order.
3) Pips
4) A text
5) Liquid repellant cloth - The inventor saw wine spilled on a tablecloth.
6) Fondue
7) Italy - An Italian pastry maker in 1946 was looking for a cheaper alternative to chocolate which was in short supply due to WWII, so he mixed hazelnuts with some cocoa.

8) Philtrum
9) It is the traditional color of Chinese royalty. In the 1890s when pencils started to be mass produced, the best graphite came from China. Manufacturers wanted people to know they used the best quality graphite, so they painted them yellow, the color of Chinese royalty.
10) Ratatouille

Quiz 24

1) In the Peanuts comic strip, what is Peppermint Patty's real name?
2) Italian painter Jacopo Robusti was better known under what name?
3) The word avocado derives from the Nahuatl Indian word "āhuacatl" meaning what?
4) In the book of Genesis in the Bible, what did God create on the fourth day?
5) What is the most money you can have in change and not be able to make change for a dollar?
6) Tashtego, Daggoo, and Fedallah are all characters in what novel?
7) What famous Italian painter spent the last four years of his life on the run from murder charges?
8) In Arthurian legend, what was the name for the empty chair at the Round Table reserved for the knight who would one day find the Holy Grail?
9) What is the name for a person with the same name who shows up in results when you Google yourself?
10) "In my younger and more vulnerable years my father gave me some advice that I've been turning over in my mind ever since. Whenever you feel like criticizing anyone, he told me, just remember that all the people in this world haven't had the advantages that you've had," is the opening line from what book?

Quiz 24 Answers

1) Patricia Reichardt
2) Tintoretto - his middle name
3) Testicle
4) Sun, Moon, and stars
5) $1.19 - three quarters, four dimes and four pennies

6) *Moby Dick* - They are harpooners.
7) Caravaggio (1571-1610)
8) Siege Perilous
9) Googleganger
10) *The Great Gatsby* – F. Scott Fitzgerald

Quiz 25

1) Written out in English, what is the second number alphabetically no matter how high you go?
2) What is the word for pocket lint?
3) Including fast food, what is the oldest restaurant chain in the U.S.?
4) Crapulous is the feeling you get from what?
5) Who was the first rock star arrested on stage?
6) What well known author created the character of the Cisco Kid?
7) Millions of Japanese treat themselves to what fast food chain food each Christmas?
8) What are the only two countries where Coca-Cola isn't sold?
9) What country originated the tradition of exchanging Christmas gifts?
10) What is a mononymous person?

Quiz 25 Answers

1) Eight billion
2) Gnurr
3) A&W – founded in Lodi, California in 1919
4) Eating or drinking too much
5) Jim Morrison - On December 9, 1967, he was arrested as he performed onstage at the New Haven Arena in Connecticut. He was arrested for an incident that took place with a police officer before the show.
6) O. Henry - The Cisco Kid appeared in his 1907 short story "The Caballero's Way."
7) KFC chicken - In 1974, KFC created a Japanese marketing campaign promoting "Kentucky for Christmas"; it gained hold quickly to the point that Christmas time KFC sales can be 10 times the normal

sales volume. Christmas dinner often requires ordering weeks in advance or waiting in line for hours.

8) Cuba and North Korea.
9) Italy - Romans
10) Someone who is known and addressed by one name

Quiz 26

1) How many letters are in the longest English word with one syllable?
2) What is the wave-like gob of toothpaste you put on your toothbrush called?
3) What country uses a 13-month calendar with 12 months of 30 days each and a 13th month of five days for regular years and six days for leap years and commemorates Christmas on January 7?
4) What was the name of the only brother of the Bronte sisters?
5) What is the oldest hamburger restaurant chain in the U.S.?
6) Which country spends more time reading per capita than any other?
7) What is probably the closest thing to a universal word because it means the same thing in every language and everybody in almost every language says it?
8) What is the word for the third to the last thing?
9) What year was the first automatically sliced commercial bread produced?
10) Coca-Cola didn't entirely remove cocaine as an ingredient until what year?

Quiz 26 Answers

1) 10 – scraunched, meaning to crush or crush noisily
2) Nurdle
3) Ethiopia
4) Branwell - He was the fourth of the Bronte children and was a poet and painter; he died at 31.
5) White Castle – It was founded in 1921 in Wichita, Kansas; the original hamburger slider was 5 cents.
6) India

7) Huh
8) Antepenultimate
9) 1928 - Missouri
10) 1929 - Most of the cocaine had been eliminated in 1903.

Quiz 27

1) What popular Christmas character was created in 1939 in a holiday coloring book created by Montgomery Ward?
2) What are the rings or spots of light you see when you rub your eyes called?
3) What is unique about the word spoonfeed?
4) What is the skin connecting your fingers and thumb called?
5) What company uses almost 1% of the world's commercial wood supply
6) What is a word that makes a completely different word spelled backwards (for example, stressed and desserts) called?
7) Who painted *The Scream*?
8) In clothing, what is the armscye?
9) What was the last letter added to the English alphabet?
10) What does defenestrate mean?

Quiz 27 Answers

1) Rudolph the Red-Nosed Reindeer
2) Phosphenes
3) It is the longest English word with letters arranged in reverse alphabetical order.
4) Purlicue
5) Ikea
6) Semordnilap - The word semordnilap is palindromes spelled backwards.
7) Edvard Munch
8) Armhole
9) J - The letters I and J were treated the same for a long time; J finally entered the alphabet in the 19th century.
10) Throw out a window

Movies

Quiz 1

1) In *Jaws*, Quint describes the sinking of a ship during WWII and how the sharks attacked the survivors. His story is based on a real event; what is the name of the ship that sank?
2) What was the number one U.S. box office film released in the 2000s?
3) What is the name of the computer in *2001: A Space Odyssey*?
4) What was the number one U.S. box office film released in the 1940s?
5) *The Rose* stars Bette Midler; the film is loosely based on the life of what singer?
6) Who plays the role of Pharaoh Rameses II in *The Ten Commandments*?
7) Who provides the voice for sultry Jessica Rabbit in *Who Framed Roger Rabbit*?
8) In *Mr. Deeds Goes to Town*, what is the title character's first name?
9) What is the name of the town that is the setting for *It's a Wonderful Life*?
10) What is the name of John Travolta's character in *Saturday Night Fever*?

Quiz 1 Answers

1) *USS Indianapolis* – After four days in the water, only 317 of the original 1,196-man crew were rescued. Estimates of how many died due to shark attacks range from a few dozen to 150; it is the U.S. Navy's single worst loss at sea and the worst shark attack in recorded history.
2) *Avatar* – 2009
3) HAL 9000 – HAL stands for heuristically programmed algorithmic computer.
4) *Bambi* – 1942
5) Janis Joplin
6) Yul Brynner

7) Kathleen Turner
8) Longfellow
9) Bedford Falls
10) Tony Manero

Quiz 2

1) What Quentin Tarantino movie is about two mob hitmen, a boxer, a gangster's wife, and a pair of diner bandits?
2) In *Coneheads*, what planet are the Coneheads from?
3) Who does James Cagney portray in *Yankee Doodle Dandy*?
4) In what science fiction movie does Kevin Spacey say, "Every being in the universe knows right from wrong, Mark"?
5) In *Fight Club*, who plays the nameless first-person narrator?
6) Who plays the title role in *The Princess Bride*?
7) What comedy that spawned two sequels is set in 1954 and has a group of Florida high school students trying to lose their virginity?
8) What two actresses play the two women whose lives are dedicated to ballet in *The Turning Point*?
9) What was the number one U.S. box office film released in the 1960s?
10) What movie has the tagline "The greatest trick the devil ever pulled was to convince the world he didn't exist"?

Quiz 2 Answers

1) *Pulp Fiction* - 1994
2) Remulak
3) George M. Cohan
4) *K-PAX* - 2001
5) Edward Norton
6) Robin Wright
7) *Porky's* - 1981
8) Anne Bancroft and Shirley MacLaine
9) *The Sound of Music* – 1965
10) *The Usual Suspects* - 1995

Quiz 3

1) What science fiction film was loosely based on Shakespeare's *The Tempest* and was the film debut of Leslie Nielsen?
2) In *Ratatouille*, what is the name of the rat who can cook voiced by Patton Oswalt?
3) What actors play the two opposing lawyers in *Inherit the Wind*?
4) Who plays the dual roles of Madeleine Elster and Judy Barton in *Vertigo*?
5) Who plays the title role in *My Man Godfrey*?
6) What was the number one U.S. box office film released in the 1930s?
7) Who won a Best Original Screenplay Oscar for *Good Will Hunting*?
8) In *300*, the Spartans fight the Persians in 480 BC at what battle?
9) What is the full name of Humphrey Bogart's character in *Casablanca*?
10) What is the only film where cartoon characters from Walt Disney and Warner Brothers appear together?

Quiz 3 Answers

1) *Forbidden Planet* - 1956
2) Remy
3) Spencer Tracy and Fredric March
4) Kim Novak
5) William Powell
6) *Gone with the Wind* – Inflation adjusted, it is the all-time U.S. box office record holder.
7) Matt Damon and Ben Affleck
8) Thermopylae
9) Rick Blaine
10) *Who Framed Roger Rabbit* – 1988

Quiz 4

1) Gregory Peck stars as Jimmy Ringo, a notorious gunman, in what movie?

2) What movie has Lana Turner convincing a drifter to help her murder her husband?
3) Who was the first actor to win the Best Actor Oscar for a musical performance?
4) What is the name of the character Katharine Ross plays in *Butch Cassidy and the Sundance Kid*?
5) Who directed *Ferris Bueller's Day Off*, *Uncle Buck*, *Weird Science*, and *Planes, Trains and Automobiles*?
6) Special Forces operative turned mercenary Wade Wilson is subjected to a rogue experiment that leaves him with new powers; what is the movie?
7) What crime drama stars Michael Douglas, Catherine Zeta-Jones, and Benicio Del Toro in a Best Supporting Actor Oscar winning performance?
8) What musical film has won the most Oscars?
9) What Best Picture Oscar winner depicts the childhood, adolescence and young adulthood of an African American gay man growing up in a rough Miami neighborhood?
10) For what film was the first posthumous Oscar of any kind awarded?

Quiz 4 Answers

1) *The Gunfighter* - 1950
2) *The Postman Always Rings Twice* - 1946
3) James Cagney – *Yankee Doodle Dandy* in 1942
4) Etta Place
5) John Hughes
6) *Deadpool* - 2016
7) *Traffic* - 2000
8) *Gigi* (1958) – nine Oscars
9) *Moonlight* - 2016
10) *Gone with the Wind* – screenwriter Sidney Howard

Quiz 5

1) With nine wins, what film holds the British Academy Awards (BAFTAs) record?
2) Who directed *A Room with a View*, *Howards End*, and *The Remains of*

the Day?

3) Who plays Julius Caesar in *Cleopatra*?
4) In *The Terminator*, what is the name of the system that became self-aware and tried to wipe out all humans?
5) What is the name of the summer camp in *Meatballs*?
6) In *Yours, Mine and Ours*, who plays the widower with 10 children and the widow with 8 children who marry?
7) In *Planes, Trains, and Automobiles*, John Candy's character Del Griffith sells what for a living?
8) Who is the only person nominated for Oscars for acting, writing, producing, and directing the same film?
9) Who has the longest screen time performance to ever win the Best Actress Oscar?
10) In *Love Actually*, who plays the aging rocker Billy Mack?

Quiz 5 Answers

1) *Butch Cassidy and the Sundance Kid* - 1969
2) James Ivory
3) Rex Harrison
4) Skynet
5) Camp North Star
6) Henry Fonda and Lucille Ball
7) Shower curtain rings
8) Warren Beatty – twice for *Heaven Can Wait* (1978) and *Reds* (1981)
9) Vivien Leigh – 2 hours 23 minutes and 32 seconds for *Gone with the Wind* (1939)
10) Bill Nighy

Quiz 6

1) Adjusted for inflation, what is the highest grossing western of all time in the U.S.?
2) Based on actual events from Virginia in 1971, what movie follows a newly appointed high school football coach and his team in their first season as a racially integrated unit?
3) What character did Basil Rathbone play in *The Adventures of Robin*

Hood?

4) Who wrote the novel on which *Breakfast at Tiffany's* is based?
5) Who plays the title role in *Gunga Din*?
6) What was the first movie based on a John Grisham novel?
7) What is the former profession of John Wayne's character in *The Quiet Man*?
8) *This Is the End* has celebrities playing themselves stuck in a house as the biblical apocalypse occurs; what celebrity's house are they stuck in?
9) What film has con man Moses Pray taking on nine-year-old Addie Loggins as his partner?
10) What is the first film by a black director to win the Best Picture Oscar?

Quiz 6 Answers

1) *Butch Cassidy and the Sundance Kid* – 1969
2) *Remember the Titans* - 2000
3) Sir Guy of Gisbourne
4) Truman Capote
5) Sam Jaffe
6) *The Firm* - 1993
7) Boxer
8) James Franco
9) *Paper Moon* - 1973
10) *12 Years a Slave* - 2013

Quiz 7

1) In *The Courtship of Eddie's Father*, who plays the young son Eddie who wants to see his father remarry?
2) In *Dances with Wolves*, who plays Stands With A Fist, a white woman who was raised by the Sioux?
3) What film has a mobster named Chili Palmer who goes to Hollywood and gets involved in the movie business?
4) In *Tremors*, what actor and actress play the survivalist couple who help battle the giant wormlike creatures?

5) What film had a 20-year gap between its release and winning an Oscar?
6) Nicolas Cage and Holly Hunter play a childless couple who steal a baby in *Raising Arizona*; who directed the film?
7) Barbra Streisand plays what real life performer in *Funny Girl*?
8) What cartoon duo won seven Oscars for best animated short film?
9) In *City Slickers*, three middle-aged friends go on an adventure holiday driving cattle; who won a Best Supporting Actor Oscar for their role as the trail boss Curly?
10) What film stars Paul Newman as a white man raised by Apaches who tries to save the passengers of a stagecoach from bandits?

Quiz 7 Answers

1) Ron Howard
2) Mary McDonnell
3) *Get Shorty* – 1995
4) Michael Gross and Reba McEntire
5) *Limelight* – It was officially released in 1952 but was not released in Los Angeles County and eligible for an Oscar until 1972. It won a Best Original Score Oscar in 1973 and is Charlie Chaplin's only competitive Oscar win.
6) Joel and Ethan Coen
7) Fanny Brice
8) Tom and Jerry
9) Jack Palance
10) *Hombre* - 1967

Quiz 8

1) What are the names of the two rival department stores in *Miracle on 34th Street*?
2) What movie beat *Citizen Kane* for the Best Picture Oscar?
3) What was the most expensive Hollywood film made during the 1930s?
4) In *Underworld*, who plays Viktor, the oldest and strongest of the elder vampires?
5) What is the name Tom Hanks gives to the volleyball he talks to in

Cast Away?

6) Who wrote and directed *The Sixth Sense*?
7) Who plays Buttons the Clown in *The Greatest Show on Earth*?
8) After *Sleeping Beauty* in 1959, what was the next fairy tale produced by Disney?
9) In *Up*, what is the South American destination that Carl wants to travel to in his house lifted by balloons?
10) What actors play the unlikely prospecting partners who also share a wife in the singing western *Paint Your Wagon*?

Quiz 8 Answers

1) Macy's and Gimbels
2) *How Green Was My Valley* - 1941
3) *Gone with the Wind* - $4 million at the time
4) Bill Nighy
5) Wilson
6) M. Night Shyamalan
7) James Stewart – He plays the entire movie in his clown makeup.
8) *The Little Mermaid* – 1989
9) Paradise Falls
10) Lee Marvin and Clint Eastwood

Quiz 9

1) Who was the first actor or actress to reject their Oscar win?
2) In *Ice Age*, Manny, Sid, and Diego are the three heroes who save the human baby; what three kinds of animals are they?
3) Who are the three singing and dancing stars of *Singin' in the Rain*?
4) What was the most expensive Hollywood film made during the 1980s?
5) In what country is the action adventure comedy *Romancing the Stone* set?
6) What South African film features a bushman in the Kalahari Desert who discovers a Coke bottle?
7) Who is the first protagonist in a Disney animated feature to have no dialogue?

8) *The Shawshank Redemption* is based on a short story by Stephen King. For the movie, they dropped the first part of the story title which is a major Hollywood star's name; what is the name?
9) What was the word's first computer animated feature film?
10) Who plays Sister Mary Benedict in *The Bells of St. Mary's*?

Quiz 9 Answers

1) George C. Scott – 1971 for *Patton*
2) Woolly mammoth, sloth, saber-toothed tiger
3) Gene Kelly, Donald O'Connor, Debbie Reynolds – Reynolds was only 19 at the time; she had no prior dance experience and commuted to the set by bus from her parent's home where she lived.
4) *Who Framed Roger Rabbit* - $70 million at the time
5) Colombia – Ironically, the story centers around an American kidnapping in Colombia, but an increase in American kidnappings in Colombia caused the filming to be moved to Mexico.
6) *The Gods Must Be Crazy* - 1980
7) Dumbo – 1941
8) Rita Hayworth – The Stephen King short story title is *Rita Hayworth and the Shawshank Redemption.* Rita Hayworth is the first poster Andy has on the wall in his cell; the prisoners are also watching the Rita Hayworth film *Gilda* in one scene.
9) *Toy Story* – 1995
10) Ingrid Bergman

Quiz 10

1) Who directed *The Lord of the Rings* trilogy?
2) What Oscar winning comedy features a famous Walls of Jericho scene?
3) What Disney film features Uncle Remus telling tales of Brer Rabbit?
4) What sports-based movie with Keira Knightley has the tagline "Sometimes, to follow your dreams... you've got to bend the rules!"?
5) Susan Sarandon won a Best Actress Oscar for her portrayal of a nun who befriends a convicted killer on death row in what movie?
6) Who is the oldest Best Director Oscar winner?

7) What movie has the Hoover family trying to get to California so that young daughter Olive can compete in a beauty pageant?
8) Who stars as Scrooge in the 1951 version of *A Christmas Carol*?
9) What Hitchcock film has two strangers trading murders?
10) *All the King's Men* is based on the life of what politician?

Quiz 10 Answers

1) Peter Jackson
2) *It Happened One Night* – Clark Gable and Claudette Colbert build a wall with a blanket hanging on a line between their beds when they share a room.
3) *Song of the South* - 1946
4) *Bend It Like Beckham* - 2002
5) *Dead Man Walking* - 1995
6) Clint Eastwood – 74 at the time for *Million Dollar Baby* in 2005
7) *Little Miss Sunshine* - 2006
8) Alastair Sim
9) *Strangers on a Train* - 1951
10) Huey Long – Louisiana governor

Quiz 11

1) What was the first film to win at least 10 Oscars?
2) In *Gremlins*, the cute, furry creature Gizmo is what kind of animal?
3) What are the names of the four turtles in *Teenage Mutant Ninja Turtles*?
4) In *Life of Pi*, what is the name of the tiger?
5) What is the first name of the possessed girl Linda Blair plays in *The Exorcist*?
6) Where is the resort where Baby and Johnny fall in love in *Dirty Dancing*?
7) What was the most expensive Hollywood film made in the 1990s?
8) What film features the line "Love means never having to say you're sorry"?
9) What was James Dean's last movie?
10) Only three Christmas movies have been nominated for the Best

Picture Oscar; what are they?

Quiz 11 Answers

1) *Ben-Hur* – 1959
2) Mogwai
3) Raphael, Leonardo, Donatello, Michelangelo
4) Richard Parker
5) Regan
6) Catskill Mountains in New York
7) *Titanic* - $200 million at the time
8) *Love Story* - 1970
9) *Giant* (1956) – He died before it was released.
10) *It's a Wonderful Life* (1946), *Miracle on 34th Street* (1947), *The Bishop's Wife* (1947)

Quiz 12

1) Who plays John Doe's traveling companion in *Meet John Doe*?
2) What town is the setting for *The Music Man*?
3) Who was the first person to win directing, writing, and best picture Oscars for the same film?
4) What 1953 Marlon Brando film was banned in British theaters for 14 years?
5) What Martin Scorsese film set in 1863 stars Leonardo DiCaprio, Daniel Day-Lewis, Cameron Diaz, Jim Broadbent, John C. Reilly, Henry Thomas, Liam Neeson, and Brendan Gleeson?
6) Abbott and Costello's first starring roles were in what movie that also features the Andrews Sisters singing "Boogie Woogie Bugle Boy"?
7) What is Jimmy Stewart's full character name in *Mr. Smith Goes to Washington*?
8) In *Guardians of the Galaxy*, who is Peter Quill's ship named after?
9) Who was the first African American to win the Best Actress Oscar?
10) What movie has disgruntled Korean War veteran Walt Kowalski setting out to reform his neighbor, a Hmong teenager?

Quiz 12 Answers

1) Walter Brennan
2) River City, Iowa
3) Billy Wilder - *The Apartment* in 1960
4) *The Wild One* (1953)– It was deemed too violent to show.
5) *Gangs of New York* - 2002
6) *Buck Privates* - 1941
7) Jefferson Smith
8) Alyssa Milano – Peter Quill's childhood crush
9) Halle Berry – *Monster's Ball* (2001)
10) *Gran Torino* - 2008

Quiz 13

1) Who plays the psychopathic character Maggott in *The Dirty Dozen*?
2) *Argo* is based on a true story about an unusual plan to rescue Americans from what country?
3) Who wrote and stars in *My Big Fat Greek Wedding*?
4) In *How to Marry a Millionaire*, what three actresses play the lead roles of the young women looking for love?
5) Kevin Smith's *Clerks* is loosely based on what classic piece of 14th century literature?
6) Adjusted for inflation, what is the highest grossing R-rated movie of all time in the U.S.?
7) *The Greatest Game Ever Played* starring Shia LaBeouf is based on a true story about what major sports championship?
8) What character says, "Today, I consider myself the luckiest man on the face of the earth"?
9) Adjusted for inflation, what is the highest grossing comedy of all time in the U.S.?
10) "Pay no attention to that man behind the curtain," is from what classic movie?

Quiz 13 Answers

1) Telly Savalas

2) Iran
3) Nia Vardalos
4) Marilyn Monroe, Betty Grable, Lauren Bacall
5) *The Divine Comedy* by Dante – The main protagonist, Dante Hicks, gets his name from this, and there are nine breaks in the film to represent the nine rings of hell.
6) *The Exorcist* – 1973
7) U.S. Open – golf
8) Lou Gehrig – played by Gary Cooper in *The Pride of the Yankees* (1942)
9) *Home Alone* – 1990
10) *The Wizard of Oz* - 1939

Quiz 14

1) What Hitchcock film features Joan Fontaine and Laurence Olivier?
2) In *The Da Vinci Code*, what is the name of the military group that is charged with protecting the descendants of Jesus?
3) Sally Field won a Best Actress Oscar for her portrayal of a single woman trying to survive on a small farm during the Great Depression; what is the film?
4) In *She Done Him Wrong*, Mae West says the famous line "Why don't you come up sometime and see me?"; what actor does she say it to?
5) What was Elvis Presley's first feature film?
6) Who won a Best Actor Oscar for their portrayal of Winston Churchill in *Darkest Hour*?
7) Who plays the junkyard tycoon Harry Brock in the original *Born Yesterday*?
8) *Erin Brockovich* is based on a true story involving one of the biggest class action lawsuits in American history; what was the company that was the target of the lawsuit?
9) Two films share the record for most Oscars by a foreign film at four each; what are the movies?
10) Who plays Mrs. Muir in *The Ghost and Mrs. Muir*?

Quiz 14 Answers

1) *Rebecca* - 1940

2) Knights Templar
3) *Places in the Heart* - 1984
4) Cary Grant
5) *Love Me Tender* - 1956
6) Gary Oldman
7) Broderick Crawford
8) Pacific Gas & Electric
9) *Fanny and Alexander* (1982) and *Crouching Tiger, Hidden Dragon* (2000)
10) Gene Tierney

Quiz 15

1) What film starring Kathleen Turner and Nicolas Cage has the tagline "Knowing what you know now, what would you do differently?"
2) Who plays the Civil War veteran father in *The Yearling*?
3) In *White Christmas*, what two actresses play the sister act who become romantically involved with Bing Crosby and Danny Kaye?
4) What is the name of Robert De Niro's character in *Taxi Driver*?
5) Who was the conductor for the music in *Fantasia*?
6) What biographical film directed by Sydney Pollack and starring Robert Redford and Meryl Streep won nine Oscars?
7) In *My Fair Lady*, who plays Colonel Pickering who bets Henry Higgins that he can't transform Eliza Doolittle?
8) Who won the only Oscar for *Cool Hand Luke*?
9) Who plays the title role in *Gypsy*?
10) What Quentin Tarantino western was nominated for Best Picture and features Christoph Waltz in the longest Best Supporting Actor Oscar winning performance ever?

Quiz 15 Answers

1) *Peggy Sue Got Married* - 1986
2) Gregory Peck
3) Rosemary Clooney and Vera-Ellen
4) Travis Bickle

5) Leopold Stokowski
6) *Out of Africa* - 1985
7) Wilfrid Hyde-White
8) George Kennedy – Best Supporting Actor Oscar
9) Natalie Wood – portrays stripper Gypsy Rose Lee
10) *Django Unchained* - 2012

Quiz 16

1) In *We Are Marshall*, a plane crash claims the lives of most of the Marshall University football team; what state is Marshall University in?
2) In *Animal House*, what is the name of the college?
3) Who plays James Dean's love interest in *Rebel Without a Cause*?
4) What character does Jackie Gleason play in *Smokey and the Bandit*?
5) Who plays the character whose dismembered body is fed into the woodchipper in *Fargo*?
6) What was the Beatles' first movie?
7) In *Edward Scissorhands*, who plays the inventor who creates Edward?
8) Who is the writer and director for both *Sleepless in Seattle* and *You've Got Mail*?
9) In *Stand by Me*, what four child actors who all went on to significant acting careers play the 12-year-old friends Gordy, Chris, Teddy, and Vern who go looking for the dead body?
10) In what city is the *Twilight* series of movies set?

Quiz 16 Answers

1) West Virginia
2) Faber College
3) Natalie Wood
4) Sheriff Buford T. Justice
5) Steve Buscemi
6) *A Hard Day's Night* - 1964
7) Vincent Price
8) Nora Ephron

9) Will Wheaton, River Phoenix, Corey Feldman, Jerry O'Connell
10) Forks, Washington – Stephenie Meyer, the author of the books, chose the city because it has the most rainfall in the contiguous 48 states and is small, out of the way, and surrounded by forest.

Quiz 17

1) For what film did Ray Milland win a Best Actor Oscar?
2) Who was the first person to win Oscars for both acting and writing?
3) What role did Clark Gable play in *Mutiny on the Bounty*?
4) Who plays the title role in *Gigi*?
5) The term blockbuster has meanings going back to large bombs in WWII, but as it is used to describe films, what was the first movie that the term was really applied to?
6) What movie stars Bud Cort as a teenager who wants to marry a 79-year-old woman played by Ruth Gordon?
7) What is the longest movie to ever win the Best Picture Oscar?
8) What film has a notorious gunman played by John Wayne being nursed back to health by a Quaker family?
9) *Quiz Show* is based on a true 1950s game show cheating scandal; Ralph Fiennes plays what real person who was a member of one of America's leading literary families and became a national celebrity based on his fraudulent wins?
10) What character does Humphrey Bogart play in *The Maltese Falcon*?

Quiz 17 Answers

1) *The Lost Weekend* - 1945
2) Emma Thompson – Best Actress Oscar for *Howards End* (1992) and Best Adapted Screenplay Oscar for *Sense and Sensibility* (1995)
3) Fletcher Christian
4) Leslie Caron
5) *Jaws* - 1975
6) *Harold and Maude* - 1971
7) *Gone with the Wind* - 238 minutes
8) *The Angel and the Badman* - 1947
9) Charles Van Doren

10) Sam Spade

Quiz 18

1) Who plays Gene Hackman's love interest in *Hoosiers*?
2) What is the highest grossing foreign language or subtitled film ever in the U.S.?
3) The creator of *Beavis and Butthead* directed the work comedy *Office Space*; who is he?
4) In *Night at the Museum*, what is Ben Stiller's character name?
5) What character does Groucho Marx play in *Duck Soup*?
6) What actor holds the record for the most years between Oscar nominations playing the same character?
7) "Bond. James Bond," is first spoken in what film?
8) What is the only remake of a regular television series to be nominated for a Best Picture Oscar?
9) Who are the only two people to direct themselves to a best actor or best actress Oscar?
10) What is the shortest film to win the Best Picture Oscar?

Quiz 18 Answers

1) Barbara Hershey
2) *The Passion of the Christ* – 2004
3) Mike Judge
4) Larry Daley
5) Rufus T. Firefly
6) Sylvester Stallone – 39 years between *Rocky* in 1976 and *Creed* in 2015
7) *Dr. No* (1962)– Sean Connery
8) *The Fugitive* (1993) – Oscar winner *Marty* (1955) was a remake of a television movie; Oscar nominated *Traffic* (2000) was adapted from a miniseries.
9) Laurence Olivier for *Hamlet* (1948) and Roberto Benigni for *Life Is Beautiful* (1997)
10) *Marty* (1955) – 90 minutes

Quiz 19

1) What was the very first film to win the Best Picture Oscar?
2) Who wrote and directed *American Graffiti*?
3) Who has won the most Best Supporting Actor or Actress Oscars?
4) What Oscar winning actress plays Tom Hanks' mother in *Philadelphia*?
5) In *Gorillas in the Mist*, Sigourney Weaver stars as what real-life scientist who went to Africa to study the vanishing mountain gorillas and fought to protect them?
6) Who plays the leader of the Russian team that goes ashore in the comedy *The Russians Are Coming! The Russians Are Coming!*?
7) What was the most expensive Hollywood film made in the 2000s?
8) Meryl Streep plays a Holocaust survivor and won her first Best Actress Oscar for what film?
9) What role did F. Murray Abraham play in *Amadeus*?
10) In *The Man Who Came to Dinner*, acerbic critic Sheridan Whiteside slips on the front steps of a prominent Ohio family's home and insists on recuperating in their home during Christmas; Bette Davis plays the critic's assistant; who plays the title role?

Quiz 19 Answers

1) *Wings* – 1927
2) George Lucas
3) Walter Brennan – three for *Come and Get It* (1936), *Kentucky* (1938), *The Westerner* (1940)
4) Joanne Woodward
5) Dian Fossey
6) Alan Arkin
7) *Pirates of the Caribbean: At World's End* (2007) - $300 million
8) *Sophie's Choice* - 1982
9) Antonio Salieri
10) Monty Woolley

Quiz 20

1) Who plays Gary Cooper's much younger wife in *High Noon*?

2) What does China syndrome refer to in *The China Syndrome*?
3) What suspense thriller stars Cary Grant, Audrey Hepburn, Walter Matthau, James Coburn, and George Kennedy?
4) In *The Shining*, novelist Jack Torrance played by Jack Nicholson takes a job as caretaker at a hotel where an evil presence drives him crazy; what is the name of the hotel?
5) Who are the only five performers to win consecutive acting Oscars?
6) What is the classical piece of music that is playing while Dudley Moore and Bo Derek are making love in *10*?
7) What film has Charlie Chaplin playing dual roles including a Jewish barber?
8) Who has the longest screen time performance to ever win the Best Actor Oscar?
9) Who plays Norman Bates in *Psycho*?
10) Marvin Hamlisch created the music for *The Sting*; much of the score is based on the work of what ragtime era composer?

Quiz 20 Answers

1) Grace Kelly
2) A hypothetical catastrophic failure where a nuclear reactor melts through the floor of its containment system and penetrates the earth's surface as if traveling through toward China.
3) *Charade* - 1963
4) Overlook Hotel
5) Luise Rainer (1936 and 1937), Spencer Tracy (1937 and 1938), Katharine Hepburn (1967 and 1968), Jason Robards (1976 and 1977), Tom Hanks (1993 and 1994)
6) *Bolero* – by Maurice Ravel
7) *The Great Dictator* (1940)– He also plays the dictator.
8) Charlton Heston – 2 hours 1 minute and 23 seconds for *Ben-Hur* (1959)
9) Anthony Perkins
10) Scott Joplin

Quiz 21

1) What country is *The King and I* set in?

2) What is the only movie to ever have three Best Actor Oscar nominations?
3) What western stars Henry Fonda, Gregory Peck, John Wayne, Richard Widmark, James Stewart, Spencer Tracy, Walter Brennan, Lee J. Cobb, Karl Malden, Eli Wallach, Robert Preston, Carroll Baker, Carolyn Jones, Debbie Reynolds, and Agnes Moorehead?
4) In *WALL-E*, what does WALL-E stand for?
5) What is Dorothy's last name in *The Wizard of Oz*?
6) What George Romero zombie flick was released in 1968?
7) Who is the only person to win an Olympic gold medal and an Oscar?
8) What movie is based on the true story of Christy Brown who was born with cerebral palsy and went on to become a writer and painter?
9) In *E.T. the Extra-Terrestrial,* what is E.T.'s candy of choice?
10) In Disney's animated *Frozen*, who provides the voice for the central character Anna?

Quiz 21 Answers

1) Siam – current day Thailand
2) *Mutiny on the Bounty* – Clark Gable, Charles Laughton, and Franchot Tone in 1936
3) *How the West Was Won* - 1962
4) Waste Allocation Load Lifter: Earth-Class
5) Gale
6) *Night of the Living Dead*
7) Kobe Bryant – Olympic basketball gold medals in 2008 and 2012 and Best Animated Short Film for *Dear Basketball* in 2018
8) *My Left Foot* - 1989
9) Reese's Pieces
10) Kristen Bell

Quiz 22

1) In the original *The Day the Earth Stood Still*, what is the name of the alien?
2) What classic film originated from a Christmas card?

3) What film stars Richard Gere as a young man at a Navy Officer Candidate School and won Louis Gossett Jr. a Best Supporting Actor Oscar?
4) Anne Bancroft won a Best Actress Oscar playing what character?
5) What was the first all color film nominated for the Best Picture Oscar?
6) What was the first animated film to win a competitive category Oscar?
7) What Alfred Hitchcock film won Joan Fontaine a Best Actress Oscar and co-stars Cary Grant as her husband she suspects is planning to kill her?
8) What is the name of Zero Mostel's character in *The Producers*?
9) What is the occupation of the title character in *Marty*?
10) What Hitchcock spy movie pairs Cary Grant and Ingrid Bergman?

Quiz 22 Answers

1) Klaatu
2) *It's a Wonderful Life* – Philip Van Doren Stern had written a short story, *The Greatest Gift*, and had unsuccessfully tried to get it published. He sent it out as a 21-page Christmas card to his closest friends; a producer at RKO Pictures got hold of it and purchased the movie rights.
3) *An Officer and a Gentleman* - 1982
4) Anne Sullivan – *The Miracle Worker* (1962)
5) *A Star is Born* – 1937
6) *Pinocchio* (1940) - Two years earlier *Snow White and the Seven Dwarfs* had won a special Oscar.
7) *Suspicion* - 1941
8) Max Bialystock
9) Butcher
10) *Notorious* - 1946

Quiz 23

1) What movie has a deranged Glenn Close boiling a bunny?
2) What was Walt Disney's first animated feature film?
3) *Breaking Away* is about a small-town teen obsessed with cycling

and the Italian cycling team; in what real town is the movie set?

4) What movie had the first Best Actress Oscar nomination for a science fiction film?
5) Who plays the title role in *Jane Eyre* opposite Orson Welles as Edward Rochester?
6) For what film, did Jean Dujardin become the first French actor ever to win the Best Actor Oscar?
7) Who was the first actress paid $20 million for a film?
8) What are the only two sequels to win Best Picture Oscars?
9) *Bye Bye Birdie* starring Dick Van Dyke, Janet Leigh, and Ann-Margret is a parody of what celebrity?
10) What musical comedy features "The Oldest Established Permanent Floating Crap Game in New York"?

Quiz 23 Answers

1) *Fatal Attraction* - 1987
2) *Snow White and the Seven Dwarfs* – 1937
3) Bloomington, Indiana – home of Indiana University
4) *Aliens* (1986)– Sigourney Weaver
5) Joan Fontaine
6) *The Artist* - 2011
7) Julia Roberts – *Erin Brockovich* (2000)
8) *The Godfather Part II* (1974) and *The Lord of the Rings: The Return of the King* (2003)
9) Elvis Presley
10) *Guys and Dolls* – 1955

Quiz 24

1) In *Hello Dolly*, what is the name of Walter Matthau's character?
2) Who plays Vito Corleone's two sons in *The Godfather*?
3) Adjusted for inflation, what was the first film to surpass the budget for *Cleopatra* in 1963?
4) *The Imitation Game* is set during WWII and stars Benedict Cumberbatch as what real-life mathematical genius?
5) Joel and Ethan Coen's *O Brother, Where Art Thou?* is loosely based on

what ancient epic poem?

6) What was the most expensive Hollywood film made during the 1940s?
7) For what film did Judy Holliday win her only Best Actress Oscar?
8) For what film did Spencer Tracy win his first Best Actor Oscar?
9) What woman has the most Oscar nominations?
10) In accepting his Best Supporting Actor Oscar, who said, "Now I know there's a Santa Claus"?

Quiz 24 Answers

1) Horace Vandergelder
2) Al Pacino and James Caan
3) *Waterworld* – 1995
4) Alan Turing
5) Homer's *Odyssey*
6) *Duel in the Sun* - $8 million at the time
7) *Born Yesterday* - 1950
8) *Captains Courageous* – 1937
9) Edith Head – 35 for costume design
10) Edmund Gwenn – for his role as Santa Claus in *Miracle on 34th Street*

Quiz 25

1) What is the theme song for *M*A*S*H*?
2) *A Christmas Story* is based on what writer's work?
3) What character said, "I just put one foot in front of the other. When I get tired, I sleep. When I get hungry, I eat. When I have to go to the bathroom, I go"?
4) *The Blind Side* is based on the true story of a family that takes in a homeless African American teen and helps him succeed in school and become an NFL first round draft pick; what is the name of the player?
5) What actor provides the voice of the lion Aslan in *The Chronicles of Narnia: The Lion, the Witch and the Wardrobe*?
6) In *Independence Day*, what is used to defeat the aliens?

7) Who plays the scarecrow in *The Wizard of Oz*?
8) A mountain climber becomes trapped under a boulder and resorts to desperate measures to survive; what is the movie?
9) What film directed by Jean-Jacques Annaud doesn't contain a single word of any modern language and traces the movements of a tribe of pre-historic humans?
10) What was the first film to feature Humphrey Bogart and Lauren Bacall?

Quiz 25 Answers

1) "Suicide is Painless"
2) Jean Shepherd
3) Forrest Gump
4) Michael Oher
5) Liam Neeson
6) Computer virus – The idea was taken from H.G. Wells' *The War of the Worlds* where the Martians are killed by bacteria and viruses.
7) Ray Bolger
8) *127 Hours* - 2010
9) *Quest for Fire* - 1981
10) *To Have and Have Not* - 1944

Quiz 26

1) In the remake *The Karate Kid*, Jackie Chan plays the kung fu master; who plays the title role?
2) Who has the most Oscar nominations?
3) Who plays the young Amish boy who witnesses a murder and is protected by Harrison Ford in *Witness*?
4) Who plays Wyatt Earp in *Gunfight at the O.K. Corral*?
5) What was the number one U.S. box office film released in the 1990s?
6) What are the nicknames of flying partners Tom Cruise and Anthony Edwards in *Top Gun*?
7) In *Four Weddings and a Funeral*, who plays the American Carrie that Hugh Grant's character falls in love with?

8) What suspense thriller has Frank Sinatra as a U.S. Army major believing that one of his men may be a brainwashed Chinese agent?
9) What science fiction film has real life married couple Hume Cronyn and Jessica Tandy playing a married couple and won Don Ameche a Best Supporting Actor Oscar?
10) In *Sister Act*, what is the stage name of Whoopi Goldberg's character?

Quiz 26 Answers

1) Jaden Smith
2) Walt Disney – 59
3) Lukas Haas
4) Burt Lancaster
5) *Titanic* – 1997
6) Maverick and Goose
7) Andie MacDowell
8) *The Manchurian Candidate* - 1962
9) *Cocoon* - 1985
10) Deloris Van Cartier

Quiz 27

1) Joel and Ethan Coen were screenwriters for *Unbroken* which is the story of Olympian Louis Zamperini who survives a plane crash in WWII and spends 47 days in a raft before he's caught by the Japanese and sent to a prisoner of war camp; what actress directed the movie?
2) In *The Maze Runner*, what are the creatures that live in the maze and attack the Gladers called?
3) Who was the first African American to win the Best Supporting Actor Oscar?
4) What Ridley Scott film about two female best friends is one of the very few films ever to produce two Best Actress Oscar nominations?
5) What film has John Wayne, Dean Martin, Ricky Nelson, and Walter Brennan trying to keep an accused murderer in jail?
6) In *The Hangover*, the three men searching for the missing groom are played by Bradley Cooper, Ed Helms, and who?

7) Who plays Gandalf in *The Lord of the Rings: The Return of the King*?
8) Who plays Will Smith's son in *The Pursuit of Happyness*?
9) Who won the most Oscars in a single year?
10) What is the only film Henry Fonda and Jane Fonda made together?

Quiz 27 Answers

1) Angelina Jolie
2) Grievers
3) Louis Gossett Jr. – *An Officer and a Gentleman* (1982)
4) *Thelma & Louise* - 1991
5) *Rio Bravo* - 1959
6) Zach Galifianakis
7) Ian McKellen
8) Jaden Smith – his real-life son
9) Walt Disney – four in 1953
10) *On Golden Pond* - 1981

Quiz 28

1) What Hitchcock film has Henry Fonda playing an innocent man mistakenly arrested for armed robbery?
2) What was the first science fiction film to win the Best Picture Oscar?
3) In *The Shootist*, John Wayne plays a terminally ill gunfighter who gets a room in a boarding house run by a woman and her son; who plays the mother and son?
4) What two actresses share the record with five consecutive Best Actress Oscar nominations?
5) Who plays the grizzled prospector in *The Treasure of the Sierra Madre*?
6) What is the only film where the top two billed actors playing a married couple won the Best Actor and Best Actress Oscars?
7) Michael Clarke Duncan plays a death row inmate who can work miracles in *The Green Mile*; what is the name of his character?
8) Who is the first character to speak in *Star Wars*?
9) In *Duel in the Sun*, Jennifer Jones is torn between two sons, one good

and the other bad; who plays the bad younger son?

10) What Woody Allen film has his character becoming president of the country of San Marcos?

Quiz 28 Answers

1) *The Wrong Man* - 1956
2) *The Shape of Water* - 2017
3) Lauren Bacall and Ron Howard
4) Bette Davis (1938-1942) and Greer Garson (1941-1945)
5) Walter Huston – His son John Huston directed the movie.
6) *On Golden Pond* – 1981 with Henry Fonda and Katharine Hepburn
7) John Coffey
8) C-3PO
9) Gregory Peck
10) *Bananas* - 1971

Quiz 29

1) In terms of tickets sold, what is the most popular James Bond film of all time?
2) What was the most expensive Hollywood film made during the 1950s?
3) What movie has the famous line "Here's looking at you kid"?
4) Peter Sellers, Alan Arkin, Roger Moore, Roberto Benigni, and Steve Martin have all played what character?
5) In *Goldfinger*, what is Goldfinger's first name?
6) What Walt Disney film has the most Oscar wins with five?
7) In *Matrix*, what is the name of the legendary hacker played by Laurence Fishburne who awakens Neo to the real world?
8) In Hitchcock's *North by Northwest*, who plays Cary Grant's love interest?
9) Who are the only two people to win both a Nobel Prize and an Oscar?
10) Who are the only sisters to win acting Oscars?

Quiz 29 Answers

1) *Thunderball* - 1965
2) *Ben-Hur* - $15 million at the time
3) *Casablanca* (1942) – Humphrey Bogart
4) Inspector Clouseau – Pink Panther movies
5) Auric – Auric is an adjective meaning of, related to, or containing gold.
6) *Mary Poppins* – 1964
7) Morpheus
8) Eve Marie Saint
9) George Bernard Shaw won the Nobel Literature Prize in 1925 and the Best Adapted Screenplay Oscar for *Pygmalion* in 1936; Bob Dylan won the Best Original Song Oscar for "Things Have Changed" from *Wonder Boys* in 2000 and the Nobel Literature Prize in 2016.
10) Olivia de Haviland and Joan Fontaine

Quiz 30

1) What is the only Walt Disney animated feature film that runs for two hours or more?
2) What film series has the most Oscar nominations?
3) What character did Spencer Tracy play in the 1938 film that won him his second consecutive Best Actor Oscar?
4) Who is the oldest winner of an acting Oscar?
5) Dean Jones starred in 11 Disney films over his career; what was the first one?
6) Peter Dinklage stars as a man born with dwarfism who moves to rural New Jersey to live a life of solitude but ends up making friends anyway; what is the movie?
7) Who plays the mother and father of the family dealing with the accidental death of its oldest son in *Ordinary People*?
8) How many movies did Spencer Tracy and Katharine Hepburn make together?
9) In *Groundhog Day*, each repeating day starts with what song on the radio?
10) Who won a Best Actor Oscar for *Gandhi*?

Quiz 30 Answers

1) *Fantasia* – 1940
2) *Lord of the Rings* trilogy – 30 nominations
3) Father Flanagan – *Boys Town*
4) Christopher Plummer – age 82 for best supporting actor in *Beginners* (2011)
5) *That Darn Cat!* - 1965
6) *The Station Agent* - 2003
7) Mary Tyler Moore and Donald Sutherland
8) Nine – *Woman of the Year* (1942), *Keeper of the Flame* (1943), *Without Love* (1945), *The Sea of Grass* (1947), *State of the Union* (1948), *Adam's Rib* (1949), *Pat and Mike* (1952), *Desk Set* (1957), *Guess Who's Coming to Dinner* (1967)
9) Sonny and Cher's "I Got You Babe"
10) Ben Kingsley

Quiz 31

1) What Oscar winning film centers on a runaway princess who falls in love with a newsman?
2) Who plays the gunslinger Jack Wilson brought in to kill the title character in *Shane*?
3) What was the number one U.S. box office film released in the 1970s?
4) The character of the boy Dill Harris who is visiting for the summer in *To Kill a Mockingbird* is based on what real life famous person?
5) Who plays Susan Walker, the little girl who doesn't believe in Santa Claus, in *Miracle on 34th Street*?
6) What British comedy has six unemployed steel workers forming a striptease act?
7) What Best Picture Oscar winner is set in Hawaii around the time of the Japanese attack on Pearl Harbor?
8) In the *National Lampoon* series of vacation movies, what is the full name of Chevy Chase's character?
9) In *Three Billboards Outside Ebbing, Missouri*, a mother challenges the local authorities to solve her daughter's murder; who won a Best Actress Oscar for her portrayal of the mother?

10) In *Black Panther*, what is the name of the fictional African nation where the action takes place?

Quiz 31 Answers

1) *Roman Holiday* (1953) – starring Gregory Peck and Audrey Hepburn
2) Jack Palance
3) *Star Wars* – 1977
4) Truman Capote – He was a childhood friend and neighbor of author Harper Lee, and they remained lifelong friends.
5) Natalie Wood
6) *The Full Monty* - 1997
7) *From Here to Eternity* - 1953
8) Clark Griswold
9) Frances McDormand
10) Wakanda

Quiz 32

1) Who plays the man James Stewart's character believes has murdered his wife in *Rear Window*?
2) What was the number one U.S. box office film released in the 1950s?
3) Who plays Fast Eddie Felson's manager in *The Hustler*?
4) What is the only film ever to have only one Oscar nomination in total and win the Best Picture Oscar?
5) What William Wyler western stars Gregory Peck, Charlton Heston, Jean Simmons, Burl Ives, and Chuck Connors?
6) What was the number one U.S. box office film released in the 1980s?
7) Based on a true story, what movie follows Carl Brashear as he attempts to become the first African American U.S. Navy diver?
8) What early Quentin Tarantino film has the tagline "Seven total strangers team up for the perfect crime. They don't know each other's name. But they've got each other's color"?
9) In *Thor*, what is the name of the bridge that connects Asgard and Earth?
10) What film stars Burt Lancaster as an aging small-time gangster

and was nominated for all five of the major Oscars?

Quiz 32 Answers

1) Raymond Burr
2) *The Ten Commandments* – 1956
3) George C. Scott
4) *Grand Hotel* - 1932
5) *The Big Country* - 1958
6) *E.T. the Extra-Terrestrial* – 1982
7) *Men of Honor* - 2000
8) *Reservoir Dogs* - 1992
9) Bifrost
10) *Atlantic City* - 1980

Quiz 33

1) In *Ocean's Eleven*, who plays the role originated by Frank Sinatra in the 1960 original?
2) What Best Picture Oscar winning film has the longest title?
3) In *Willy Wonka and the Chocolate Factory*, what is the last name of the protagonist Charlie?
4) What was the first of 14 Sherlock Holmes films starring Basil Rathbone and Nigel Bruce?
5) Who was the first actor or actress to win a competitive acting Oscar for a Walt Disney film?
6) In *Slumdog Millionaire*, what is the final answer Jamal gives to win the grand prize?
7) In *Good Morning Vietnam*, Robin Williams' character is based on a real-life disc jockey on U.S. Armed Forces Radio in Saigon during the Vietnam War; what is his name?
8) What Francis Ford Coppola film stars Martin Sheen, Marlon Brando, Robert Duvall, Laurence Fishburne, Dennis Hopper, and Harrison Ford?
9) What western features Steve McQueen playing a teen hunting down the killers of his parents?
10) Who won a Best Adapted Screenplay Oscar for *Sense and Sensibility* and was nominated for a Best Actress Oscar for her performance in

the film?

Quiz 33 Answers

1) George Clooney – plays Danny Ocean
2) *The Lord of the Rings: The Return of the King* - 2003
3) Bucket
4) *The Hound of the Baskervilles* - 1939
5) Julie Andrews – *Mary Poppins* (1964)
6) Aramis – the third musketeer in *The Three Musketeers*
7) Adrian Cronauer
8) *Apocalypse Now* - 1979
9) *Nevada Smith* - 1966
10) Emma Thompson

Quiz 34

1) Adjusted for inflation, what is the earliest movie made that has grossed $1 billion in the U.S.?
2) What actor holds the record with four consecutive Best Actor Oscar nominations?
3) David Niven has the record for the shortest screen time performance to ever win the Best Actor Oscar; what film was it in?
4) In *Ghost*, what does Sam always say instead of saying "I love you"?
5) What was Bruce Lee's final film?
6) In *The Social Network*, what is the name of the website Mark Zuckerberg initially creates to rate the attractiveness of female Harvard students and in the process gets a six-month academic probation?
7) What movie has Tobie Maguire and Reese Witherspoon zapped back to the 1950s?
8) In *The Lord of the Rings: The Fellowship of the Ring*, how many are in the original fellowship?
9) What movie features Charlie Chaplin struggling in an industrialized world?
10) What is the name of James Stewart's character in *Harvey*?

Quiz 34 Answers

1) *Snow White and the Seven Dwarfs* – 1937
2) Marlon Brando (1951-1954)
3) *Separate Tables* (1958)– Niven was on screen for 23 minutes and 39 seconds.
4) Ditto
5) *Enter the Dragon* - 1973
6) FaceMash
7) *Pleasantville* - 1998
8) Nine – Frodo, Gandalf, Legolas, Gimli, Aragorn, Boromir, Merry, Pippin, Samwise
9) *Modern Times* - 1936
10) Elwood P. Dowd

Quiz 35

1) Who directed *Mystic River* about three childhood friends whose lives are shattered when one of their daughters is murdered?
2) What movie features Karl Childers, a simple man hospitalized since childhood for murder, who is released to start a new life in a small town?
3) Ma and Pa Kettle first appeared in supporting roles in *The Egg and I* in 1947 and went on to star in nine movies of their own starting with *Ma and Pa Kettle* in 1949; who played Ma and Pa Kettle?
4) What musical stars Emma Watson, Kevin Kline, Ewan McGregor, Emma Thompson, Ian McKellen, and Stanley Tucci?
5) In the film *In the Heat of the Night*, Virgil Tibbs is a homicide detective in what city?
6) Adjusted for inflation, what is the only horror film to gross $1 billion in the U.S.?
7) Who plays the role of Big Daddy in *Cat on a Hot Tin Roof*?
8) Directed by Gene Kelly, what was the last film starring James Stewart and Henry Fonda?
9) What film set primarily in New Zealand won a Best Supporting Actress Oscar for Anna Paquin and a Best Actress Oscar for Holly Hunter?
10) What movie has the record for the largest Oscar sweep – winning

every category it was nominated for?

Quiz 35 Answers

1) Clint Eastwood
2) *Sling Blade* - 1996
3) Marjorie Main and Percy Kilbride
4) *Beauty and the Beast* - 2017
5) Philadelphia
6) *The Exorcist* – 1973
7) Burl Ives
8) *The Cheyenne Social Club* – 1970
9) *The Piano* - 1993
10) *The Lord of the Rings: Return of the King* (2003) – It won all 11 Oscars it was nominated for.

Quiz 36

1) What is the name of the adventurer Stewart Granger plays in *King Solomon's Mines*?
2) What actor says, "You fell victim to one of the classic blunders - the most famous of which is never get involved in a land war in Asia - but only slightly less well-known is this: Never go in against a Sicilian when death is on the line"?
3) What was Clint Eastwood's character called in *The Good, the Bad and the Ugly*?
4) What film stars Warren Beatty, Julie Christie, and Goldie Hawn and was also Carrie Fisher's screen debut?
5) What 1982 movie is based on Philip K. Dick's book *Do Androids Dream of Electric Sheep*?
6) The first film Steven Spielberg produced was a horror film which he also co-wrote starring Craig T. Nelson and JoBeth Williams; what is the movie?
7) Adjusted for inflation, what is the highest grossing animated movie of all time in the U.S.?
8) What film has news anchorman Howard Beale threatening to kill himself on live television after learning he is being forced to retire?
9) What is the only Best Picture Oscar winner without any female

speaking roles?

10) What is the name of Humphrey Bogart's character in *The Caine Mutiny*?

Quiz 36 Answers

1) Allan Quartermain
2) Wallace Shawn – as Vizzini in *The Princess Bride* (1987)
3) Blondie
4) *Shampoo* - 1975
5) *Blade Runner*
6) *Poltergeist* - 1982
7) *Snow White and the Seven Dwarfs* – 1937
8) *Network* - 1976
9) *Lawrence of Arabia* - 1962
10) Captain Queeg

Quiz 37

1) What film includes the famous scene where Jack Nicholson's character tries to order toast which isn't on the menu?
2) In Best Picture Oscar winner *The King's Speech*, Colin Firth plays what English king who needed a speech therapist to overcome his stammer?
3) What is the name of Cary Grant's character in *Arsenic and Old Lace*?
4) What was the last film John F. Kennedy saw before his assassination?
5) In *Back to the Future*, what year does Marty McFly go back to?
6) In *Close Encounters of the Third Kind*, what is the real location that Richard Dreyfuss' character builds in mashed potatoes and is drawn to?
7) Who plays the title role in *The Buddy Holly Story*?
8) Jessica Tandy plays elderly Ninny Threadgoode who tells stories about people she used to know in what movie?
9) In Monty Python's *Life of Brian*, Brian is born at the same time as Jesus but in a different stable and is constantly being mistaken for him; who plays Brian?

10) Who are the four actors who play the friends on a canoe trip in *Deliverance*?

Quiz 37 Answers

1) *Five Easy Pieces* – 1970
2) King George VI
3) Mortimer Brewster
4) *Tom Jones* – 1963
5) 1955
6) Devils Tower National Monument in Wyoming
7) Gary Busey
8) *Fried Green Tomatoes* – 1991
9) Graham Chapman
10) Burt Reynolds, Jon Voight, Ned Beatty, Ronny Cox

Quiz 38

1) For what movie did Katharine Hepburn win her first Best Actress Oscar?
2) Who plays General Savage who takes over a bomber unit during WWII and whips them into shape in *Twelve O'Clock High*?
3) In *The Sound of Music*, what branch of the military does Captain von Trapp belong to?
4) What is the name of the town where *Bill and Ted's Excellent Adventure* is set?
5) What is the name of Uma Thurman's assassin character in *Kill Bill: Volume 1*?
6) In *Stand and Deliver*, who plays the teacher in a tough high school who inspires his students to learn calculus?
7) Besides the cartoon character, what is *The Pink Panther* in the movie of the same name?
8) In what movie does Marilyn Monroe's iconic scene with her white dress blowing upward while she stands on a subway grate take place?
9) What 1999 independent film had a $60,000 budget and grossed almost $250 million worldwide?
10) In *Stripes*, who plays Bill Murray's best friend that he convinces to

enlist in the army?

Quiz 38 Answers

1) *Morning Glory* – 1933
2) Gregory Peck
3) Navy – Even though Austria is landlocked, there was a combined Austro-Hungarian Navy at the time.
4) San Dimas
5) The Bride
6) Edward James Olmos
7) Diamond
8) *The Seven Year Itch* - 1955
9) *The Blair Witch Project*
10) Harold Ramis

Quiz 39

1) What crime drama stars Russell Crowe, Guy Pearce, Kevin Spacey, James Cromwell, Danny DeVito and won Kim Basinger a Best Supporting Actress Oscar?
2) What are the names of the three tunnels being dug in *The Great Escape*?
3) In *National Velvet*, Velvet's mother provides the entrance fee for the horse race out of her prize money for doing what?
4) Elizabeth Taylor plays a middle-aged wife in an abusive relationship and won her second Best Actress Oscar for what film?
5) A lion, zebra, giraffe, and what animal find themselves unexpectedly in the wild in *Madagascar*?
6) What is the name of the dog owned by Nick and Nora Charles in *The Thin Man*?
7) In *The Jerk*, what is the name of Steve Martin's idiot character?
8) What film won a Best Actress Oscar for Jane Fonda and a Best Actor Oscar for Jon Voight?
9) What western stars John Wayne as Ethan Edwards looking for his abducted niece?
10) What Alfred Hitchcock film centers on a serial killer who is strangling women with a necktie?

Quiz 39 Answers

1) *L.A. Confidential* - 1997
2) Tom, Dick, Harry
3) Swimming the English Channel
4) *Who's Afraid of Virginia Woolf?* - 1966
5) Hippopotamus
6) Asta
7) Navin Johnson
8) *Coming Home* - 1978
9) *The Searchers* - 1956
10) *Frenzy* – 1972

Science and Nature

Quiz 1

1) What is the study of movement in relation to human anatomy called?
2) What year was the drug ecstasy invented?
3) What is the mass in grams of one cubic centimeter of water at 4 degrees Celsius (temperature water is at its maximum density)?
4) What year was the fax machine patented?
5) What country has the highest percentage of natural redheads?
6) What ingredient makes vinegar taste sour or bitter?
7) What are the three types of human twins?
8) What plant produces about one-half of the Earth's oxygen?
9) What is the full name of the SARS virus?
10) What year was the first active communications satellite launched?

Quiz 1 Answers

1) Kinesiology
2) 1912 - Merck wanted to develop something to stop abnormal bleeding, and it synthesized MDMA to avoid a Bayer patent. They didn't have any real interest in it at the time, and it wasn't until 1975 that the psychoactive effects of the drug were seriously considered.
3) One gram
4) 1843 - The fax machine is older than the telephone and was patented the same year the first wagon train crossed the Oregon Trail. The original patent for an electric printing telegraph or fax was in 1843 by Scottish inventor Alexander Bain, and the first commercial use of a fax machine was in France in 1865, 11 years before the telephone was invented and the year the American Civil War ended.
5) Scotland - about 13%
6) Acetic acid - Vinegar typically contains 5-20% acetic acid.
7) Identical, fraternal, and sesquizygous or semi-identical - Identical or monozygotic twins result from a single fertilized egg that splits

in two and forms two identical boys or two girls who share 100% of their DNA. Fraternal or dizygotic twins form from two eggs that have been fertilized by two of the father's sperm creating two genetically unique siblings that share 50% of their DNA. Semi-identical twins are so rare that only two cases have ever been identified; they share between 50% and 100% of their DNA and are formed when a single egg is fertilized by two sperm. This shouldn't happen because once a sperm enters the egg, the egg locks down to prevent another sperm from entering. Even if a second sperm entered, an embryo with three rather than the normal two sets of chromosomes won't survive. To produce semi-identical twins, the egg splits the three sets of chromosomes into two separate cell sets.

8) Phytoplankton
9) Severe acute respiratory syndrome
10) 1962 - Telstar 1 was a medium Earth orbit satellite.

Quiz 2

1) What is the point in the orbit of the Moon or a satellite when it is nearest the Earth called?
2) Table sugar from sugar cane or beets is what kind of sugar?
3) At normal atmospheric pressure, what is the only element in the universe that can't freeze?
4) Lyme disease gets its name from a small coastal town where several cases were identified in 1975 in what state?
5) What is the southern version of the aurora borealis (northern lights) called?
6) N_2O is more commonly known as what?
7) What element is named after the Moon?
8) What plant's name comes from the Turkish word for turban?
9) What type of galaxy is the most common in the universe?
10) Even though it makes up about 2.4% of the Earth's crust, what element is never found in its pure form in nature?

Quiz 2 Answers

1) Perigee
2) Sucrose

3) Helium - Its freezing point is -458 degrees Fahrenheit.
4) Connecticut
5) Aurora australis
6) Laughing gas - nitrous oxide
7) Selenium - Selene means moon in Greek.
8) Tulip
9) Elliptical
10) Potassium - It is so reactive that it is never found in its pure form in nature; it must be isolated artificially by separating it from its compounds.

Quiz 3

1) In humans, which lung (right or left) is always larger?
2) By what common name is calcium oxide (CaO) known?
3) What metal melts in your hand?
4) What is the more common name for red corundum?
5) What is the scientific name for the Moon?
6) An aphyllous plant doesn't have what?
7) Humans have a depression in the right atrium of the heart that is a result of our fetal development; what is it called?
8) What celestial object gets its name from a Greek word meaning long-haired?
9) In computers, the smallest unit of data is a bit which has a binary value of 0 or 1; what is the term "bit" short for?
10) Our current North Star is Polaris, it will be replaced by what star in about 13,000 years?

Quiz 3 Answers

1) Right - The left lung is smaller to leave enough room for your heart.
2) Quicklime - used in cement, making glass, manufacturing steel, etc.
3) Gallium - It melts at 85.6 degrees Fahrenheit.
4) Ruby - Corundum is a very hard mineral composed of aluminum oxide that is the source for both rubies and sapphires. If it is red in

color, it is a ruby; if it is any other color, it is a sapphire although the most popular and valued sapphire color is blue.

5) Moon - Unlike other moons in our solar system, it doesn't have any other official name.
6) Leaves
7) Fossa ovalis - An unborn child receives oxygen from its mother, so blood goes directly from the right to the left atrium through the foramen ovale; after birth, the opening closes, creating the fossa ovalis.
8) Comet - from the Greek kometes
9) Binary digit
10) Vega - The change is due to a change in the direction the Earth's axis points due to a motion called precession. If you think of a spinning top given a slight nudge, the top traces out a cone pattern; that is how the Earth moves on its axis. The Earth bulges out at the equator, and the gravitational attraction of the Moon and Sun on the bulge cause the precession which repeats in a 26,000-year cycle which will make Polaris the North Star again in about 26,000 years.

Quiz 4

1) What kind of fruit is a pineapple?
2) What tree that is native to tropical southern North America and northern South America is extremely toxic in all forms and can cause blistering even from standing beneath the tree during rain?
3) On the human body, what is the niddick?
4) What is a device used to measure the amount of moisture in the atmosphere called?
5) What year did people first recognize that dinosaurs had existed?
6) In physics, mass multiplied by acceleration gives you what?
7) Where in the human body would you find the round window and the oval window?
8) What psychologist coined the terms introvert and extrovert?
9) What planet in our solar systems rotates the slowest?
10) Scheelite is an important ore of what element?

Quiz 4 Answers

1) Berry - It produces hundreds of flowers within a small space which produce fruits which coalesce into a single larger fruit.
2) Manchineel tree - Burning the tree can cause eye injuries, and the fruit is possibly fatal producing internal bleeding.
3) Nape of the neck
4) Hygrometer
5) 1824 - Even though the name dinosaur wasn't applied until 1842, William Buckland, a geology professor as Oxford, was the first person to recognize dinosaurs for what they were in 1824 when he used the name Megalosaurus to describe an extinct carnivorous lizard fossil.
6) Force
7) Ear - The round window is an opening from the middle ear to the inner ear; the oval window is an opening that leads from the middle ear to the inner ear.
8) Carl Jung - 1920s
9) Venus - At the equator, Venus rotates 4 mph; the Earth rotates 1,038 mph at the equator.
10) Tungsten

Quiz 5

1) What is the thickest layer of the Earth's four layers?
2) How many sides does an enneadecagon have?
3) In the human body, what is produced by the parotid glands?
4) Who originated the quantum theory and won the 1918 Nobel Prize in Physics for his work?
5) In nature, what are drupelets?
6) Who developed the system we use today for classifying plants and animals?
7) What element is named after a village in Scotland?
8) What is the name for the part of the human ear that receives sound vibrations and converts them into nerve impulses?
9) Brass is an alloy of what two metals?
10) What body part does a cicada use to make their loud sound?

Quiz 5 Answers

1) Mantle - It is about 1,802 miles thick and makes up about 84% of the Earth's volume.
2) 19 sides
3) Saliva
4) Max Planck
5) The individual bumps forming a fleshy aggregate fruit such as a blackberry or raspberry
6) Carolus Linnaeus - In the first half of the 18th century, he developed a taxonomy for naming and classifying plants and animals.
7) Strontium - It is named after the village of Strontian, Scotland.
8) Cochlea
9) Copper and zinc
10) Ribs - They flex their muscles to buckle a series of ribs one after another to produce their loud sound. Every time a rib buckles, it produces a click; many clicks produce the buzzing sound. The series of ribs are called a tymbal and can produce a sound over 100 decibels that can be heard over a mile and a half away.

Quiz 6

1) What is the second largest moon in our solar system?
2) What is the smallest thing ever photographed?
3) Who developed the first antibiotic, penicillin?
4) Because of the speed the Sun moves at, what is the maximum possible length for a solar eclipse to the nearest minute?
5) What is the study of life in outer space called?
6) What is the second largest moon of Jupiter?
7) What is a two-dimensional image of a slice through a three-dimensional object called?
8) Gunpowder is made up of a mixture of sulfur, charcoal, and what?
9) What are the only two non-silvery pure metals in the world?
10) What is the name of the prolific meteor shower that peaks in August each year?

Quiz 6 Answers

1) Titan - 3,200-mile diameter moon of Saturn
2) The shadow of a single atom - In 2012, scientists were able to take a picture of the shadow produced by a single atom. Using an electrical field, they suspended the atom in a vacuum chamber and shot a laser beam at it to produce the shadow.
3) Alexander Fleming - 1928
4) Eight minutes - 7 minutes and 58 seconds
5) Exobiology
6) Callisto - 2,996-mile diameter, third largest moon in our solar system
7) Tomogram - used in radiology, archaeology, biology, geophysics, oceanography, etc.
8) Potassium nitrate
9) Gold and copper
10) Perseids meteor shower

Quiz 7

1) In what century did the practice of quarantine begin?
2) In our solar system, there are three types of planets - terrestrial, gas giants, and what?
3) Glass is neither a liquid nor a solid; what is it called?
4) Who was the first American to orbit the Earth in space?
5) What is the largest cell in the human body?
6) For humans, what is the rarest hair and eye color combination?
7) Up to about 10,000 years ago, all humans had what eye color?
8) What brand name is sildenafil citrate marketed under?
9) In trigonometry, what is calculated as adjacent divided by hypotenuse?
10) What element has the symbol Pb?

Quiz 7 Answers

1) 14th century - Ships arriving in Venice from plague infected ports were required to sit at anchor for 40 days before landing. The word quarantine derives from the Italian words "quaranta giorni" which

mean 40 days.

2) Ice giants - Uranus and Neptune
3) Amorphous solid - a state somewhere between liquid and solid
4) John Glenn - 1962
5) Female egg
6) Red hair and blue eyes - Only about 0.17% of the population has the combination because both red hair and blue eyes are recessive traits where both parents must carry the gene for the child to have it.
7) Brown - A genetic mutation at about that time produced blue eyes.
8) Viagra
9) Cosine
10) Lead - Pb comes from the Latin word "plumbum" meaning waterworks; in ancient times, lead was widely used in the construction of water pipes.

Quiz 8

1) What was the name of the first orbiting space station?
2) In terms of mass, what is the most abundant element in the human body?
3) What is the branch of medicine concerned with disease as it affects a community of people called?
4) Pewter is an alloy of what two metals?
5) What is the longest number of days a human has ever gone without sleep voluntarily without any artificial stimulants?
6) What planet in our solar system is big enough to fit over 1,300 Earths inside it?
7) What periodic table element has the shortest name?
8) What is the name of the chemical process used to harden rubber by treating it with sulfur?
9) What is the international standard unit of work or energy?
10) What is the small bump on the inner corner of your eye called?

Quiz 8 Answers

1) *Salyut 1* - launched by the Soviet Union in April 1971

2) Oxygen
3) Epidemiology
4) Tin and lead
5) 11 days
6) Jupiter - It has a diameter of about 88,695 miles and is the largest planet in our solar system.
7) Tin
8) Vulcanization - invented by Charles Goodyear
9) Joule
10) Caruncula

Quiz 9

1) What is the rarest hair color in the world?
2) What does an ichthyologist study?
3) About 1 in every 200 people is born with an extra rib which forms above the first rib at the base of the neck just above the collarbone; what is it called?
4) What year was the first internet search engine created?
5) In astronomy, who coined the term "Big Bang"?
6) In the electromagnetic spectrum, what comes between microwaves and visible light?
7) What astronomy unit of measure is about 93 million miles?
8) Who was the marine biologist and author of *Silent Spring* who was one of the first people to warn of the dangers of pesticides like DDT?
9) Under daylight conditions, the human eye is most sensitive to what color?
10) What is H_2SO_4 the chemical formula for?

Quiz 9 Answers

1) Red - less than 2% of the population
2) Fish
3) Cervical rib - You can have a cervical rib on either or both sides, and it can be a fully formed bony rib or a thin strand of tissue fibers.

4) 1990 - It was called Archie which stood for archive without the v and was created by a small group of computer science students at McGill University in Montreal, Quebec, Canada.
5) Fred Hoyle - He was an English astronomer and coined it in 1949 on a BBC radio broadcast.
6) Infrared
7) Astronomical unit - defined by the distance from the Earth to the Sun
8) Rachel Carson
9) Green - Light at this wavelength produces the impression of highest brightness compared to light at other wavelengths.
10) Sulfuric acid

Quiz 10

1) Harvard didn't offer calculus classes for the first few years; why?
2) What are the most luminous objects in the known universe?
3) In the human body, what is otalgia?
4) What planet is the largest of the terrestrial planets in our solar system?
5) Where on your body would you find rascette lines?
6) In humans, which ear is better at receiving sounds from speech?
7) What is the name for the point in a planet's orbit when it is furthest from the Sun?
8) In 1999, NASA estimated that what material cost $28 quadrillion per pound to produce?
9) What was the first Apollo mission to orbit the Moon?
10) How many planets in our solar system have rings?

Quiz 10 Answers

1) Calculus hadn't been invented yet. Harvard was established in 1636; calculus wasn't developed until the mid-1600s.
2) Quasars - They are highly luminous radio galaxies with a supermassive black hole; the nearest known quasar is 600 million light-years away.
3) Earache
4) Earth - Terrestrial planets are the inner, rocky planets - Mercury,

Venus, Earth and Mars.

5) Inner wrist creases
6) Right ear - The left ear is more sensitive to sounds of music.
7) Aphelion
8) Antimatter
9) *Apollo 8* - December 1968
10) Four - Jupiter, Saturn, Uranus, Neptune - Galileo discovered Saturn's rings in 1610; the rings on the other planets weren't discovered until the 1970s.

Quiz 11

1) Sphalerite is the primary ore of what metal?
2) What synthetic drug was first produced in 1897 by Felix Hoffman, a German chemist for Bayer?
3) What is the medical name for the human butt crack?
4) What type of galaxy is the Milky Way?
5) As a gas, oxygen is odorless and colorless; what color is it in its liquid and solid forms?
6) The surface area of Pluto is only about 3% larger than what country?
7) What is the only human internal organ that can regenerate itself?
8) What common spice can be toxic in a dose of two teaspoons or more inducing hallucinations, convulsions, pain, nausea, and paranoia that can last for several days?
9) What principle states that the position and the velocity of an object cannot both be measured exactly at the same time?
10) What is your pollex?

Quiz 11 Answers

1) Zinc
2) Aspirin
3) Intergluteal cleft
4) Spiral
5) Pale blue
6) Russia

7) Liver - You can lose up to 75 percent of your liver, and the remaining portion can regenerate into a whole liver.
8) Nutmeg - It comes from the seed of a tropical evergreen.
9) Heisenberg uncertainty principle
10) Thumb

Quiz 12

1) Steel is made by alloying iron with what?
2) What tree native to Africa, Australia, and India can grow to almost 100 feet tall with a trunk diameter up to 36 feet, live for thousands of years, and store up to 32,000 gallons of water in its trunk?
3) What element is named after the Earth?
4) What function does the sinoatrial node in the human heart serve?
5) What is the scientific study of trees call?
6) What is the standard international unit of electrical current?
7) What element is named after a U.S. university?
8) What is the heaviest element produced by fusion in a star?
9) The physiological sense called equilibrioception is known by what more common term?
10) What is the study of freshwater environments, particularly lakes, called?

Quiz 12 Answers

1) Carbon - usually less than 1%
2) Baobab - Because it stores such large volumes of water in its trunk, elephants, eland and other animals chew the bark during dry seasons.
3) Tellurium - Tellus is Latin for Earth.
4) Pacemaker - It is specialized muscle tissue in the wall of the right atrium that produces a contracting signal at regular intervals.
5) Dendrology
6) Ampere - named after French mathematician and physicist André-Marie Ampère
7) Berkelium - It was first made in 1950 at the University of California, Berkeley.

8) Iron
9) Sense of balance
10) Limnology

Quiz 13

1) According to research by Johns Hopkins, where do medical errors rank as a cause of death in the U.S.?
2) What planet in our solar system has a diameter just 397 miles smaller than the Earth?
3) What was the first man-made element?
4) The Big Dipper isn't a constellation; what is it?
5) What was the first Apollo mission to use a lunar rover?
6) What is the second most common element in the universe?
7) What creates the sound you hear when you hold a seashell to your ear?
8) In humans, what is the stage before frostbite called?
9) Linseed oil comes from what plant?
10) What plants did Gregor Mendel use for his genetics experiments?

Quiz 13 Answers

1) Third - behind heart disease and cancer.
2) Venus
3) Technetium - 1937
4) Asterism - There are 88 official constellations in the night sky; any other grouping of stars that isn't one of the 88 is an asterism. In the Big Dipper's case, it is part of the Ursa Major or Great Bear constellation.
5) *Apollo 15* - July 1971
6) Helium - about 25% of universe by mass
7) Surrounding environmental noise resonating in the seashell cavity - In a soundproof room, you don't hear anything when you hold a seashell to your ear.
8) Frostnip - There is skin irritation causing redness and cold feeling followed by numbness, but there is no permanent damage.
9) Flax

10) Pea plants

Quiz 14

1) What unit of measure is equal to about 3.26 light-years?
2) What does outer space smell most like?
3) Who is widely credited with saving more lives than any other medical scientist of the 20th century?
4) In March 1965, Alexei Leonov was the first person to do what?
5) In the human body, what tube connects the kidney to the bladder?
6) On your body, where would you find your lunula?
7) What was the first country to adopt the metric system?
8) What is the farthest object visible to the naked human eye?
9) What is the study of plants called?
10) In physics, mass multiplied by velocity gives you what?

Quiz 14 Answers

1) Parsec
2) Burning odor of hydrocarbons - like gunpowder, diesel, and barbecue
3) Maurice Ralph Hilleman (1919-2005) - He was an American microbiologist who specialized in developing vaccines and developed over 40 in his career including 8 of the 14 vaccines routinely recommended: measles, mumps, hepatitis A, hepatitis B, chickenpox, meningitis, pneumonia, and Haemophilus influenzae.
4) Spacewalk
5) Ureter
6) White crescent near the base of your fingernail
7) France - 1795
8) Andromeda Galaxy - It is 2.6 million light-years away and is visible as a dim, large gray cloud almost directly overhead in a clear night sky.
9) Botany
10) Momentum

Quiz 15

1) The number zero with its own unique value and properties did not exist until what century?
2) What century was the telescope invented?
3) What kind of organism is the largest single living organism on Earth?
4) What is the manipulation of matter on an atomic, molecular, and supramolecular scale called?
5) What part of the human brain regulates involuntary functions?
6) If you wrapped a rope around the Earth's equator so that it was tightly hugging the ground, how much additional rope would you need for it to hover one foot above the ground all the way around the Earth?
7) $C_{10}H_{14}N_2$ is a poisonous alkaloid consumed by millions daily; what is it?
8) What state of matter does the Sun largely consist of?
9) How many months after conception do human embryos develop fingerprints?
10) What fibrous protein is the main constituent of hair and nails?

Quiz 15 Answers

1) 7th century - Early counting systems only saw zero as a placeholder, not a true number.
2) 17th century - 1608
3) Mushroom - It is a honey mushroom in Malheur National Forest in Oregon that covers more than three square miles, weighs at least 7,500 tons, and is at least 2,000 years old. DNA testing has confirmed it is the same organism that has spread from a single location thousands of years ago.
4) Nanotechnology
5) Medulla oblongata
6) 6.3 feet - Circumference = 2 x Pi x radius = 2 x Pi x (1 additional foot of radius) = 6.3 feet
7) Nicotine
8) Plasma
9) Three months

10) Keratin

Quiz 16

1) Who won the 1922 Nobel Prize in Physics for their research on the structure of the atom and the development of the quantum theory?
2) What did Marie Curie name the first element she discovered?
3) What two physicists first split the atom in 1932 and went on to win a Nobel Prize for their work?
4) What plant was originally called Georgium Sidus or the Georgian Planet in honor of King George III of England?
5) What was the first Apollo mission to get to space and orbit the Earth?
6) Based on the arrangement of their molecules, there are two types of solids - crystalline and what?
7) If you yawn and have saliva shoot out of your mouth, what is it called?
8) Even though it is one of the most common elements in the Earth's crust, what metal was more valuable than gold in the 1800s?
9) What century did Nicolaus Copernicus develop the heliocentric model?
10) When poured, does hot water have a higher or lower pitch than cold water?

Quiz 16 Answers

1) Niels Bohr
2) Polonium - after her native country of Poland
3) John Cockcroft and Ernest Walton
4) Uranus
5) *Apollo* 7 - October 1968
6) Amorphous - Crystalline solids have an orderly molecule structure; amorphous solids like glass have a random structure.
7) Gleeking - The salivary glands underneath your tongue become stimulated and shoot a concentrated jet of pure saliva; it typically happens when yawning.
8) Aluminum - It is almost never found in its pure form and is difficult to extract from ores, so prior to more efficient processes being developed to extract it, aluminum was quite rare. In the

1850s, aluminum was priced at $1,200 per kilogram, and gold was priced at about half that at $664 per kilogram.

9) 16th century - published in 1543
10) Higher - Water changes viscosity with temperature which affects the sound when poured.

Quiz 17

1) The atomic bomb dropped on Nagasaki used what kind of nuclear material?
2) What year was the world's first artificial satellite, *Sputnik* 1, launched?
3) What gas makes up most of the Earth's atmosphere?
4) What planet's moons are named after characters created by William Shakespeare and Alexander Pope?
5) What is the common name for Fe_2O_3?
6) After the Sun, what is the closest star to Earth?
7) Bananas along with foods like spinach, apricots, salmon, avocados, and mushrooms are very mildly radioactive; what element makes them radioactive?
8) Where does the Moon rank in size among all the moons in our solar system?
9) An angle that is more than 90 degrees and less than 180 degrees is called what?
10) The word scuba is an acronym for what?

Quiz 17 Answers

1) Plutonium - The Hiroshima bomb used uranium-235; Nagasaki used plutonium-239.
2) 1957
3) Nitrogen - about 78%
4) Uranus - 27 moons: Cordelia, Ophelia, Bianca, Cressida, Desdemona, Juliet, Portia, Rosalind, Cupid, Belinda, Perdita, Puck, Mab, Miranda, Ariel, Umbriel, Titania, Oberon, Francisco, Caliban, Stephano, Trinculo, Sycorax, Margaret, Prospero, Setebos, Ferdinand.
5) Rust- iron oxide
6) Proxima Centauri - 4.22 light-years away

7) Potassium K-40 - A very small fraction of potassium atoms are K-40 radioactive atoms that spontaneously decay releasing beta radiation and gamma rays which are both capable of tissue damage. However, K-40 is not very radioactive with a half-life of 1.3 billion years, so you would have to eat about 10 million bananas to die of radiation poisoning.
8) Fifth - behind Ganymede, Titan, Callisto, and Io
9) Obtuse
10) Self-contained underwater breathing apparatus

Quiz 18

1) What piece of computer equipment was invented by Douglas Engelbart at Stanford Research Institute in the early 1960s?
2) What two elements make up most of the Earth's core?
3) The uppermost region of the Sun is called what?
4) What part of the human brain is most responsible for motor functions?
5) What famous actress was one of the inventors of spread spectrum and frequency hopping technology that is the basis for current cellular communications?
6) What is the only human organ that can float in water?
7) The point at which a liquid can exist simultaneously as a liquid, solid, and gas is called its what?
8) What is the fastest spinning planet in our solar system?
9) Why don't people sneeze in their sleep?
10) What is the third largest planet in our solar system?

Quiz 18 Answers

1) Mouse
2) Iron and nickel
3) Corona - It is 1 to 2 million degrees Kelvin
4) Cerebellum
5) Hedy Lamarr - at the beginning of WWII
6) Lungs - They contain about 300 million balloon-like structures called alveoli which replace the carbon-dioxide waste in your blood with oxygen.

7) Triple point - It is the temperature and pressure that puts the three states of matter into thermodynamic equilibrium where no one state is trying to change into any other state. The boiling liquid causes high energy molecules to rise as a gas which lowers the temperature of the boiling liquid and makes it freeze. The cycle continues if the triple point temperature and pressure are maintained. For water, the triple point is at 32.02 degrees Fahrenheit and 0.006 atmospheres (normal pressure is one atmosphere).
8) Jupiter - 28,273 mph at the equator compared to 1,038 mph for the Earth
9) The brain shuts down the reflexes that would result in a sneeze through a process called REM atonia.
10) Uranus - It has a diameter of 31,765 miles; its volume is about 63 times larger than the Earth.

Quiz 19

1) What is the standard international unit of capacitance?
2) How many playing cards would you need to have in a deck to have more possible unique sequences than there are stars in the observable universe?
3) What law states that equal volumes of all gases at the same temperature and pressure have the same number of molecules?
4) Only one side of the Moon is visible from the Earth because the Moon rotates on its axis at the same rate that it orbits the Earth; what is this known as?
5) Copper gets its name from what island country?
6) What disease was called the white plague in the 1700s due to the paleness of the patients and was commonly called consumption in the 1800s?
7) In physics, force multiplied by velocity gives you what?
8) The ability of litmus paper to change color when exposed to an acid or base is a result of it being infused with what organisms?
9) What periodic table element has the longest name?
10) The first telescope used for astronomy purposes by Galileo Galilei was what kind of telescope?

Quiz 19 Answers

1) Farad - named after English physicist Michael Faraday
2) 25 - There are 1.55 x 10^{25} possible sequences for 25 cards; there are only about 10^{24} stars in the observable universe. A full deck of 52 cards has 8.07 x 10^{67} possible sequences.
3) Avogadro's law - developed by Amedeo Avogadro in 1811
4) Synchronous rotation or tidal locking
5) Cyprus - The name comes from the Latin word "cuprum" meaning "from the island of Cyprus." In ancient Rome, most copper was mined in Cyprus.
6) Tuberculosis
7) Power
8) Lichens
9) Rutherfordium
10) Refractor

Quiz 20

1) What is the division sign (short horizontal line with a dot above and below) in math called?
2) What part of the human body produces more than 90% of your serotonin, the neurotransmitter that contributes to feelings of well-being and happiness?
3) What European country has two elements on the periodic table named after it?
4) Magnetite, hematite, limonite and siderite are the primary ores of what metal?
5) The atomic number for an element is determined by what?
6) When you read to yourself, your tongue and vocal cords still get movement signals from the brain in a process called what?
7) Why do human testicles hang outside the body?
8) Who developed the 1869 Periodic Law which forms the basis for the periodic table?
9) What are the three main types of galaxies?
10) Although it had been proposed in some form for over 50 years, the scientific community didn't agree on plate tectonics until what year?

Quiz 20 Answers

1) Obelus
2) Digestive tract
3) France - Francium (Fr) and gallium (Ga) are named for France; gallium comes from the Latin Gallia, the region we now know as France.
4) Iron
5) Number of protons in the atom's nucleus
6) Subvocal speech - It is characterized by minuscule movements in the larynx and other muscles involved in the articulation of speech; the movements are undetectable without the aid of machines.
7) Sperm dies at body temperature.
8) Dmitry Mendeleev
9) Elliptical, spiral, irregular
10) 1967

Quiz 21

1) Lettuce is a member of what plant family?
2) In humans, what prevents the stomach acids from dissolving the stomach?
3) Most members of the nightshade family that includes tomatoes, potatoes, eggplants, and green peppers contain small quantities of what stimulant?
4) What element is named after a U.S. state?
5) When you peel a banana, what are the strings that come off called?
6) If you are locked in a completely sealed room, what will kill you first?
7) What is the smallest cell in the human body?
8) What is the name of the process where a solid turns directly into a gas without passing through the liquid phase?
9) About 90% of the coal we burn today comes from what historical period before wood eating bacteria evolved?
10) After going deaf, what method did Beethoven use to hear almost perfectly?

Quiz 21 Answers

1) Sunflower
2) Mucus lining
3) Nicotine
4) Californium
5) Phloem bundles - They distribute nutrients up and down the banana as it grows.
6) Carbon dioxide poisoning - It will kill you before you die from lack of oxygen.
7) Male sperm
8) Sublimation
9) Carboniferous Period - This era from 359 to 299 million years ago is known as the Carboniferous Period because of the large amounts of coal formed during the period.
10) Bone conduction - He discovered that if he bit on a metal pole connected to the piano he was playing; he could hear almost perfectly. Vibrations are transferred into our bones, and our ears pick up the signal with no sound distortion bypassing the eardrums. We all hear sounds through both our bones and our eardrums; most sounds are air conducted where the eardrum converts sound waves to vibrations and transmits them to the inner ear; however, in some cases vibrations are heard directly by the inner ear bypassing your eardrums. This is one of the ways you hear your own voice.

Quiz 22

1) What is the better-known name for the poison prussic acid?
2) What Swedish scientist has a temperature scale named after him?
3) If a scuba diver suffers from the bends, what gas is being rapidly released from the blood and tissues?
4) How many muscles are in your fingers?
5) Galvanizing is the process of applying a protective coating of what metal to steel or iron to prevent rusting?
6) What element is named after the seventh planet from the Sun?
7) What unit of measure is equal to about 5.88 trillion miles?
8) On what two planets in our solar system do scientists believe it

rains diamonds?

9) What is the name for the second lowest layer of the Earth's atmosphere from about 7-31 miles altitude?
10) What is the largest living structure in the world?

Quiz 22 Answers

1) Cyanide or hydrogen cyanide
2) Anders Celsius
3) Nitrogen
4) None - The muscles which bend the finger joints are in the palm and in the mid forearm and are connected to the finger bones by tendons which pull on and move the fingers.
5) Zinc
6) Uranium
7) Light year
8) Jupiter and Saturn - Lightning storms turn methane into soot which under pressure hardens into chunks of graphite and then diamond as it falls. The largest diamonds would likely be about a centimeter in diameter and would eventually melt in the hot planet core.
9) Stratosphere
10) Great Barrier Reef - Situated off the northeastern coast of Australia, it stretches for 1,429 miles and covers an area of approximately 133,000 square miles.

Quiz 23

1) Two angles that add up to 180 degrees are called what?
2) What century was the idea of the atom first introduced?
3) What is the only major nut tree indigenous to North America?
4) In terms of number of atoms, what is the most abundant element in the human body?
5) What is the three-line symbol you typically find in the upper corner of a screen that you click or tap to get to a menu called?
6) Beriberi disease is caused by a deficiency of what vitamin?
7) In 2009, what famous scientist threw a champagne party for time travelers?

8) Albert Einstein's 1921 Nobel Prize in Physics wasn't for his work on relativity; what was if for?
9) What English scientist is credited with inventing the World Wide Web in 1989?
10) What is the most common radioactive element in the human body?

Quiz 23 Answers

1) Supplementary
2) 5th century BC – Around 450 BC, the Greek philosopher Democritus introduced the idea of the atom as the point where matter could not be cut into still smaller pieces. Atom comes from the Greek word "atomos" meaning uncuttable.
3) Hydrogen
4) Hamburger button - It looks like a hamburger.
5) B1 - thiamine
6) Stephen Hawking - He didn't put out invitations until after the party hypothesizing that if someone showed up it would be proof of time travel. No one came.
7) Photoelectric effect - He suggested for the first time that light is both a wave and a particle and established the existence of photons.
8) Tim Berners-Lee
9) Potassium-40 (K-40) - It makes up about 0.012% of the potassium found in nature, and we ingest it in foods containing potassium.

Quiz 24

1) What is the term for the tendency of an object in motion to remain in motion, or an object at rest to remain at rest unless acted upon by a force?
2) The Julian calendar that was used prior to the current calendar had 365.25 days per year; to the nearest minute, how much longer was that than the actual year as measured by the time from one vernal equinox to the next?
3) If you average out the colors of all the different stars we can see, what color is the universe?
4) What is the second most abundant element in the earth's crust?
5) In humans, what is the only muscle not attached on both ends?
6) What NASA space flight was the last manned mission to the Moon?

7) What is the largest herb plant?
8) What is the name for the third major layer of the Earth's atmosphere from about 31-50 miles altitude?
9) What four planets in our solar system are Jovian planets?
10) What is the lightest metallic element?

Quiz 24 Answers

1) Inertia
2) 11 minutes - 11 minutes and 14 seconds to be more exact which amounts to a day every 128 years
3) Beige
4) Silicon - 27.7%
5) Tongue
6) *Apollo* 17
7) Banana - Some species grow up to 100 feet; it doesn't have a true woody trunk like a tree and behaves like a perennial.
8) Mesosphere
9) Jupiter, Saturn, Uranus, Neptune - The term is derived from Jupiter; planets are considered Jovian if they are like Jupiter.
10) Lithium - It floats in water.

Quiz 25

1) What two scientists discovered the double-helix structure of DNA in 1953?
2) What was the first planet discovered by telescope?
3) What science deals with the structure of the universe and its origin?
4) Morton's toe is what condition?
5) Who discovered that there is an increase (or decrease) in the frequency of sound, light, or other waves as the source and observer move toward (or away from) each other?
6) The commonly stated low end for human hearing is 20 hertz; what is the upper end?
7) Who discovered the law that the volume of a given mass of gas at a constant temperature is inversely proportional to its pressure?

8) In 1898, who created the first remote control that could control mechanical devices at a distance with radio waves?
9) What gas is the second most common in the Earth's atmosphere?
10) What is the most abundant element in the Earth's crust?

Quiz 25 Answers

1) James Watson and Francis Crick
2) Uranus - Sir William Herschelin in 1781
3) Cosmology
4) Your second toe is longer than your big toe - It occurs in 10-20% of the population.
5) Christian Doppler - Doppler effect
6) 20,000 hertz
7) Robert Boyle - 17th century
8) Nikola Tesla - The first electronic television wasn't invented until 29 years later in 1927, and the first wireless television remote wasn't created until 1956.
9) Oxygen - about 21%
10) Oxygen - 46.6%

Quiz 26

1) What standard international unit for measuring area is equal to 2.471 acres?
2) What is the most abundant element in Mar's atmosphere?
3) In the human body, what is the common name for the laryngeal prominence?
4) The asteroid belt is a region that contains most of the asteroids in our solar system; it is located between the orbits of what two planets?
5) What are the only two letters that don't appear in any official element names on the periodic table?
6) What element is named after the creator of dynamite?
7) What is the largest part of the human brain?
8) Fluorine, chlorine, bromine, and iodine belong to what group of elements?

9) What is the property called where two particles are inextricably linked together no matter their physical separation?
10) What is an atom or molecule with a net electric charge due to the loss or gain of one or more electrons called?

Quiz 26 Answers

1) Hectare - It is equal to the area of a square with 100-meter sides or 10,000 square meters.
2) Carbon dioxide - about 96%
3) Adam's apple - The thyroid cartilage that surrounds the larynx tends to protrude outward.
4) Mars and Jupiter
5) J and Q
6) Nobelium - named after Alfred Nobel
7) Cerebrum - It makes up about 85% of the brain's weight.
8) Halogens - They are reactive nonmetallic elements.
9) Quantum entanglement - Albert Einstein described it as "spooky action at a distance" and didn't believe nature would be so unreasonable, but quantum entanglement that occurs when two particles are inextricably linked together no matter their physical separation has been proven repeatedly in experiments. Although entangled particles are not physically connected, they are still able to share information with each other instantaneously breaking the rule that no information can be transmitted faster than the speed of light. Entangled particles 750 miles apart have shown that any change in one is instantly reflected in the other; this would be true even if they were separated by light-years of distance.
10) Ion

Sports

Quiz 1

1) Who was the first American NHL player with 50 goals in a season?
2) What sport originated the term southpaw?
3) Who won gold medals in the 5000-meter, 10,000-meter, and marathon races in the 1952 games despite never having run a marathon in competition before?
4) What was the first team to appear in four consecutive Super Bowls?
5) Who has held the MLB season RBI record since 1930?
6) While in college, Jim Brown was an All-American in what other sport besides football?
7) What male or female singles figure skater has won the most U.S. Championships?
8) What was the first NBA team to win 10 championships?
9) At what age did Wayne Gretzky become a professional?
10) Who was the first person to win four consecutive MLB Cy Young Awards?

Quiz 1 Answers

1) Bobby Carpenter - 1984-85 Washington Capitals
2) Boxing - Left-handed fighters were said to use a southpaw stance; no one is quite sure why but hitting someone with a left came to be known as a southpaw punch.
3) Emil Zatopek - Czechoslovakia
4) Buffalo Bills – 1991 to 1994
5) Hack Wilson - 191 in 1930
6) Lacrosse - Syracuse University
7) Dick Button - seven consecutive from 1946-1952
8) Boston Celtics - 10th championship in 1967-68 season
9) 17
10) Gregg Maddux - 1992 to 1995

Quiz 2

1) What batter holds the MLB record for being walked the most times in a season?
2) Who holds the NFL career record for most extra points made?
3) Who holds the NBA record for most career free throws made?
4) What was the first team to win three consecutive cricket World Cups?
5) What were the only Olympics where distances were measured in yards?
6) Who has the most career NBA MVP awards?
7) What were golf balls originally made of?
8) What is the NHL record for career goals by a goalie?
9) Where did ice hockey originate?
10) Who was the first quarterback to win Super Bowl MVP without throwing a touchdown?

Quiz 2 Answers

1) Barry Bonds - 232 in 2004
2) George Blanda - 943 from 1949-1975
3) Karl Malone - 9,787
4) Australia - 1999, 2003, 2007
5) 1904 St. Louis
6) Kareem Abdul-Jabbar - six
7) Wood - In the early 17th century, wood was replaced by a feather ball consisting of boiled feathers compressed inside a stitched leather cover.
8) Two - Ron Hextall and Martin Brodeur
9) United Kingdom - There are references to similar games being played on ice in England, Scotland, and Ireland going back 200 years before the first documented game in Canada.
10) Joe Namath - 1969

Quiz 3

1) What male alpine skier has the most World Cup race wins?

2) Who was the first baseball player to win the ESPY award for best male athlete?
3) How many gold medals did Usain Bolt win in the 100 and 200-meter sprints and the 4 x 100-meter relay between 2008 and 2016?
4) What female alpine skier has the most World Cup downhill season titles?
5) Who was the first MLB player to hit 400 home runs and steal 400 bases?
6) Who was the first coach with four Super Bowl wins?
7) What player holds the record for most NHL career penalty minutes?
8) Who was the first MLB pitcher to strike out a side with nine pitches in both leagues?
9) What year did the last undefeated team win the NCAA Division I basketball championship?
10) Who was the first pitcher in MLB history to throw four no hitters?

Quiz 3 Answers

1) Ingemar Stenmark (Sweden) - 86 wins from 1973-1989
2) Barry Bonds - 1994
3) Eight - He initially won all nine events over the three Olympics, but his 2008 4 x 100 gold was taken away due to a doping violation by a teammate.
4) Lindsey Vonn – U.S.
5) Barry Bonds - 1998
6) Chuck Noll - Pittsburgh Steelers - 1975, 1976, 1979,1980
7) David "Tiger" Williams - 3,971 minutes from 1974-1988
8) Nolan Ryan
9) 1976 - Indiana
10) Sandy Koufax - 1965

Quiz 4

1) What NHL team set a record for most consecutive playoff appearances with 25 seasons from 1979-2004?
2) Who is the only person named a first team high school All-American in football, basketball, and baseball?

3) What metal currently makes up 92.5% of an Olympic gold medal?
4) Where is the Olympic torch originally lit to start its relay to the host site?
5) Who was the last filly to win the Kentucky Derby?
6) How many horses have won racing's Triple Crown?
7) How many fillies have won the Kentucky Derby?
8) What is the longest period any sports trophy has been successfully defended?
9) Who was the first American woman to win three gold medals in a single Olympics?
10) Who was the last woman to win a calendar year tennis Grand Slam?

Quiz 4 Answers

1) St. Louis Blues
2) Danny Ainge - He went to high school in Eugene, Oregon.
3) Silver
4) Temple of Hera in Olympia, Greece
5) Winning Colors - 1988
6) 13 - Sir Barton (1919), Gallant Fox (1930), Omaha (1935), War Admiral (1937), Whirlaway (1941), Count Fleet (1943), Assault (1946), Citation (1948), Secretariat (1973), Seattle Slew (1977), Affirmed (1978), American Pharoah (2015), Justify (2018).
7) Three - 1915, 1980, 1988
8) 132 years - The America's Cup for sailing was held by the United States from its start in 1851 until Australia won in 1983.
9) Wilma Rudolph - track and field at the 1960 Rome Olympics
10) Steffi Graf - 1988

Quiz 5

1) Who was the first NFL rusher to run for 25 touchdowns in a season?
2) What year was hockey's Stanley Cup first awarded?
3) Who is the only person to win Olympic gold medals in both indoor and beach volleyball?
4) What Olympic sport allowed professionals for the first time in

2016?

5) What has won the most track and field gold medals in a single Olympics?
6) What international incident prompted the 1980 Moscow Olympics boycott?
7) Who was the first track and field athlete to win four consecutive Olympic gold medals in the same event?
8) Who won the 2018 men's soccer World Cup?
9) In the post 1968 open era, who was the first woman to win a calendar year tennis Grand Slam?
10) Who is the only person to win gold medals in both the winter and summer Olympics?

Quiz 5 Answers

1) Emmitt Smith - 1995 Dallas Cowboys
2) 1893
3) Karch Kiraly (U.S.) - 1984 and 1988 indoor volleyball gold medals and 1996 beach volleyball gold
4) Boxing
5) Paavo Nurmi (Finland) - 5 golds in 1924 Paris games
6) Soviet Union's 1979 invasion of Afghanistan
7) Al Oerter - discus from 1956 to 1968
8) France
9) Margaret Court - 1970
10) Eddie Eagan (U.S.) - boxing (1920) and bobsled (1932)

Quiz 6

1) What is the only year in men's or women's NCAA Division I basketball that two undefeated teams have met for the national championship?
2) Who is the first tennis player to win all four Grand Slam tournaments and an Olympic gold medal in tennis in the same calendar year?
3) With a minimum of 3,000 plate appearances, who are the only three MLB players ever with career batting averages over .350?
4) Who holds the NBA record for most seasons leading the league in

points?
5) Which Olympics was the first where every participating country had at least one female athlete on their team?
6) The Olympic triathlon consists of a 40-kilometer bike ride, a 10-kilometer run, and how long of a swim?
7) Who was the first college player to be a three-time unanimous, consensus All-American?
8) What driver has the most consecutive NASCAR championships?
9) In 2000, what did the Cincinnati Reds do for the first time in MLB baseball's 162 game season history?
10) How many seasons did Wayne Gretzky win the Art Ross Trophy for leading the NHL in scoring?

Quiz 6 Answers

1) 2014 women's tournament - Connecticut beat Notre Dame 79-58.
2) Steffi Graf - 1988
3) Ty Cobb (.366), Rogers Hornsby (.359), Shoeless Joe Jackson (.356)
4) Michael Jordan - 11
5) 2012 London - Saudi Arabia, Qatar, and Brunei sent female athletes for the first time.
6) 1.5 kilometer
7) Herschel Walker - 1980, 1981, 1982 for Georgia
8) Jimmie Johnson - five from 2006-2010
9) They went the entire season without being shutout.
10) 10

Quiz 7

1) Who was the first American woman to win the Olympic women's gymnastics all-around gold medal?
2) What player holds the record for most career points in the men's NCAA Division I basketball tournament?
3) Who was the first person to win a gold medal in three different Olympics?
4) Who was the first African American Heisman Trophy winner?
5) Who was the first athlete to win the same Olympic running event

three times?

6) What is the oldest college football bowl game?
7) Who has the second most career Olympic medals?
8) What bowler has the most career PBA wins?
9) What sport originated the term home run?
10) What is the oldest of horse racing's Triple Crown races?

Quiz 7 Answers

1) Mary Lou Retton - 1984 Los Angeles
2) Christian Laettner - 407 for Duke 1989-1992
3) Sonja Henie - figure skating in 1928, 1932, 1936
4) Ernie Davis - 1961 Syracuse University
5) Usain Bolt - 100 and 200-meter races in 2008, 2012, 2016
6) Rose Bowl - 1902
7) Larisa Latynina (Soviet Union) - 18 medals in gymnastics from 1956-1964
8) Walter Ray Williams Jr. - 47 wins
9) Cricket
10) Belmont Stakes - 1867

Quiz 8

1) Who was the first professional boxer to win world titles in three weight divisions?
2) What jockey rode Secretariat to his 1973 Triple Crown win?
3) Who was the first pitcher to win an MLB Cy Young Award in both leagues?
4) Who holds the NHL season points record for a defenseman?
5) Ski jumping and cross-country skiing are combined into what Olympic sport?
6) When Mark Spitz won seven swimming gold medals in a single Olympics, in how many of the events did he break the world record?
7) Who has the most career World Series home runs?
8) Who is the only male to win six consecutive Grand Slam singles tennis tournaments?

9) Who is the oldest player ever in an NFL game?
10) What is the only country to win a gold medal at every Summer Olympics?

Quiz 8 Answers

1) Bob Fitzsimmons - middleweight (1891), heavyweight (1897), light heavyweight (1903)
2) Ron Turcotte
3) Gaylord Perry - 1978
4) Bobby Orr - 139 points (102 assists, 37 goals) for 1970-71 Boston Bruins
5) Nordic combined
6) Seven
7) Mickey Mantle - 18
8) Don Budge – 1937 Wimbledon to 1938 U.S. Championships
9) George Blanda - 48
10) Great Britain - Due to boycotts, only Great Britain, France, Australia, Greece, and Switzerland have participated in every Summer Olympics.

Quiz 9

1) Since Joe DiMaggio's record, who has the longest MLB consecutive game streak with at least one hit?
2) Who is the only American who has won an overall cross-country skiing World Cup championship?
3) What country hosted the first Winter Olympics?
4) What female alpine skier has the most overall World Cup titles?
5) At what age did Gordie Howe play his last professional hockey game?
6) What year were women first allowed to compete in the modern Olympics?
7) What golfer has the most PGA tour victories?
8) Who were the second pair of NFL teammates to each rush for 1,000 yards in the same season?
9) Who is the first NBA player ever to average a triple-double over a season twice?

10) Who was the first NHL player to score 100 points in six consecutive seasons?

Quiz 9 Answers

1) Pete Rose - 44 in 1978
2) Bill Koch - 1981-82 season
3) France – Chamonix in 1924
4) Annmarie Moser-Proll (Austria) - six
5) 52
6) 1900
7) Sam Snead - 82 wins from 1936-1965
8) Franco Harris and Rocky Bleier - 1976 Pittsburgh Steelers
9) Russell Westbrook - Oklahoma City Thunder in 2016-17 and 2017-18
10) Bobby Orr - 1969 to 1975

Quiz 10

1) What bowler has won the PBA Player of the Year the most times?
2) Who is the youngest male track and field Olympic gold medalist ever?
3) Who was the first NBA player with more than 3,000 steals?
4) Who was the first NFL player to have 1,000 yards rushing and 1,000 yards receiving in a season?
5) Who is the first driver to ever complete the Triple Crown of Motorsport consisting of winning the Indianapolis 500, 24 Hours of Le Mans, and the Monaco Grand Prix over a career?
6) How old was the youngest Olympic medalist ever in an individual event?
7) Who holds the NBA record for highest season points per game?
8) What woman golfer has the most career LPGA tour wins?
9) What year did Wilt Chamberlain score his 100 points in one NBA game?
10) What will be the first city to host both the summer and winter Olympics?

Quiz 10 Answers

1) Walter Ray Williams Jr. - seven times
2) Bob Mathias (U.S.) - He was 17 years old when he won the 1948 decathlon.
3) John Stockton
4) Roger Craig - 1985 San Francisco 49ers
5) Graham Hill (Great Britain) - 1963 Monaco Grand Prix, 1966 Indianapolis 500, 1972 Le Mans
6) 12 - 200-meter women's breastroke swimming in 1936
7) Wilt Chamberlain - 50.4 ppg in 1961-62 season
8) Kathy Whitworth - 88
9) 1962
10) Beijing - 2008 summer and 2022 winter

Quiz 11

1) What two teammates finished one and two in the NHL scoring race five times?
2) What were the first Olympics held in Asia?
3) Who holds the NBA career record for assists?
4) Who was named MVP of the first Super Bowl in 1967?
5) Who held the MLB record for stolen bases in a season for 47 years?
6) What pitcher has the most career shutouts?
7) What NHL player was the first to win one of the major NHL trophies eight consecutive years?
8) If you include the Canadian Football League, who was the first professional quarterback with 70,000 career passing yards?
9) What Super Bowl winning NFL head coach also won a NASCAR Cup series championship as an owner?
10) What year did the first NFL indoor game take place?

Quiz 11 Answers

1) Phil Esposito and Bobby Orr
2) Tokyo, Japan - 1964
3) John Stockton - 15,806

4) Bart Starr - Green Bay Packers
5) Ty Cobb – 96 set in 1915
6) Walter Johnson - 110
7) Bobby Orr - won eight Norris Trophies from 1968-1975
8) Warren Moon - 21, 228 yards in the CFL and 49,325 yards in the NFL
9) Joe Gibbs - 2000 NASCAR Cup
10) 1932 - With temperatures of 30 below in Chicago, the Bears played a game indoors against the Portsmouth Spartans in the Chicago Stadium which was used mainly for horse shows; they played on a modified 80-yard field.

Quiz 12

1) Who was the first quarterback to lead his team to four Super Bowl titles?
2) Why was Brazil allowed to permanently keep the men's soccer World Cup trophy after their 1970 victory?
3) Who holds the NBA career record for highest rebounds per game average?
4) Who was the first person to swim 100 meters in under one minute?
5) Which NBA team set a record of 33 consecutive regular season wins in the 1971-72 season?
6) Who won the 2014 men's field hockey World Cup?
7) What year was the famous "Battle of the Sexes" tennis match between Billie Jean King and Bobby Riggs?
8) Who was the first NFL quarterback to throw for 5,000 yards in a season?
9) At the time he retired, how many NHL records did Wayne Gretzky hold?
10) What year was the first Olympic athlete disqualified for drug use?

Quiz 12 Answers

1) Terry Bradshaw - 1975, 1976, 1979, 1980
2) It was Brazil's third win. It was stipulated at the time the tournament was set up that if any nation won the trophy three times, they would be allowed to keep it permanently.

3) Wilt Chamberlain - 22.9 rebounds per game
4) Johnny Weissmuller - 58.6 seconds in the 100-meter freestyle in 1922
5) Los Angeles Lakers
6) Australia
7) 1973
8) Dan Marino - 1984 Miami Dolphins
9) 61
10) 1968 Mexico City - excessive alcohol

Quiz 13

1) What was the first Summer Olympics to be held entirely during the winter?
2) Who is the only person to hit an MLB home run and score an NFL touchdown in the same week?
3) With a minimum of 3,000 plate appearances, who has the highest MLB career batting average?
4) Who pitched in 1,252 MLB games over 24 years?
5) Who scored the winning goal for the United States in the "Miracle on Ice" hockey game against the Soviet Union in 1980?
6) Who was the first NHL player to use a slapshot?
7) Who was the first NHL goaltender to create and wear a practical mask?
8) The actor who played Jethro on television's *The Beverly Hillbillies* was the son of a famous athlete; who was his father?
9) How long was UCLA's NCAA record men's basketball consecutive game win streak which ended in 1974?
10) Who holds the NBA career record for most triple-doubles?

Quiz 13 Answers

1) Rio de Janeiro (2016) - The other two Summer Olympics in the southern hemisphere had taken place at least partly in the spring.
2) Deion Sanders - September 1989
3) Ty Cobb - .366 over 24 seasons
4) Jesse Orosco - He played from 1979-2003 for the Mets, Dodgers,

Indians, Brewers, Orioles, Cardinals, Padres, Yankees, and Twins.

5) Mike Eruzione
6) Bernie Geoffrion - 1951
7) Jacques Plante - 1959
8) Max Baer Sr. - world heavyweight boxing champion in 1934
9) 88 games
10) Oscar Robertson - 181

Quiz 14

1) Who was the first person to ever play for 25 years in the NFL?
2) Who won the first women's soccer World Cup?
3) Who was the 20-year-old amateur American golfer who won the U.S. Open in 1913 and started a golf boom in the U.S.?
4) How many times in NHL history has a goalie been credited with scoring a goal against an opposing goalie (not an empty net goal)?
5) In what event did Baron Pierre de Coubertin, founder of the modern Olympics, win a gold medal at the 1912 Olympic games?
6) Who is the only MLB player to hit two grand slams in one inning?
7) Who holds the NBA career record for most steals?
8) Who was the first NHL player to score 100 points in a season?
9) Frenchwoman Micheline Ostermeyer won the shot put and discus at the 1948 London Olympics. She also had a demanding day job; what was it?
10) How many times has the United States hosted either the Summer or Winter Olympics?

Quiz 14 Answers

1) George Blanda - He played from 1949-1975 taking off the 1959 season.
2) United States - 1991
3) Francis Ouimet
4) Once - On March 21, 2013 during a game between the New Jersey Devils and Carolina Hurricanes, a delayed penalty was called against New Jersey. Carolina goalie Dan Ellis headed for the bench for the extra attacker, but after he left the crease, the Hurricanes accidentally sent the puck the length of the ice back toward their

empty net. Ellis tried to race back but was too late. Because Devils goalie Martin Brodeur had been the last to touch the puck, he was given credit for the goal, and because Ellis was on the ice when the puck went in, the goal went on his record.

5) Mixed literature - Art competition was introduced in 1912 and continued in the Olympics through 1948; Coubertin won for a poem.
6) Fernando Tatis - April 23, 1999
7) John Stockton - 3,265
8) Phil Esposito - 126 points (49 goals, 77 assists) for 1968-69 Boston Bruins
9) Concert pianist - She had never picked up a discus until a few weeks before winning the Olympic title; she also won bronze in the 80-meter hurdles.
10) Eight (4 summer, 4 winter) - 1904 St. Louis, 1932 Lake Placid, 1932 Los Angeles, 1960 Squaw Valley, 1980 Lake Placid, 1984 Los Angeles, 1996 Atlanta, 2002 Salt Lake City

Quiz 15

1) What are the only two countries that have won consecutive men's soccer World Cups?
2) What NCAA Division I school has the record for most consecutive national championships in any men's or women's sport?
3) Who was the first winner of the women's Olympic marathon?
4) When was the last time the Summer and Winter Olympics were held in the same year?
5) Who was the first player to hit 50 or more home runs in four consecutive seasons?
6) What country won the first men's rugby World Cup?
7) Who has won the most gymnastics gold medals at a single Olympics?
8) What golfer holds the record for most PGA tour wins in a season?
9) How many NHL teams did Wayne Gretzky play for?
10) Who is the youngest man to ever win a tennis Grand Slam singles title?

Quiz 15 Answers

1) Italy (1934, 1938) and Brazil (1958, 1962)
2) Arkansas - 12 straight men's indoor track and field championships from 1984-1995
3) Joan Benoit - Los Angeles Olympics in 1984
4) 1992
5) Mark McGwire - 1996 to 1999
6) New Zealand - 1987
7) Vitaly Scherbo (Unified Team) - 6 golds in 1992 Barcelona games
8) Byron Nelson – 18 wins in 1945
9) Four - Edmonton, Los Angeles, St. Louis, New York Rangers
10) Michael Chang - 17 years, 110 days old when he won the 1989 French Open

Quiz 16

1) What is the only country to win a gold medal at every Winter Olympics?
2) Who was the first pitcher to have 3,000 career strikeouts?
3) Who was the first American driver to win the Formula One World Championship?
4) Who stunned Kentucky to win the NCAA Division I men's basketball championship in one of the greatest tournament upsets ever in 1966?
5) What sport originated the term hat trick?
6) What male alpine skier has the most overall World Cup titles?
7) What are the five events in an alpine skiing World Cup competition?
8) Who are the only two NBA players with more than 50 rebounds in a game?
9) In what was dubbed as "The Match of the Century," Seabiscuit defeated what 1937 Triple Crown winner in 1938?
10) What college has won the most NCAA Division I women's basketball titles?

Quiz 16 Answers

1) United States
2) Walter Johnson - 1923
3) Phil Hill - 1961
4) Texas Western – It was the first all African American lineup to win a national championship.
5) Cricket - The term first appeared in 1858 in cricket when H. H. Stephenson took three wickets with three consecutive balls; fans held a collection for him and presented him with a hat bought with the proceeds.
6) Marcel Hirscher - Austria
7) Slalom, giant slalom, super giant slalom, downhill, and combined (downhill and slalom)
8) Bill Russell and Wilt Chamberlain
9) War Admiral
10) Connecticut

Quiz 17

1) What year was the first NFL night game?
2) What MLB pitcher has the career record for most wins?
3) The famous black power salute of Tommie Smith and John Carlos at the 1968 Mexico City Olympic games took place at the medal ceremony for what event?
4) What is the record for the fewest pitches ever for a complete MLB game?
5) What is the record for most gold medals won in a single Olympics?
6) Who are the only two females to win all four tennis Grand Slam singles tournaments during their career plus the Olympic singles gold medal?
7) What driver has won the most Formula One World Championships?
8) What country has won the most cricket World Cups?
9) How many NCAA Division I men's basketball teams have gone undefeated in winning the national championship?
10) Who is the only MLB player who has won an MVP with two different teams at two different positions??

Quiz 17 Answers

1) 1929
2) Cy Young - 511
3) 200-meter sprint - Tommie Smith won the gold; John Carlos won the bronze.
4) 58 - Charles Barrett in 1944
5) Eight - Michael Phelps in swimming at the 2008 Beijing games
6) Steffi Graf and Serena Williams
7) Michael Schumacher (Germany) - seven from 1994-2004
8) Australia
9) Seven - San Francisco (1956), North Carolina (1957), UCLA (1964), UCLA (1967), UCLA (1972), UCLA (1973), Indiana (1976)
10) Alex Rodriguez - Rangers at shortstop and Yankees at third base

Quiz 18

1) What five disciplines make up the modern Olympic pentathlon?
2) What is the lowest score ever recorded for an 18-hole round in a women's LPGA tournament?
3) In the 1908 London Olympics, a team of eight London policemen beat a team of Liverpool policemen for the gold medal, and a third team of British policemen won the bronze in what sport that was discontinued in 1920?
4) Who was the first PGA golfer to shoot their age in a tournament round?
5) In which Winter Olympics team sport is pebbling part of the preparation?
6) Who is the only MLB player to hit a home run in every inning from the 1st to the 16th over their career?
7) Although no woman has completed a four or five major calendar Grand Slam in golf, one woman won all three majors that were contested in a calendar year; who was she?
8) Who has won the most Vezina Trophies as the NHL's best goaltender?
9) Who holds the NBA career record for most blocks?
10) Who has the highest NCAA Division I men's basketball career scoring average?

Quiz 18 Answers

1) Shooting, swimming, fencing, equestrian show jumping, and running
2) 59 - Annika Sorenstam in 2001
3) Tug of war - There was no limit on the number of teams a nation could enter which resulted in the British sweep of the medals.
4) Sam Snead - He shot a 67 at the 1979 Quad Cities Open.
5) Curling - Pebbling the ice is done to create friction for the stone to curl; they sprinkle the ice with tiny water droplets which freeze on the surface to create a pebbled texture.
6) Willie Mays
7) Mildred "Babe" Didrikson Zaharias - 1950
8) Jacques Plante - seven in the 1950s and 1960s
9) Hakeem Olajuwon - 3,830
10) Pete Maravich - 44.2 ppg for LSU from 1967-1970

Quiz 19

1) What are the colors of the five rings on the Olympic flag?
2) How many male golfers have completed a double career Grand Slam by winning each of the four major championships at least twice?
3) From 1900 to 1908, Ray Ewry won eight track and field gold medals in what jumping events that were discontinued in 1912?
4) What country did the U.S. defeat in the men's hockey gold medal game in Lake Placid Olympics in 1980?
5) Who set a long jump world record at the 1968 Mexico City Olympics that would stand for 23 years?
6) What NHL player has the second most career regular season points?
7) What player has the most MLB World Series wins?
8) Who were first pair of NFL teammates to each rush for 1,000 yards in the same season?
9) What are the seven events in the women's track and field heptathlon?
10) What triple Olympic gold medalist had a daughter who became a princess?

Quiz 19 Answers

1) Blue, yellow, black, green, red
2) Two - Jack Nicklaus and Tiger Woods
3) Standing long jump, standing high jump, and standing triple jump - They were the same as today's events, but the athlete started in the standing position with no approach run.
4) Finland - They defeated the Soviet Union 4-3 in the semi-final "Miracle on Ice" game.
5) Bob Beamon (U.S.) - His jump of 29 feet 2 1/2 inches was more than 21 inches better than the prior world record.
6) Jaromir Jagr - 1,921 points
7) Yogi Berra - 10
8) Mercury Morris and Larry Csonka - 1972 Miami Dolphins
9) 100-meter hurdles, high jump, shot put, 200 meters, long jump, javelin, 800 meters
10) John B. Kelly Sr. - He won golds in the single and double sculls in 1920 Antwerp and gold in the double sculls in 1924 Paris and was the father of actress Grace Kelly who became the Princess of Monaco.

Quiz 20

1) The Army vs. Navy football game was the first time instant replay was used in any sports broadcast; what year was it?
2) Who has the MLB record for most runs scored in a season?
3) Who was the first woman to win gold medals in two different sports at the same Winter Olympics?
4) How long was the longest consecutive game win streak in U.S. high school football?
5) Who was the first African American to win a Wimbledon singles title?
6) Who is the only MLB player to hit 60 or more home runs in a season three times?
7) At which Olympics did Jean-Claude Killy win three skiing gold medals?
8) What was the name of the terrorist group responsible for the violence at the 1972 Munich Olympics?

9) Who was the first NFL quarterback to complete 400 passes in a season?
10) How many basketball players have won NCAA, Olympic, and NBA championships?

Quiz 20 Answers

1) 1963
2) Babe Ruth - 179 in 1921
3) Ester Ledecka (Czech Republic) - 2018 PyeongChang Olympics in skiing and snowboarding
4) 151 games - De La Salle Spartans from Concord, California from 1991-2004
5) Althea Gibson - 1957
6) Sammy Sosa - in 1998, 1999, 2001
7) 1968 - Grenoble, France
8) Black September
9) Warren Moon - 1991 Houston Oilers
10) Seven - Clyde Lovellette, Bill Russell, K.C. Jones, Jerry Lucas, Quinn Buckner, Michael Jordan, Magic Johnson

Quiz 21

1) What two athletes are tied for the most track and field career Olympic gold medals?
2) What year was the oldest recorded ancient Olympics?
3) What is the only jersey number retired league wide by the NHL?
4) Who has the most career World Series RBIs?
5) Who was the first athlete to appear on the front of the Wheaties box?
6) How many times did Wayne Gretzky score 50 NHL goals in the first 50 games of the season?
7) In 1931, what female pitcher became the first woman in professional baseball to strikeout Babe Ruth and Lou Gehrig in an exhibition game?
8) Who has the NFL career record for most fumbles?
9) Who was the first player in MLB history to steal 100 bases in a season?

10) The United States lost the men's basketball gold medal for the first time ever at what Olympics?

Quiz 21 Answers

1) Paavo Nurmi (Finland) - 9 golds from 1920 to 1928 and Carl Lewis (U.S.) - 9 golds from 1984 to 1996
2) 776 BC
3) 99 - Wayne Gretzky
4) Mickey Mantle - 40
5) Bob Richards in 1958 - He was the 1952 and 1956 Olympic pole vault gold medalist.
6) Three - 1981-82, 1983-84, 1984-85
7) Jackie Mitchell - In an exhibition game between the New York Yankees and the Chattanooga Lookouts, a class AA minor league team, she struck out Ruth and Gehrig in succession; she was 17 years old at the time. Baseball commissioner Kenesaw Mountain Landis banned women from the sport later that year.
8) Brett Favre - 166
9) Maury Wills – 104 steals in 1962
10) 1972 Munich

Quiz 22

1) What were the first Olympics ever televised?
2) Who was the first NHL player with 500 career goals?
3) Ichiro Suzuki broke the MLB single season hits record with 262 in 2004; whose 84-year-old record did he break?
4) Who did Miami beat to win the Super Bowl and retain their perfect undefeated season?
5) What was the first professional hockey team Wayne Gretzky played for?
6) Who is the only MLB player to ever hit a walk-off inside-the-park grand slam?
7) Who was the first goalie with 500 career wins?
8) How old was the youngest player in MLB history?
9) What hall of fame player won the MLB batting Triple Crown with only nine home runs?

10) Who was the first NFL player to score 200 career touchdowns?

Quiz 22 Answers

1) Berlin - 1936
2) Maurice Richard - 500th in 1957
3) George Sisler - 257 hits in 1920
4) Washington Redskins
5) Indianapolis Racers - He only played eight games with the Racers before being traded to the Edmonton Oilers.
6) Roberto Clemente - 1956
7) Patrick Roy
8) 15 - Joe Nuxhall for the 1944 Cincinnati Reds
9) Ty Cobb - 1909
10) Jerry Rice

Quiz 23

1) What Winter Olympics athlete has the most career medals?
2) Who was the first MLB pitcher to reach 20 wins in a season with only 1 loss?
3) Who was the first NBA player to score 20,000 career points?
4) What was the first country to win consecutive women's rugby World Cups?
5) Who won the 2015 cricket World Cup?
6) How many male golfers have held all four major championships at the same time?
7) Who is the career WNBA scoring leader?
8) Who was the second NHL player with 500 career goals?
9) Who was the first NFL quarterback with 6,000 career completions?
10) Who won the 2015 women's soccer World Cup?

Quiz 23 Answers

1) Marit Bjorgen (Norway) - 15 cross country skiing medals from 2002-2018
2) Roger Clemens – He finished the season 20-3 in 2001.

3) Bob Pettit - 1965
4) New Zealand - 1998 and 2002
5) Australia
6) Two - Bobby Jones and Tiger Woods
7) Diana Taurasi
8) Gordie Howe - 500th in 1962
9) Brett Favre - 2009 Minnesota Vikings
10) United States

Quiz 24

1) Who was the first African American to be named Associated Press female athlete of the year?
2) What is the only team that was part of the ABA for its entire nine years without ever moving or changing its name and joined the NBA and still has not moved or changed its name?
3) Who was the first player with 20,000 receiving yards in their NFL career?
4) Who were the first two NBA teammates to both score 2,000 points in a season?
5) What is the only Olympic sport that still bans professionals?
6) Who was the first NFL player to intercept 80 passes in their career?
7) What was the first U.S. men's professional sport to have female referees for regular season play?
8) What two players share the NBA career record for most consecutive seasons leading the league in points?
9) Who was the first MLB player to hit home runs in his teens and in his forties?
10) What American has the most Winter Olympics medals?

Quiz 24 Answers

1) Althea Gibson - tennis in 1957
2) Indiana Pacers
3) Jerry Rice - 2001 Oakland Raiders
4) Jerry West and Elgin Baylor - Los Angeles Lakers 1964-65 season
5) Wrestling

6) Paul Krause - Washington Redskins and Minnesota Vikings from 1964-1979
7) NBA - 1997
8) Wilt Chamberlain and Michael Jordan - seven
9) Ty Cobb - He played form 1905-1928 and started in MLB at age 18.
10) Apolo Anton Ohno - eight medals from 2002 to 2010 in short track speed skating

Quiz 25

1) What were the first Olympics held in the southern hemisphere?
2) What Pro Football Hall of Fame player once led the NFL in passing, interceptions, and punting in the same season?
3) What team won the first college football BCS Championship?
4) Who was the first African American to play Major League Baseball?
5) Who is the oldest golfer to win a PGA tour event?
6) In what country did volleyball originate?
7) Who was the first freshman to win the Heisman Trophy?
8) Who is the only person to win the Olympic marathon twice in a row?
9) Who were the first NFL quarterback and running back teammates to each rush for 1,000 yards in the same season?
10) What is the record for the most Olympic games anyone has ever competed in?

Quiz 25 Answers

1) Melbourne, Australia - 1956
2) Sammy Baugh - 1943 Washington Redskins
3) University of Tennessee - 1998
4) Moses Fleetwood Walker - On May 1, 1884, he became the first African American in the major leagues; he played 42 games for the Toledo Blue Stockings before suffering an injury and returning to the minor leagues. This was 63 years before Jackie Robinson's major league debut. The Blue Stockings were formed as a minor league team in 1883 and moved to the major league for the 1884 season; they moved back to the minor leagues for the 1885 season which was their last season.

5) Sam Snead - He was 52 years old when he won the 1965 Greater Greensboro Open.
6) United States
7) Johnny Manziel - 2012
8) Abebe Bikila - 1960 and 1964
9) Michael Vick and Warrick Dunn - 2006 Atlanta Falcons
10) 10 - A Canadian equestrian rider competed in every Olympics from 1972 to 2012 except the boycotted 1980 games; he has one silver medal in 2008.

Quiz 26

1) Who has the highest season batting average ever for a starting pitcher?
2) What was the first team sport added to the Olympics?
3) What Olympics were the first to feature active NBA players on the U.S. team?
4) Who has the most career MLB batting titles?
5) Who holds the record with seven MLB MVP Awards?
6) What is the name of the biennial men's golf competition between teams from Europe and the United States?
7) What MLB player has the highest career on-base percentage?
8) Who won the 2018 women's field hockey World Cup?
9) What boxer won world titles in the largest number of weight divisions?
10) What 10 events make up the decathlon?

Quiz 26 Answers

1) Walter Johnson - .433 in 1925
2) Soccer - 1900
3) 1992 - Barcelona
4) Ty Cobb - 11
5) Barry Bonds
6) Ryder Cup - established in 1927
7) Ted Williams - .482
8) Netherlands

9) Manny Pacquiao - Eight divisions - flyweight, super bantamweight, featherweight, super featherweight, lightweight, light welterweight, welterweight, super welterweight
10) 100, 400, and 1500-meter runs, 110 hurdles, long jump, high jump, pole vault, shot put, discus, javelin

Quiz 27

1) Who is the youngest jockey ever to win horse racing's Triple Crown?
2) Who duplicated Jesse Owens' feat by winning four track and field Olympic gold medals in 1984?
3) Who is the first world boxing champion to hold a PhD degree?
4) Who has the most career World Series hits?
5) What was the first sport to be filmed?
6) Who was the first NFL running back to rush for 100 career touchdowns?
7) Who was the first woman to repeat as Olympic champion in the heptathlon?
8) What was the first country to win two consecutive men's rugby World Cups?
9) How many times did Babe Ruth hit four MLB home runs in one game?
10) What was the first city to host the modern Olympics twice?

Quiz 27 Answers

1) Steve Cauthen - He was 18 years old when he won the Triple Crown aboard Affirmed in 1978.
2) Carl Lewis – He won the 100, 200, 4 x 100, and long jump
3) Vitali Klitschko - He was a three-time world heavyweight champion starting in 1999 and ending in 2013 and got his PhD in sports science in 2000. He has also served as mayor of Kiev and in the Ukrainian parliament.
4) Yogi Berra - 71
5) Boxing - 1894
6) Jim Brown - Cleveland Browns from 1957-1965
7) Jackie Joyner-Kersee (U.S.) - 1988 Seoul and 1992 Barcelona

8) New Zealand - 2011 and 2015
9) 0
10) Paris – 1900 and 1924

Quiz 28

1) Since Ted Williams' .406 season in 1941, what MLB player has had the highest season batting average?
2) In the post 1920 era, who has the most consecutive MLB batting titles leading both leagues?
3) Since the start of the Winter Olympics, how many athletes have won medals at both the winter and summer games?
4) How many players have won more than one MLB batting Triple Crown?
5) Who is the only person to have both a reception and an interception in the Super Bowl?
6) In 1930, who won the first Sullivan Award given to the most outstanding U.S. amateur athlete?
7) What team has the most consecutive NBA championships?
8) What is the name of the biennial women's golf competition between teams from Europe and the United States?
9) Who hit a home run from both sides of the plate in the same game 10 times over their MLB career?
10) What year were professionals allowed to compete in the Olympics?

Quiz 28 Answers

1) Tony Gwynn - .394 with San Diego in 1994
2) Rod Carew - three from 1973-1975
3) Five - Eddie Eagan (U.S.), Jacob Tullin Thams (Norway), Christa Luding-Rothenburger (East Germany), Clara Hughes (Canada), Lauryn Williams (U.S.)
4) Two - Rogers Hornsby and Ted Williams each won two.
5) Deion Sanders – He had an interception in Super Bowl XXIX and a reception in Super Bowl XXX.
6) Bobby Jones - golf
7) Boston Celtics - eight from 1959-1966
8) Solheim Cup – started in 1990

9) Mickey Mantle
10) 1984

Quiz 29

1) Among countries that have won at least one Olympic medal, what country has the lowest number of medals per capita?
2) Who won the 2017 women's rugby World Cup?
3) Who was the first player in the WNBA to dunk?
4) What is the maximum number of dogs a musher can have on their team at the start of the Iditarod Trail Sled Dog Race?
5) Who was the first athlete to win gold medals in five consecutive Olympics?
6) Who is the first person to win a medal in six straight Summer Olympics?
7) What is the name of one of the oldest trophies in college football contested between Minnesota and Michigan?
8) Who was the oldest player to lead the NBA in scoring?
9) What player won 11 NBA championships and 5 MVP awards?
10) What was the first MLB franchise to move to three different states during their history?

Quiz 29 Answers

1) India
2) New Zealand
3) Lisa Leslie - 2002
4) 16
5) Steven Redgrave – British rower from 1984–2000
6) Kim Rhode - U.S. skeet shooter from 1996–2016
7) Little Brown Jug – started in 1892
8) Michael Jordan - 35
9) Bill Russell
10) Baltimore Orioles - formerly Milwaukee Brewers (1901), St. Louis Browns (1902), and then Baltimore Orioles (1954)

Quiz 30

1) What MLB pitcher has the most career losses?
2) Professional bowler Walter Ray Williams Jr. is also a nine-time world champion in what other sport?
3) Who was the first woman to have her name engraved on the Stanley Cup?
4) Who was the first NBA player to average a triple-double for a season?
5) Who was the first NFL punter to average over 50 yards a punt for a season?
6) Who was the second NFL player ever to have 1,000 yards rushing and 1,000 yards receiving in a season?
7) What is the world's oldest tennis tournament?
8) What woman golfer has the most career LPGA Majors wins?
9) To allow visitors to travel safely to Olympia, what was put in place before and during each of the ancient Olympic games?
10) Who was the second NBA player ever to average a triple-double over a season?

Quiz 30 Answers

1) Cy Young – 316 losses
2) Horseshoes
3) Marguerite Norris - In 1952, she became the first female chief executive in NHL history after inheriting the Detroit Red Wings presidency from her father, James Norris Sr., on his death. In 1954, the Red Wings defeated the Montreal Canadiens making her the first woman to have her name engraved on the Stanley Cup.
4) Oscar Robertson - 30.8 points, 12.5 rebounds, and 11.4 assists in 1961-62
5) Sammy Baugh – He had 51.4 yards per punt for the 1940 Washington Redskins while also playing quarterback.
6) Marshall Faulk - 1999 St. Louis Rams
7) Wimbledon - 1877
8) Patty Berg - 15 from 1937-1958
9) A truce or ekecheiria - Wars were suspended; legal disputes were put on hold, and no death penalties were carried out during this

time.

10) Russell Westbrook - Oklahoma City Thunder in 2016-17

Quiz 31

1) Who is the first player ever in both the Pro Football Hall of Fame and the Canadian Football Hall of Fame?
2) Who is the only six-time winner (male or female) of the Associated Press Athlete of the year?
3) In one Olympics, what is the largest number of different sports a single competitor has won medals in?
4) What country won the first women's rugby World Cup?
5) According to USGA rules, how many clubs can a golfer have in their bag?
6) Who was the first woman to win the Sullivan Award given annually to the most outstanding U.S. amateur athlete?
7) Lacrosse was invented in what country?
8) How old was the oldest Summer Olympics medalist?
9) What is the New Zealand rugby team called?
10) In any NCAA division, what is the record for most consecutive team national championships in any men's or women's sport?

Quiz 31 Answers

1) Warren Moon
2) Babe Didrikson Zaharias - 1932, 1945, 1946, 1947, 1950, 1954
3) Three – American Frank Kugler won medals in freestyle wrestling, weightlifting, and tug of war in the 1904 St. Louis games.
4) United States - 1991
5) 14
6) Ann Curtis - 1944 for swimming
7) United States - Native Americans invented the game.
8) 72 - shooting in 1920
9) All Blacks
10) 31 years - Kenyon College in division III men's swimming and diving from 1980-2010

Quiz 32

1) Who was the first MLB player to hit 500 home runs and steal 500 bases?
2) Who holds the NBA career record for most minutes played?
3) Who is the only male diver to ever sweep the diving events at consecutive Olympic games?
4) Who was the first person to repeat as Olympic decathlon gold medalist?
5) Who is the only MLB pitcher with three Triple Crowns leading both leagues?
6) What two MLB players hold the record for playing the most consecutive seasons with the same team?
7) In 1965, Satchell Paige pitched three innings for the Kansas City Athletics against the Boston Red Sox; how old was Paige?
8) Who has the most Stanley Cup wins combined as player and non-player?
9) Who was the first MLB player to steal 1,000 bases?
10) What father and son drivers were both Formula One World Champions?

Quiz 32 Answers

1) Barry Bonds - 2003
2) Kareem Abdul-Jabbar - 57,446 minutes
3) Greg Louganis - 1984 Los Angeles and 1988 Seoul
4) Bob Mathias (U.S.) - 1948 and 1952
5) Sandy Koufax - 1963, 1965, 1966
6) Brooks Robinson (Baltimore Orioles) and Carl Yastrzemski (Boston Red Sox) - 23 seasons
7) 59
8) Jean Beliveau - 17 wins with 10 as player and 7 as non-player with the Montreal Canadiens
9) Rickey Henderson
10) Graham and Damon Hill - Graham in 1962 and 1968 and son Damon in 1996

Quiz 33

1) In the 22 seasons between 1980-81 and 2001-02, three NHL players won 21 of the 22 Art Ross Trophies for scoring; who were they?
2) Who was the lone college player on the 1992 Olympic basketball Dream Team?
3) In what two Olympic sports do men and women compete head to head?
4) Who was the first person to win the *Sports Illustrated* Sportsperson of the Year twice?
5) What are the only two days during the year where there are no MLB, NFL, NHL or NBA games played?
6) Who was the first NCAA Division I football player to rush for 2,000 yards in a season?
7) Who was the only Olympic medalist to also win a Nobel Prize?
8) Who was the first NFL quarterback to throw 3,000 completions?
9) Who is the only person to win six consecutive tennis Grand Slam singles tournaments and not complete a calendar year Grand Slam?
10) Who holds the NBA career record for highest points per game?

Quiz 33 Answers

1) Wayne Gretzky (10 times), Jaromir Jagr (5 times), Mario Lemieux (6 times)
2) Christian Laettner
3) Equestrian and sailing
4) Tiger Woods - 1996 and 2000
5) The Monday before and the Wednesday after the MLB All-Star Game - The All-Star Game is always played on a Tuesday in July, and there are no MLB games the day before or after, and MLB is the only professional sport played in July.
6) Marcus Allen - 1981 USC
7) Philip Noel-Baker (Great Britain) - He won a silver medal in the 1500-meter run in 1920 and the Nobel Peace Prize in 1959.
8) Fran Tarkenton - 1976 Minnesota Vikings
9) Martina Navratilova – 1983 Wimbledon to 1984 U.S. Open
10) Michael Jordan - 30.1 ppg

Quiz 34

1) In 1935, what athlete set world records in three different events in 45 minutes?
2) What two teams played in the first college football game?
3) Who was head of the committee that organized the opening day ceremonies for the 1960 Squaw Valley Winter Olympics?
4) What NASCAR driver has the most career victories?
5) Who was the first president of the NFL?
6) Who was the first tennis player ever expelled from a Grand Slam tournament?
7) What year did Roger Bannister run the first sub-four-minute mile?
8) What Australian was the first woman to swim the 100-meter freestyle in under one minute in the Olympics?
9) Who is the only pitcher in MLB history to throw consecutive no hitters?
10) Who was the first NBA player drafted number one who never played U.S. high school or college basketball?

Quiz 34 Answers

1) Jesse Owens - At a Big Ten track and field meet, he set world records in the long jump, 220-yard sprint, and 220-yard low hurdles and tied the world record for the 100-yard dash.
2) Rutgers and Princeton - In 1869, Rutgers beat Princeton 6-4 in a game that had 25 players on each side and one-point touchdowns; the first team to reach six points was declared the winner.
3) Walt Disney
4) Richard Petty – 200 wins
5) Jim Thorpe
6) John McEnroe - 1990 Australian Open
7) 1954
8) Dawn Fraser - 1964 Tokyo
9) Johnny Vander Meer - 1938 Cincinnati Reds
10) Yao Ming

Quiz 35

1) What famous philosopher was a two-time winner at the ancient Olympics?
2) How many events were there in the first ancient Olympics?
3) Who is the only NBA player with 40 points and 40 rebounds in a game?
4) How many times have the Winter and Summer Olympic games been held in the same country in the same year?
5) Who was the first woman to appear in any NHL game?
6) Who was the first NHL player to score 50 goals in a season?
7) Who won the 2015 men's rugby World Cup?
8) What NHL player has the second most career regular season goals?
9) Who was the first NFL player to score 2,000 points?
10) What country won the first men's soccer World Cup?

Quiz 35 Answers

1) Plato - He won in plankration which was a submission sport combining elements of wrestling and boxing but with very few rules; only eye gouging and biting were banned.
2) One - a foot race
3) Wilt Chamberlain - 1968
4) Three - 1924 Paris and Chamonix, 1932 Los Angeles and Lake Placid, 1936 Berlin and Garmisch-Partenkirchen
5) Manon Rheaume - She goaltended for the Tampa Bay Lightning in a pre-season game against the St. Louis Blues in September 1992.
6) Maurice Richard
7) New Zealand
8) Gordie Howe - 801 goals
9) George Blanda
10) Uruguay - 1930

Quiz 36

1) Who was the first NHL player with 100 assists in a season?
2) Who was the first MLB player with 3,000 hits and 500 home runs

in their career?

3) In 1994, Pete Rose broke the MLB most games played record; whose record did he break?
4) Who was the first player to lead the NBA in scoring and assists in the same season?
5) Who was the lightest boxer to ever hold the world heavyweight title?
6) What college was the first to have seven Heisman Trophy winners?
7) Why are MLB umpires required to wear black underwear?
8) What MLB pitcher led his league the most times in strikeouts?
9) Who was the first non-Canadian player to have a 100-point NHL season?
10) Who was the first NBA player to get a quadruple-double in a game?

Quiz 36 Answers

1) Bobby Orr - 1970-71 Boston Bruins
2) Willie Mays - 1970
3) Carl Yastrzemski
4) Nate Archibald - 34 ppg and 11.4 assists per game in 1971-72
5) Bob Fitzsimmons - 167 pounds when he won the title in 1897
6) Notre Dame - Angelo Bertelli, John Lujack, Leon Hart, John Lattner, Paul Hornung, John Huarte, Tim Brown
7) In case their pants split
8) Walter Johnson - 12 times
9) Kent Nilsson (Sweden) - 131 points for 1980-81 Calgary Flames
10) Nate Thurmond - 1974

Quiz 37

1) Who holds the career record for most NBA games played?
2) Who was the first female jockey to win a Triple Crown race?
3) What NHL player never missed a regular season game in his career and holds the record for most consecutive games played at 964?
4) Who is the only person named Associated Press athlete of the year in two different sports?
5) In addition to his Olympic swimming medals, Johnny Weissmuller

won an Olympic medal in what other sport?

6) Who has the highest MLB career slugging percentage?
7) Who holds the MLB record reaching base in 84 consecutive games?
8) In which three Olympic games were there boycotts by various teams?
9) What were the first Olympics televised in the U.S.?
10) Who was the last person to win an MLB batting Triple Crown?

Quiz 37 Answers

1) Robert Parish - 1,611 games
2) Julie Krone - 1993 Belmont Stakes aboard Colonial Affair
3) Doug Jarvis - played from 1975-1987
4) Babe Didrikson Zaharias - track and field in 1932; golf in 1945, 1946, 1947, 1950, 1954
5) Water polo - bronze in 1924
6) Babe Ruth - .690
7) Ted Williams - 1949
8) 1976 Montreal in protest of a New Zealand rugby tour of South Africa, 1980 Moscow in protest of the Soviet Union's invasion of Afghanistan, 1984 Los Angeles where the Soviet Union withdrew in retaliation for 1980 boycott
9) 1960 Squaw Valley Winter Olympics
10) Miguel Cabrera - 2012

Quiz 38

1) What is the lowest score ever recorded for an 18-hole round of golf in a PGA tournament?
2) In the ancient Olympics, women weren't allowed to participate or even be in the stadium, but they could still win the Olympic prize in what event?
3) Who was the first NFL quarterback with 70,000 career passing yards?
4) Who was the first American born NHL player to score 100 points in a season?
5) Who was the last man to win a calendar year tennis Grand Slam?

6) Who has the most career regular season points for an NHL defenseman?
7) What college has won the most consecutive NCAA Division I women's basketball titles?
8) What coach leads the NFL in career wins?
9) What player has been named to the most MLB All-Star rosters?
10) In 1932, what athlete won the team championship single-handedly at the AAU national track and field meet?

Quiz 38 Answers

1) 58 - Jim Furyk in 2016
2) Chariot racing - The prize went to the owner of the chariot and horse, so women could and did win the prize.
3) Brett Favre - 2010 Minnesota Vikings
4) Neal Broten - 105 points with the 1985-86 Minnesota North Stars
5) Rod Laver - 1969
6) Ray Bourque - 1,579 points
7) Connecticut - four consecutive from 2013-2016
8) Don Shula - 347 with Baltimore Colts and Miami Dolphins
9) Hank Aaron - 21 times
10) Mildred "Babe" Didrikson Zaharias - She competed in 8 out of 10 events; she won 5 and tied for first in a sixth event. She won the team championship despite being the only member of her team.

Quiz 39

1) What country has won the most Summer Olympics medals?
2) What was the first country to win two consecutive women's soccer World Cups?
3) What was the first Olympics to include competitors from all six continents?
4) Who is the only driver to win five consecutive Formula One World Championships?
5) Who was the first American born NHL player to reach 500 career goals?
6) What MLB player has won the most Gold Glove Awards?

7) At the first modern Olympics, what was awarded to winners?
8) Who was the first female to win individual gold medals at four consecutive Olympics?
9) Who holds the NBA career record for most seasons leading the league in rebounds?
10) Who holds the NBA career record for most points?

Quiz 39 Answers

1) United States
2) Germany - 2003 and 2007
3) Stockholm - 1912
4) Michael Schumacher (Germany) - 2000 to 2004
5) Joey Mullen - 500th in 1997
6) Gregg Maddux - 18
7) Silver medal - Second place received bronze medals.
8) Kaori Icho - Japanese wrestler from 2004 to 2016
9) Wilt Chamberlain - 11
10) Kareem Abdul-Jabbar - 38,387

Television

Quiz 1

1) What series starred Keri Russell as a girl fresh out of high school who follows her high school crush to college to be near him?
2) Martin Caldin, a U.S. Air Force pilot and NASA public relations person, wrote the novel *Cyborg* which was the source material for what show?
3) What year was the first *Today* broadcast?
4) What line follows "You are traveling through another dimension, a dimension not only of sight and sound but of mind. A journey into a wondrous land of imagination"?
5) Who played the talk show sidekick on *The Larry Sanders Show*?
6) Who played Joey Potter on *Dawson's Creek*?
7) Who played the title role in *Doogie Howser, M.D.*?
8) What year were the first Emmy Awards?
9) What sitcom starred Ricky Gervais as an actor reduced to working as an extra whose attempts to boost his career end in failure and embarrassment?
10) What was the first soap opera to expand to 60 minutes?

Quiz 1 Answers

1) *Felicity* (1998-2002)
2) *The Six Million Dollar Man* (1974-1978)
3) 1951
4) Next stop, the Twilight Zone!
5) Jeffrey Tambor
6) Katie Holmes
7) Neil Patrick Harris
8) 1949
9) *Extras* (2005-2007)
10) *Another World* - 1975

Quiz 2

1) On *Game of Thrones*, the seven kingdoms are part of what continent?
2) What is the only television show that was made into a Best Picture Oscar winner?
3) What was the first weekly U.S. television series budgeted at over $1 million per episode?
4) What supernatural series had brothers Stefan and Damon Salvatore returning to their home of Mystic Falls, Virginia?
5) Who played Lois Lane on *Lois & Clark: The New Adventures of Superman*?
6) In *Mad About You*, what was Paul Buchman's occupation?
7) What were the three main competing syndicated newsmagazine shows that all debuted in the late 1980s?
8) What crime drama focuses on Baltimore's inner-city drug scene?
9) Who played the agent Ari Gold on the sitcom *Entourage*?
10) What was the name of the original DCI on the British detective drama *Midsomer Murders*?

Quiz 2 Answers

1) Westeros
2) *Marty* - 1955
3) *Battlestar Galactica* - 1978
4) *The Vampire Diaries* (2009-2017)
5) Teri Hatcher
6) Filmmaker
7) *A Current Affair* (1986), *Inside Edition* (1988), *Hard Copy* (1989)
8) *The Wire* (2002-2008)
9) Jeremy Piven
10) Tom Barnaby

Quiz 3

1) What series followed police officers Mike Danko, Willie Gillis, and Terry Webster?

2) Who plays the title character in *Have Gun - Will Travel*?
3) What was the first series set in Hawaii?
4) What drama starred Leo McKern as a portly eccentric London criminal law barrister?
5) In what city was *Matlock* set?
6) What was the first U.S. dramatic series to feature an African American actor in a lead role.
7) What sitcom centered on a church deacon and his assistant who disagreed on what was best for their congregation?
8) What was the first U.S. show to broadcast 1,000 episodes?
9) What children's series had a family that is thrown back in time and must survive in the age of dinosaurs?
10) What was the make and model of Rockford's car on *The Rockford Files*?

Quiz 3 Answers

1) *The Rookies* (1972-1976)
2) Richard Boone
3) *Hawaiian Eye* (1959-1963) - It wasn't filmed there.
4) *Rumpole of the Bailey* (1978-1992)
5) Atlanta
6) *I Spy* - starring Bill Cosby in 1965
7) *Amen* (1986-1991)
8) *The Howdy Doody Show* (1947-1960)
9) *Land of the Lost* (1974-1977)
10) Pontiac Firebird

Quiz 4

1) What was the name of the hospital on *St. Elsewhere*?
2) What year was cigarette advertising banned from U.S. television?
3) What is the family name on *Everybody Loves Raymond*?
4) Who played the title role in the private eye series *Barnaby Jones*?
5) What show had John Davidson, Fran Tarkenton, and Cathy Lee Crosby as hosts?

6) Who played the title role in *The Life and Legend of Wyatt Earp*?
7) What U.S. show has aired the most episodes?
8) What sitcom character's real name was Exigius 12½?
9) In *77 Sunset Strip*, what was the character name of the restaurant valet played by Edd Byrnes?
10) Who played the title role in the sitcom *Blossom*?

Quiz 4 Answers

1) St. Eligius
2) 1971
3) Barone
4) Buddy Ebsen
5) *That's Incredible!* (1980-1984)
6) Hugh O'Brian
7) *SportsCenter* - over 50,000 unique episodes since 1979
8) Uncle Martin, the Martian on *My Favorite Martian* (1963-1966)
9) Kookie
10) Mayim Bialik

Quiz 5

1) What was the first show to earn Emmys for all its principal cast members?
2) What science fiction series about an extraterrestrial race arriving on Earth was a reboot of a 1980s miniseries and series?
3) What talent show was originally hosted by Ed McMahon?
4) How did the name Muppet originate for the characters on *The Muppet Show*?
5) What show had the last theme song to make it to number one on Billboard's Hot 100?
6) What series starred Lloyd Bridges as scuba diver Mike Nelson?
7) What was Kyra Sedgwick's character name on *The Closer*?
8) What sitcom was based on the childhood experiences of comedian Chris Rock?
9) What sitcom featured a recovering alcoholic who becomes the manager of a big city bus station?

10) What series centered on the lives of three young alien/human hybrids with extraordinary gifts?

Quiz 5 Answers

1) *All in the Family* (1971-1979)
2) *V* (2009-2011)
3) *Star Search* (1983-2004)
4) It is a combination of the words marionette and puppet.
5) *Miami Vice* - "Theme from Miami Vice" (1985)
6) *Sea Hunt* (1958-1961)
7) Brenda Johnson
8) *Everybody Hates Chris* (2005-2009)
9) *The John Larroquette Show* (1993-1996)
10) *Roswell* (1999-2002)

Quiz 6

1) What state was *Twin Peaks* set in?
2) What quiz show was the center of the 1950s scandal involving Charles Van Doren and Herb Stempel?
3) What police drama features two Oscar winners in its lead roles?
4) What series centered on the members of a dysfunctional California family that runs an independent funeral home?
5) Who was the first African American to win the Outstanding Lead Actress in a Comedy Series Emmy?
6) What was the name of the house where Mrs. Muir lived with her children on *The Ghost & Mrs. Muir*?
7) What was the nickname of the Dwight Schultz character on *The A-Team*?
8) Who played the title role in *Dr. Quinn, Medicine Woman*?
9) What actress won six consecutive Outstanding Lead Actress in a Comedy Series Emmys from 2012-2017?
10) Who plays President Conrad Dalton on the political drama *Madam Secretary*?

Quiz 6 Answers

1) Washington
2) *Twenty-One* (1956-1958)
3) *The Streets of San Francisco* (1972-1977) - starring Karl Malden and Michael Douglas
4) *Six Feet Under* (2001-2005)
5) Isabel Sanford - *The Jeffersons* (1981)
6) Gull Cottage
7) "Howling Mad" Murdock
8) Jane Seymour
9) Julia Louis-Dreyfus - *Veep*
10) Keith Carradine

Quiz 7

1) What sitcom featured Frank Lambert, a construction worker, and Carol Foster, a beautician, who each have three children and must learn to live together after spontaneously getting married?
2) In *The Prisoner*, all the characters are assigned numbers rather than names; what is the number assigned to the title character?
3) What is the only primetime drama to be spun off from two separate shows?
4) What sitcom was known for obliterating the fourth wall to the point of casually chatting with the studio audience and cast members either in or out of character?
5) Who was a co-host and correspondent on *Entertainment Tonight* for 29 years?
6) Who played Balki Bartokomous on *Perfect Strangers*?
7) What was the name of the all-knowing, all-seeing artificial intelligence created by Harold Finch on *Person of Interest*?
8) Who was the original host of the daytime version of *Wheel of Fortune*?
9) What year did Walt Disney have its first series?
10) The series *GLOW* is set in the 1980s and features women in what activity?

Quiz 7 Answers

1) *Step by Step* (1991–1998)
2) Six
3) *Law & Order: Special Victims Unit* – It spun off from *Law & Order*, and the character of Detective John Munch came from *Homicide: Life on the Street.*
4) *It's Garry Shandling's Show* (1986–1990)
5) Mary Hart
6) Bronson Pinchot
7) The Machine
8) Chuck Woolery
9) 1954 – *Disneyland* which later became *Walt Disney's Wonderful World of Color*
10) Professional wrestling

Quiz 8

1) What was the first hour long western on U.S. television?
2) What sitcom starred Ricky Schroeder as spoiled rich kid Ricky Stratton?
3) What U.S. live action sitcom character appeared for the most consecutive years?
4) What drama was based on five siblings who are left to find their own way after their parents are killed by a drunk driver?
5) What award-winning songwriter appeared in the western *Laramie*?
6) Who was the first person to win Emmys for acting, writing, and directing for the same series?
7) What series centered on cases of an FBI unit specializing in missing persons investigations and starred Anthony LaPaglia and Poppy Montgomery?
8) What show has the most Emmy wins for a drama?
9) Who starred in the title role of Dr. Sam Waters in the crime drama *Profiler*?
10) On *Richard Diamond, Private Detective*, a future famous actress played the role of Sam, the switchboard operator, who only ever had her legs and hands visible on camera; who played the role?

Quiz 8 Answers

1) *Cheyenne* (1955-1963)
2) *Silver Spoons* (1982-1987)
3) Frasier Crane - Between *Cheers* and *Frasier*, Kelsey Grammer played the character for 20 consecutive years.
4) *Party of Five* (1990-2000)
5) Hoagy Carmichael - composer of "Stardust" and "Georgia on My Mind"
6) Alan Alda - *M*A*S*H*
7) *Without a Trace* (2002-2009)
8) *Game of Thrones* (2011-2019) - 59 wins
9) Ally Walker
10) Mary Tyler Moore

Quiz 9

1) What sitcom had Martin Lawrence playing a total of 10 characters over the series run?
2) What two series are tied for the most consecutive Outstanding Comedy Series Emmys at five?
3) Who co-starred with Michael Landon on *Little House on the Prairie* and *Highway to Heaven*?
4) What was the first nationally televised children's show in the U.S.?
5) Who starred as firefighter Tommy Gavin who deals with the fears of his job and his personal problems in the comedy drama *Rescue Me*?
6) Who was the only female comedy regular on *Your Show of Shows*?
7) What show originated the term "jumped the shark" indicating a show has had a sharp drop in quality or has inserted desperate attempts for ratings?
8) Tim Roth starred as Dr. Cal Lightman, the world's leading deception expert who studies facial expressions and involuntary body language, in what series?
9) Who was the first African American to win the Outstanding Lead Actress in a Drama Series Emmy?
10) Who was the first African American to win the Outstanding Lead Actor in a Comedy Series Emmy?

Quiz 9 Answers

1) *Martin* (1992-1997)
2) *Frasier* (1994-1998) and *Modern Family* (2010-2014)
3) Victor French
4) *The Howdy Doody Show* (1947-1960)
5) Dennis Leary
6) Imogene Coca
7) *Happy Days* - During the season five opener, Fonzie jumped a shark while water-skiing which marked the beginning of a sharp decline in the show's quality.
8) *Lie to Me* (2009-2011)
9) Viola Davis - *How to Get Away with Murder* (2015)
10) Robert Guillaume - *Benson* (1985)

Quiz 10

1) What stop motion animation series features voice work by Seth Green who is also one of the creators?
2) What were the names of the two main characters on *The Wild Wild West*?
3) What sitcom featured Mr. Floppy, a boozing, chain-smoking stuffed rabbit voiced by Bobcat Goldthwait, whom the lead character consults for advice?
4) What is the only U.S. primetime series to be on for at least 14 years without winning an Emmy?
5) What was the name of the late-night music show hosted by Wolfman Jack?
6) What was the first primetime series starring a female private eye?
7) What was the name of the housekeeper played by Miyoshi Umeki on *The Courtship of Eddie's Father*?
8) What was the first *Law & Order* spin-off?
9) *Boston Legal* was a spin-off of what series?
10) What was the name of Christopher Lloyd's character on *Taxi*?

Quiz 10 Answers

1) *Robot Chicken* - debuted in 2005

2) James West and Artemus Gordon
3) *Unhappily Ever After* (1995-1999)
4) *Supernatural* - debuted in 2005
5) *The Midnight Special* (1972-1981)
6) *Honey West* (1965-1966)
7) Mrs. Livingston
8) *Law & Order: Special Victims Unit* (1999)
9) *The Practice* (1997-2004)
10) Jim Ignatowski

Quiz 11

1) What is the longest running game show in the U.S.?
2) What sitcom marked the acting debut of Jerry Seinfeld?
3) What was the last U.S. show to have its entire run filmed in black and white?
4) What series is set 97 years after a nuclear war when a spaceship housing humanity's last survivors sends a group of juvenile delinquents back to Earth in hopes of re-populating the planet?
5) Who plays the alcoholic father Frank Gallagher on *Shameless*?
6) Who was the original host of *Candid Camera*?
7) Who played the title roles in *Kate & Allie*?
8) The characters played by Jim Parsons and Johnny Galecki on *The Big Bang Theory* are named after who?
9) What series was a remake of the British show *Steptoe and Son*?
10) For what series did Rachel Brosnahan win the 2018 Outstanding Lead Actress in a Comedy Series Emmy?

Quiz 11 Answers

1) *The Price is Right* - started in 1972
2) *Benson* - 1980
3) *The Dick Van Dyke Show* (1961-1966)
4) *The 100* - debuted 2014
5) William H. Macy
6) Allen Funt

7) Susan Saint James and Jane Curtin
8) Sheldon Leonard - famous television producer and actor
9) *Sanford and Son* (1972-1977)
10) *The Marvelous Mrs. Maisel* - debuted 2017

Quiz 12

1) What series showed the aftermath of a nearby nuclear explosion on a small peaceful town?
2) What star of one of the favorite family dramas of the 1970s played Frank Gaad, a supervisor in the FBI counter-intelligence department, who is dedicated to identifying the Soviet spies in *The Americans*?
3) What game show featured Ben Stein as host and Jimmy Kimmel as co-host?
4) Who is the creator and star of the comedy *Master of None* about the life of a young actor in New York?
5) What series was spun off from *The Carol Burnett Show*?
6) What television show cast holds the record for most Billboard Hot 100 hit song entries?
7) On the prison drama *Oz*, what is the name of the experimental unit of the prison?
8) What series had charming con artist Neal Caffrey helping the FBI catch elusive criminals in exchange for his freedom?
9) Which three series have won Emmys for all their main cast members?
10) What year did Nielsen start providing television ratings data?

Quiz 12 Answers

1) *Jericho* (2006-2008)
2) Richard Thomas - John Boy of *The Waltons*
3) *Win Ben Stein's Money* (1997-2002)
4) Aziz Ansari
5) *Mama's Family* (1983-1990)
6) *Glee* (2009-2015) - 207 entries
7) Emerald City

8) *White Collar* (2009-2014)
9) *All in the Family, The Golden Girls, Will & Grace*
10) 1950

Quiz 13

1) What comedy drama featured Hank Moody, a self-loathing, narcissistic author, drug user, alcoholic, and borderline sex addict?
2) What series was part of the *NBC Wednesday Mystery Movie* rotation and starred George Peppard as a suave, Polish American freelance investigator who solved seemingly impossible thefts?
3) What was the first television family with a computer in their home?
4) On *Bonanza*, what was Ben Cartwright's occupation before becoming a rancher?
5) What long running series featured movie stars such as Jane Wyman, Cliff Robertson, Lana Turner, and Kim Novak?
6) What science documentary series debuted in 1974?
7) Who played the title role in *Dennis the Menace*?
8) What drama is about politics in New York high finance and features U.S. Attorney Chuck Rhoades and hedge fund king Bobby Axelrod?
9) What was the first show ever to air on Fox primetime?
10) What sitcom starred Thomas Jane as a struggling suburban Detroit high school coach who resorts to male prostitution?

Quiz 13 Answers

1) *Californication* (2007-2014)
2) *Banacek* (1972-1974)
3) *The Addams Family* (1964-1966) - They had a huge UNIVAC computer.
4) Ship's captain
5) *Falcon Crest* (1981-1990)
6) *Nova*
7) Jay North
8) *Billions* - debuted 2016
9) *Married with Children* - April 15, 1987
10) *Hung* (209-2011)

Quiz 14

1) Who played the title roles in *McMillan & Wife*?
2) Who played the original Clarabell the Clown on *The Howdy Doody Show*?
3) What well known disc jockey, radio personality, voice actor and actor provided the voice for Shaggy on *Scooby Doo, Where Are You*?
4) What is the longest running variety show in the U.S.?
5) What reality series has the theme song "Bad Boys"?
6) The characters on *The Honeymooners* first appeared on what show?
7) What Jack Webb series had real life husband and wife Julie London and Bobby Troup?
8) What anthology crime drama was Jessica Biel's first leading role in a television series?
9) What series was based on the 1970s British show *Man About the House*?
10) What was the longest running *All in the Family* spin-off?

Quiz 14 Answers

1) Rock Hudson and Susan Saint James
2) Bob Keeshan - He went on to play Captain Kangaroo.
3) Casey Kasem
4) *Saturday Night Live* - started in 1975
5) *Cops* - debuted in 1989
6) *The Jackie Gleason Show* - It featured sketches with *The Honeymooners*.
7) *Emergency!* (1972-1979)
8) *The Sinner* - debuted 2017
9) *Three's Company* (1976-1984)
10) *The Jeffersons* - 11 seasons from 1975-1985

Quiz 15

1) Gene Barry played a Los Angeles chief of detectives who was also a millionaire and lived a high-wheeling lifestyle on what series?
2) What actor on the sitcom *Superstore* is a former cast member of *The*

Kids in the Hall and *Saturday Night Live*?

3) What sitcom was based on a 1978 Walter Matthau and Glenda Jackson film of the same name?
4) What show has a Guinness World Record for most swearing in an animated series?
5) What series features a brilliant college dropout who finds himself working as a lawyer for one of New York City's top attorneys?
6) Who played detective Virgil Tibbs in the series *In the Heat of the Night*?
7) What dramatic series had the first romantic kiss between two women on primetime U.S. television?
8) What animated show featured the adventures of a cowardly dog who must defend his unknowing farmer owners from all kinds of dangers?
9) What animated science fiction comedy had character Tad Ghostal hosting his own late-night talk show filmed in outer space along with his cohost and former villain Zorak interviewing Earth celebrities through their videophone?
10) What was the first western to have all its episodes broadcast in color?

Quiz 15 Answers

1) *Burke's Law* (1963-1966)
2) Mark McKinney - He plays the store manager Glenn and was one of *The Kids in the Hall* and on *SNL* from 1995 to 1997.
3) *House Calls* (1979-1982) - starring Wayne Rogers and Lynn Redgrave
4) *South Park* – debuted 1997
5) *Suits* - debuted 2011
6) Howard E. Rollins Jr.
7) *L.A. Law* - In 1991, female characters Abby played by Michele Greene and C.J. played by Amanda Donohoe kissed.
8) *Courage the Cowardly Dog* (1999-2002)
9) *Space Ghost Coast to Coast* (1993-2008)
10) *Bonanza* (1959-1973)

Quiz 16

1) Bea Arthur costarred with what actress for 13 years over two different series?
2) What is the longest running animated children's show in the U.S.?
3) What series features Joel the janitor, Tom Servo, and Crow T. Robot watching and commenting on bad movies?
4) What show is generally credited as the inventor of the rerun?
5) What series featured E.G. Marshall and Robert Reed as a father and son tackling challenging legal cases often involving critical issues for the times?
6) The sweaters children's television star Mr. Rogers wore on his show were created by whom?
7) What two male dramatic characters appeared for the most consecutive years in American live action primetime television?
8) Who was the only cast member to win an award for *Green Acres*?
9) The actors playing what two characters on the U.S. version of *The Office* went to high school together in real life?
10) Who was the first African American woman to win a primetime acting Emmy?

Quiz 16 Answers

1) Rue McClanahan - *Maude* and *The Golden Girls*
2) *Arthur* - started on PBS in 1996
3) *Mystery Science Theater 3000* (1988-1999)
4) *I Love Lucy* (1951-1957) - during Lucille Ball's pregnancy
5) *The Defenders* (1961-1965)
6) His mother
7) Matt Dillon - played by James Arness on *Gunsmoke* from 1955 to 1975 and Detective John Munch played by Richard Belzer on *Homicide: Life on the Street* from 1993 to 1999 and on *Law & Order: Special Victims Unit* from 1999 to 2013
8) Arnold the pig - He won a Patsy Award for best animal performance in 1967.
9) Jim Halpert and Ryan Howard - John Krasinski and B.J. Novak both went to Newton South High School in Newton, Massachusetts, and both graduated in 1997. They were even on the same little league

baseball team.

10) Gail Fisher - *Mannix* (1970) for Outstanding Supporting Actress in a Drama Series

Quiz 17

1) What were the first names of the four *Designing Women*?
2) What show had the first interracial couple on regular primetime U.S. television?
3) *This Is Your Life* surprised a celebrity each week and told the story of their life; who was the host?
4) What was the name of the groundbreaking 26-part documentary series narrated by Laurence Olivier about WWII?
5) After 227 in 1985, what 1990s sitcom was the second ever to feature four African American females as lead characters?
6) Who is generally credited with inventing the television as we know it and giving the world's first public demonstration of a true television set?
7) What sketch comedy starred Dave Foley, Bruce McCulloch, Kevin McDonald, Scott Thompson, and Mark McKinney?
8) Who played the Beast in the original 1980s *Beauty and the Beast*?
9) What year did the U.S. begin transitioning to color television?
10) In *A Charlie Brown Christmas*, what Christmas carol do all the children sing at the end?

Quiz 17 Answers

1) Julia, Suzanne, Mary Jo, Charlene
2) *The Jeffersons* - neighbors Tom and Helen Willis in 1975
3) Ralph Edwards
4) *The World at War* (1973-1976)
5) *Living Single* (1993-1998)
6) John Logie Baird - He demonstrated a television set in 1926.
7) *The Kids in the Hall* (1988-1994)
8) Ron Perlman
9) 1953
10) "Hark! The Herald Angels Sing"

Quiz 18

1) What was the first cable series to win the Outstanding Drama Series Emmy?
2) What actress received an Emmy nomination for Best Lead Actress in a Drama Series for each of the 12 seasons her show ran but never won?
3) On *Seinfeld*, what is Kramer's first name?
4) What science fiction series featured former galactic war veteran Malcolm Reynolds as captain of the transport ship *Serenity*?
5) What former movie Superman plays the part of The Atom on *Arrow*?
6) What children's series is based on the books by Marc Brown and features the adventures of an eight-year-old aardvark and his family and friends?
7) On *Longmire*, Walt Longmire is the dedicated sheriff of Absaroka County who is dealing with the death of his wife; what state is the show set in?
8) What was the name of the small town plagued by bizarre and violent crimes in *Picket Fences*?
9) Who was the first detective character that was created specifically for television and had not appeared in any other media?
10) To prevent continuity problems and allow the episodes to be shown in any order, what 1960s sitcom was always set during winter?

Quiz 18 Answers

1) *The Sopranos* - 2006
2) Angela Lansbury - *Murder, She Wrote* (1984-1996)
3) Cosmo
4) *Firefly* (2002-2003)
5) Brandon Routh - He starred as Superman in *Superman Returns* (2006).
6) *Arthur* - started in 1996
7) Wyoming
8) Rome, Wisconsin
9) Peter Gunn - 1958
10) *Hogan's Heroes* (1965-1971)

Quiz 19

1) Who was the first president to hold a televised news conference?
2) Who was the original host of Comedy Central's *The Daily Show*?
3) What was the name of the police informant played by Antonio Fargas on *Starsky and Hutch*?
4) What series featured nurses and doctors in a Vietnam War field hospital?
5) The number one song "Johnny Angel" debuted on a sitcom and was sung by the actress who played the daughter on the show; what was the series?
6) What science fiction series featured two U.S Secret Service agents who must retrieve supernatural objects called artifacts?
7) Who played the ethically challenged attorney Alan Shore on the crime drama *Boston Legal*?
8) In *Buffy the Vampire Slayer*, what is Buffy's last name?
9) What was the name of the evil organization the agents were always battling on *The Man from U.N.C.L.E.*?
10) *This Old House* debuted in 1979; who was the original master carpenter on the show?

Quiz 19 Answers

1) Dwight D. Eisenhower
2) Craig Kilborn
3) Huggy Bear
4) *China Beach* (1988-1991)
5) *The Donna Reed Show* - Shelley Fabares played the daughter and sang the song.
6) *Warehouse 13* (2009-2014)
7) James Spader
8) Summers
9) Thrush
10) Norm Abram

Quiz 20

1) Who plays Joyce Byers, the mother of the missing boy, on *Stranger*

Things?

2) What was the first name of Chuck Norris' title character on *Walker, Texas Ranger*?
3) What mystery crime drama starred a real-life father and son playing father and son?
4) What show has the most Emmy wins for a comedy?
5) What was the name of the Ewing ranch on *Dallas*?
6) What show popularized and may have originated the phrase "Whoa Nelly!"?
7) What is the name of *The Walking Dead* spin-off that follows two families banding together to survive?
8) Who is the only Star Trek character to appear regularly on two different Star Trek series?
9) *The Partridge Family* was based on what real-life musical family?
10) What comedy series holds the record for most acting Emmy wins?

Quiz 20 Answers

1) Winona Ryder
2) Cordell
3) *Diagnosis Murder* (1993-2001) - starred Dick and Barry Van Dyke
4) *Frasier* (1993-2004) - 37 wins
5) Southfork
6) *The Roy Rogers Show* (1951-1957) - On nearly every show, Pat Brady would yell the phrase while racing after villains or rushing for help in his Jeep named Nellybelle.
7) *Fear the Walking Dead* - debuted 2015
8) Worf - He was played by Michael Dorn and appeared on both *Star Trek: The Next Generation* and *Star Trek: Deep Space Nine*.
9) The Cowsills - They were considered for the show, but the children were older than the parts written for the series.
10) *The Mary Tyler Moore Show* (1970-1977) - 16 wins

Quiz 21

1) What is the longest running live action primetime spin-off series ever on American television?

2) In what city did *The Oprah Winfrey Show* originate?
3) What was the name of the think tank MacGyver worked for in the original *MacGyver*?
4) Donald Glover became only the second African American to win the Outstanding Lead Actor in a Comedy Series Emmy for what show?
5) Who played the title role on *Trapper John, M.D.*?
6) What year was the first paid television advertisement broadcast in the U.S.?
7) What year did Fox become the first new national television network since the 1950s?
8) Who played the role of Nell Harper in *Gimme a Break!*?
9) Who played Sgt. Morgan O'Rourke on *F Troop*?
10) Who played the two brothers and title characters of the miniseries *Rich Man, Poor Man*?

Quiz 21 Answers

1) *Law & Order: Special Victims Unit* – debuted in 1999
2) Chicago
3) Phoenix Foundation
4) *Atlanta* (2017)
5) Pernell Roberts
6) 1941
7) 1993
8) Nell Carter
9) Forrest Tucker
10) Peter Strauss and Nick Nolte

Quiz 22

1) The sitcom *30 Rock* centers around the creation of a sketch comedy show; what is the name of the show they are creating?
2) Who played the boss in the original British series *The Office*?
3) What drama features teenager Clay Jensen as he tries to uncover the reason behind his classmate's suicide?
4) What was the first regularly scheduled broadcast network in the U.S.?

5) What do the title initials stand for on *JAG*?
6) How many different actors on *The Mary Tyler Moore Show* won Emmys?
7) What office place sitcom was based on a movie of the same name and starred the sister of one of the movie's stars?
8) Who stars in the title role in the series *Sherlock*?
9) What American primetime scripted show has been the longest running show on the air for the longest time?
10) What anthology series was created by Steven Spielberg and featured many famous actors and had episodes directed by Spielberg, Clint Eastwood, Martin Scorsese, and Robert Zemeckis?

Quiz 22 Answers

1) *TGS* - It was originally titled *The Girlie Show* before they brought in Tracy Jordan.
2) Ricky Gervais
3) *13 Reasons Why* - debuted 2017
4) NBC - 1945
5) Judge Advocate General
6) Six - Mary Tyler Moore, Ted Knight, Betty White, Cloris Leachman, Ed Asner, Valerie Harper
7) *Nine to Five* (1982-1988) - Rachel Dennison, Dolly Parton's sister, played the role of Doralee that Parton played in the movie.
8) Benedict Cumberbatch
9) *The Simpsons* - It has been the longest running show since July 1998.
10) *Amazing Stories* (1985-1987)

Quiz 23

1) What was the first U.S. daily soap opera offered in syndication?
2) What series starred Robert Conrad as Gregory "Pappy" Boyington, squadron leader of a group of fighter pilots stationed on a Pacific island during WWII?
3) What character on *Family Guy* is voiced by the show's creator Seth MacFarlane in his natural speaking voice?
4) What is the name of the underwater city where SpongeBob lives on

SpongeBob SquarePants?

5) What year did *The Tonight Show* debut?
6) What British sitcom was about two best friends, Edina Monsoon and Patsy Stone, who are constantly drugged up and outrageously selfish?
7) Who was the original host for *Unsolved Mysteries* which had re-enactments, interviews and updates, about real mysteries?
8) What was the first name of Dr. Niles Crane's wife who was frequently talked about but never seen on *Frasier*?
9) What are the two main non-human races on *Babylon 5*?
10) Who played the title role in the series *Nurse Jackie*?

Quiz 23 Answers

1) *Dark Shadows* (1966-1971)
2) *Black Sheep Squadron* (1976-1978)
3) Brian - the dog
4) Bikini Bottom
5) 1954
6) *Absolutely Fabulous* (1992-2012)
7) Robert Stack
8) Maris
9) Minbari and Centauri
10) Edie Falco

Quiz 24

1) Who was the first woman to run a major television studio?
2) The early career of Dr. Phil McGraw of the *Dr. Phil* show inspired what crime drama series?
3) What series had this opening "He awoke and found himself trapped in the past, facing mirror images that were not his own, and driven by an unknown force to change history for the better"?
4) Who is the youngest person to have a self-titled U.S. television show?
5) What sitcom follows a group of old friends in a fantasy football league?

6) What was George and Louise's only child's name on *The Jeffersons*?
7) What comedy series had Jim Carrey, Jamie Foxx, and Jennifer Lopez?
8) On *Who's the Boss*, what was Tony's occupation before becoming a housekeeper?
9) What action series featured characters Reno Raines, Bobby Sixkiller, and Cheyenne Phillips working as bounty hunters?
10) Who starred as Carl Kolchak, a Chicago reporter who always got into situations involving the supernatural, in *Kolchak: The Night Stalker*?

Quiz 24 Answers

1) Lucille Ball - She ran Desilu Studio starting in 1962; the studio produced many popular shows including *Mission Impossible* and *Star Trek.*
2) *Bull* - McGraw earned his PhD in psychology from the University of North Texas in 1979 and founded Courtroom Sciences, Inc., a trial sciences firm, in 1980.
3) *Quantum Leap* (1989-1993)
4) Patty Duke - She was 16 years old when *The Patty Duke Show* debuted in 1963.
5) *The League* (2009-2015)
6) Lionel
7) *In Living Color* (1990-1994)
8) Baseball player
9) *Renegade* (1992-1997)
10) Darren McGavin

Quiz 25

1) Who was the first African American to win the Outstanding Lead Actor in a Drama Series Emmy?
2) On *Charmed*, what was the name of the book of witchcraft that was passed down to the sisters?
3) Who was the first U.S. president to be televised?
4) What drama centers around the exploits of Colombian drug lord Pablo Escobar?

5) What is the first name of the grizzled old cook played by Frank McGrath on *Wagon Train*?
6) *Maude* was a spin-off from *All in the Family*; what was Maude's relationship to the Bunkers?
7) What is the name of the magic school the central characters attend in *The Magicians*?
8) Who hosted *Night Gallery*?
9) Who played the title role in *The Nanny*?
10) Who played head detective Mac Taylor on *CSI: NY*?

Quiz 25 Answers

1) Bill Cosby - *I Spy* (1966)
2) *Book of Shadows*
3) Franklin D. Roosevelt - opening ceremonies of the 1939 New York World's Fair
4) *Narcos* (2015-2017)
5) Charlie
6) She was Edith's cousin.
7) Brakebills
8) Rod Serling
9) Fran Drescher
10) Gary Sinise

Quiz 26

1) What anthology horror series was based on the EC Comics books of the 1950s?
2) The writers office in *The Dick Van Dyke Show* is based on Carl Reiner's experience on *Your Show of Shows* where he worked as a writer. Dick Van Dyke's character is based on Carl Reiner; Morey Amsterdam's character of Buddy Sorrell is based on what famous writer, director and actor who was also a writer on *Your Show of Shows*?
3) What children's animated series features Tommy Pickles, Chuckie Finster, and Phil and Lil Deville as four babies?
4) What were the names of the Ewing couple who starred on *Knots Landing*?

5) What year did the first television sitcom in the world debut?
6) What series featured Mia Farrow, Ryan O'Neal, Dorothy Malone, and Ed Nelson?
7) What future national television figure was the first person to play Ronald McDonald in three 1963 television advertisements?
8) What sitcom starred identical twins Tia and Tamera Mowry as twins separated at birth who are reunited as teenagers?
9) What was the first television series to feature a final episode where all plot lines were resolved, and all questions were answered?
10) What action drama stared Jessica Alba as Max Guevera, a genetically enhanced superhuman prototype, searching for others like her and battling corruption in a post-apocalyptic Pacific Northwest?

Quiz 26 Answers

1) *Tales from the Crypt* (1989-1996)
2) Mel Brooks
3) *Rugrats* (1990-2006)
4) Gary and Valene Ewing - played by Ted Shackelford and Joan Van Ark
5) 1946 - *Pinwright's Progress* debuted on November 29, 1946 on the BBC. It featured the adventures of the smallest store in the world and included the store proprietor, his pretty daughter, a nemesis, and helpful staff who end up making things worse.
6) *Peyton Place* (1964-1969)
7) Willard Scott - The future *Today Show* weatherman was a local radio personality in Washington, D.C. and had played Bozo the Clown on television from 1959-1962.
8) *Sister, Sister* (1994-1999)
9) *The Fugitive* - 1967
10) *Dark Angel* (2000-2002)

Quiz 27

1) Who played the title role in *House*?
2) What is the name of the cruise ship on *The Love Boat*?
3) On *Supergirl*, what is the name of Supergirl's alter ego?

4) What year did U.S. commercial networks first broadcast most of their primetime shows in color?
5) What streaming drama is set in a theocratic dictatorship in a dystopian future after a second American civil war?
6) *Wonder Woman* was based on the character created by William Moulton Marston who was also a psychologist and inventor of what well known device?
7) What series has the most Emmy wins in a single year?
8) What are the names of Lucy and Ricky's landlords and friends in *I Love Lucy*?
9) On *The Patty Duke Show*, what was the reason given that Patty and her cousin looked so much alike?
10) U.S. television allows alcohol to be advertised if what?

Quiz 27 Answers

1) Hugh Laurie
2) *Pacific Princess*
3) Kara Danvers
4) 1965
5) *The Handmaid's Tale* - debuted 2017
6) Lie detector – consequently, Wonder Woman's Lasso of Truth
7) *Game of Thrones* - 12 wins in 2015, 2016, and 2019
8) Fred and Ethel Mertz
9) Their fathers were identical twins.
10) No alcohol is consumed in the commercial – It isn't a law or FCC regulation, just a broadcasting standard.

Quiz 28

1) On the superhero drama *Agents of S.H.I.E.L.D.*, what does S.H.I.E.L.D. stand for?
2) What sitcom featured a free-spirited yoga instructor and a conservative lawyer who get married on their first date?
3) What is the name of the town that is the setting for *Parks and Recreation*?
4) What is the longest running television show of any kind in the U.S.?

5) What children's animated series featured Lily Tomlin as Ms. Frizzle?
6) What series had the largest number of performers nominated for lead, supporting, or guest actress or actor Emmys over its run?
7) Who was host of the true crime series *America's Most Wanted*?
8) What is the name of the character played by two-time Oscar winner Maggie Smith in *Downton Abbey*?
9) What crime drama had a mathematician helping his FBI brother solve crimes?
10) What town is *Father Knows Best* set in?

Quiz 28 Answers

1) Strategic Homeland Intervention, Enforcement and Logistics Division
2) *Dharma & Greg* (1997-2002)
3) Pawnee, Indiana
4) *Meet the Press* - started in 1947 and still running
5) *The Magic School Bus* (1994-1997)
6) *ER* (1994-2009)- 31 separate performers
7) John Walsh
8) Violet Crawley - Dowager Countess of Grantham
9) *Numb3rs* (2005-2010)
10) Springfield

Quiz 29

1) What was the first American series shown on British television?
2) Who played the title role on *Julia* about a widowed nurse?
3) What are the first names of the title characters in *2 Broke Girls*?
4) What was the first U.S. primetime soap opera?
5) Who played the title role in the sitcom *Malcolm in the Middle*?
6) Who plays the role of Jackie Harris on *Roseanne*?
7) What action adventure character's real name is Don Diego de la Vega?
8) Who was the first African American to win the Outstanding Supporting Actress in a Comedy Series Emmy?

9) The British historical drama *Poldark* features a soldier returning home to England after fighting in the American Revolution; what area of England is the series set in?
10) Who was the narrator and voice of the adult Kevin on *The Wonder Years*?

Quiz 29 Answers

1) *Dragnet*
2) Diahann Carroll
3) Max and Caroline
4) *Peyton Place* (1964-1969)
5) Frankie Muniz
6) Laurie Metcalf
7) Zorro
8) Jackee Harry - 227 (1987)
9) Cornwall
10) Daniel Stern

Quiz 30

1) Who starred as Captain Dylan Hunt who is frozen in time for 300 years and along with his sentient warship Andromeda sets out to restore peace to the universe on *Andromeda*?
2) What were the names of the trio of angels on *Touched by an Angel*?
3) What was the occupation of Marlo Thomas' boyfriend on *That Girl*?
4) What was the first streaming series to win the Outstanding Comedy Series Emmy?
5) What series has the most watched episode in U.S. television history?
6) What comedy adventure starred Greg Evigan as a trucker who travels the highways of America with his pet chimpanzee?
7) What British comedy drama centers on a socially challenged doctor who moves from London to Cornwall?
8) What author created the character of *The Saint*?
9) What was the name of the hospital on *Scrubs*?
10) What was the name of Groucho Marx's game show?

Quiz 30 Answers

1) Kevin Sorbo
2) Monica, Tess, Andrew
3) Magazine reporter
4) *The Marvelous Mrs. Maisel* (2018) - Amazon
5) *M*A*S*H* - series finale in 1983 with over 105 million viewers
6) *B.J. and the Bear* (1978-1981)
7) *Doc Martin* - debuted 2004
8) Leslie Charteris - He wrote a series of books and stories starting in the 1930s.
9) Sacred Heart
10) *You Bet Your Life* (1950-1961)

Quiz 31

1) What is the oldest network newscast in the U.S.?
2) What were the names of the five children on *The Cosby Show*?
3) What series centers on a young surgeon with autism and savant syndrome who joins a prestigious hospital?
4) What was Ted Knight's final series?
5) Who was the first automaker to advertise on network television?
6) What was the first animated series after *The Flintstones* in 1961 to be nominated for the Outstanding Comedy Series Emmy?
7) What action comedy starring David Rasche was a parody of the *Dirty Harry* movies?
8) In *Buck Rogers in the 25th Century*, what was the empire the Earth is battling?
9) What series had the host delivering lines such as "I hope you'll join us again next week when we will present you with another story of gripping, spine-tingling suspense, and three boring commercials to take the edge off of it"?
10) What sitcom starred Danny McBride as a burned-out MLB pitcher who goes home to North Carolina to work as a gym teacher at his old middle school?

Quiz 31 Answers

1) *CBS Evening News* - started in 1948
2) Sondra, Denise, Vanessa, Rudy, Theo
3) *The Good Doctor* - debuted 2017
4) *Too Close for Comfort* (1980-1987) - He died during the series.
5) Chevrolet - 1946
6) *Family Guy* - 2009
7) *Sledge Hammer!* (1986-1988)
8) Draconian
9) *Alfred Hitchcock Presents* (1955-1962)
10) *Eastbound & Down* (2009-2013)

Quiz 32

1) Where was the crime drama *Silk Stockings* set?
2) Who played the title role in *The Farmer's Daughter* which was based on a 1947 Loretta Young movie of the same name?
3) What was the name of the title character on *The Mentalist*?
4) What was the first show to end while it was still at the top of the Nielsen Ratings?
5) What actor played Dr. Jerry Robinson on *The Bob Newhart Show* and went on to become an award-winning director of hundreds of television episodes for a variety of shows?
6) What actor led the WWII commando squad on *Rat Patrol*?
7) Who played the title roles in *Nanny and the Professor*?
8) What series that started in 1999 won the Outstanding Drama Series Emmy each of its first four seasons?
9) At the time they were cast, which of *The Monkees* were musicians?
10) What state was the sitcom *The Middle* set in?

Quiz 32 Answers

1) Palm Beach, Florida
2) Inger Stevens
3) Patrick Jane
4) *I Love Lucy* (1951-1957)

5) Peter Bonerz
6) Christopher George
7) Juliet Mills and Richard Long
8) *The West Wing* (1999-2006)
9) Peter Tork and Michael Nesmith
10) Indiana

Quiz 33

1) Who played Myrna Turner, Oscar Madison's secretary, on the original *The Odd Couple*?
2) In *How the Grinch Stole Christmas!*, what is the name of the Grinch's dog?
3) What is the longest running children's show in the U.S.?
4) Who plays the brilliant criminal defense professor Annalise Keating on *How to Get Away with Murder*?
5) What is the name of Jane Lynch's cheer leading coach character on *Glee*?
6) The entire series *How I Met Your Mother* is told from the perspective of what character?
7) What actress has played the same role for the longest time in American live action primetime television?
8) What was the captain's name in *Star Trek: Enterprise*?
9) What was the name of the character Howard Hesseman played in *WKRP in Cincinnati*?
10) On the sitcom *The Good Place*, who plays Michael, the architect of the good place?

Quiz 33 Answers

1) Penny Marshall
2) Max
3) *Sesame Street* - started in 1969
4) Viola Davis
5) Sue Sylvester
6) Ted Mosby
7) Mariska Hargitay - She has played Olivia Benson on *Law & Order:*

Special Victims Unit since 1999.

8) Jonathan Archer
9) Dr. Johnny Fever
10) Ted Danson

Quiz 34

1) What character does Sean Hayes play on *Will & Grace*?
2) Who was the first host of *Saturday Night Live* in 1975?
3) Who plays Detective Jake Peralta on the crime comedy *Brooklyn Nine-Nine*?
4) What drama is based on the Israeli series *Prisoners of War*?
5) What is the name of the FBI unit the team works for on *Criminal Minds*?
6) What is the first primetime U.S. series starring an Asian American family since Margaret Cho's *All-American Girl* in 1994?
7) What fantasy drama centers on a homicide detective who discovers he is a descendant of hunters who fight supernatural forces?
8) Who were the original co-hosts of *Good Morning America* when it debuted in 1975?
9) Who is regarded as the first television entertainer to step out of character and break the fourth wall by talking directly to the television audience?
10) What was the original name of the advertising firm at the center of *Mad Men*?

Quiz 34 Answers

1) Jack McFarland
2) George Carlin
3) Andy Samberg
4) *Homeland* - debuted 2011
5) Behavioral Analysis Unit (BAU)
6) *Fresh Off the Boat* - debuted 2015
7) *Grimm* (2011-2017)
8) David Hartman and Nancy Dussault
9) George Burns - on *The George Burns and Gracie Allen Show* from

1950-1958

10) Sterling Cooper

Quiz 35

1) What series had 25 different actors fill the six regular roles on the show over its run?
2) Who played the title role on the private detective series *Honey West*?
3) What Oscar winner plays the title role in the sitcom *Mom*?
4) How many continuous years was *American Bandstand* on the air?
5) What sports drama series was based on a 2004 movie of the same name?
6) What was the character name of the vampire on the cult soap opera *Dark Shadows*?
7) What crime drama anthology is inspired by a Coen brothers film?
8) Who sang the theme song and was the narrator on *The Dukes of Hazzard*?
9) Who plays Los Angeles area college professor Mort Pfefferman who decides to transition from being a male to a female in the comedy *Transparent*?
10) What was the name of the space station leader in *Star Trek: Deep Space Nine*?

Quiz 35 Answers

1) *Law & Order* (1990-2010)
2) Anne Francis
3) Allison Janney
4) 37 years
5) *Friday Night Lights* (2006-2011)
6) Barnabas Collins
7) *Fargo* - debuted 2014
8) Waylon Jennings
9) Jeffrey Tambor
10) Benjamin Sisko

Quiz 36

1) What actor and actress play the mother and father on *Leave It to Beaver*?
2) What animated comedy features Bob Belcher and his wife and three children trying to run a restaurant?
3) On *Castle*, what was the name of the fictional heroine Castle created based on working with Kate?
4) After *Doctor Who*, what is the second longest running science fiction or fantasy series?
5) What Hollywood legend played Robert Wagner's father in a recurring role on *It Takes a Thief*?
6) Who was the first African American to host a nationwide show?
7) What was the first show in producer Dick Wolf's set of four Chicago based series?
8) What town was the setting for *Little House on the Prairie*?
9) What series at its height aired in 148 countries on every inhabited continent and was called the most watched television show in the world by *The Guinness Book of World Records*?
10) What was the first sitcom where the theme song was sung by the leading actors?

Quiz 36 Answers

1) Hugh Beaumont and Barbara Billingsley
2) *Bob's Burgers* - debuted 2011
3) Nikki Heat
4) *Supernatural* - debuted in 2005
5) Fred Astaire
6) Nat King Cole - 1956
7) *Chicago Fire* - It debuted in 2012 and was followed by *Chicago P.D.*, *Chicago Med*, and *Chicago Justice*.
8) Walnut Grove, Minnesota
9) *Baywatch* (1989-2001)
10) *Green Acres* (1965-1971)- Eddie Albert and Eva Gabor

Quiz 37

1) Who played agent Jim Hardie in *Tales of Wells Fargo*?
2) Who starred in the title role on *The Life and Times of Grizzly Adams* about a falsely accused man who must flee into the mountains?
3) What BBC crime series follows a fish out of water British police inspector working on the Caribbean island of Saint-Marie solving murders?
4) Who played the young Kunta Kinte on the miniseries *Roots*?
5) Who was the first African American to win a primetime Emmy?
6) On the crime comedy *Monk*, what was Monk's first name?
7) What actor on *Night Court* won four consecutive Emmys for their role?
8) Who was the only actor to appear in both the 1970s and 2000s versions of *Battlestar Galactica*?
9) What series starred Burt Reynolds as a homicide detective in his hometown of Santa Luisa, California?
10) What drama focused on three generations of women living together in Hartford, Connecticut with one of them working as a family court judge?

Quiz 37 Answers

1) Dale Robertson
2) Dan Haggerty
3) *Death in Paradise* - debuted 2010
4) Levar Burton
5) Harry Belafonte - *Tonight with Harry Belafonte* (1960)
6) Adrian
7) John Larroquette
8) Richard Hatch
9) *Dan August* (1970-1971)
10) *Judging Amy* (1999-2006)

Quiz 38

1) In what year did the first television couple share a bed?

2) What western series starred Richard Boone as an ex-gunfighter who uses contemporary methods of solving crimes?
3) What science fiction drama dealt with decades of missing persons returned by a ball of light without any signs of aging and with many of them having heightened abilities?
4) What series is based on a book of the same name and centers on a public relations executive who is sentenced to a minimum-security women's prison in Connecticut?
5) What was the name of the electronics store Chuck works at as a cover while he is a spy on *Chuck*?
6) What year did *Gunsmoke* debut?
7) In what year was the first color television system demonstrated?
8) What was Earl's last name in the sitcom *My Name is Earl*?
9) What drama series was about the reign and marriages of King Henry VIII?
10) Between the two leads, what series had the Outstanding Actress in a Drama Series Emmy winner six straight years?

Quiz 38 Answers

1) 1947 - on *Mary Kay and Johnny* which was the first American sitcom
2) *Hec Ramsey* (1972-1974)
3) The 4400 (2004-2007)
4) *Orange Is the New Black* (2013-2019)
5) Buy More
6) 1955
7) 1928
8) Hickey
9) *The Tudors* (2007-2010)
10) *Cagney & Lacey* (1981-1988) - Sharon Gless and Tyne Daly

Quiz 39

1) What is the longest running Superman series?
2) What sitcom centers on a young obstetrician-gynecologist trying to balance her personal and professional life?
3) Who was the host of the game show *Password*?

4) What role does *Seinfeld* co-creator Larry David play in *Curb Your Enthusiasm*?
5) What year was the first NFL game televised?
6) What is the longest running sitcom in the U.S.?
7) Who was the musical director on *Late Night with David Letterman*?
8) What sitcom starred Donna Pescow as a middle-class Italian American who marries into a wealthy family?
9) Lucille Ball played a secretary for her brother-in-law in what kind of business in *Here's Lucy*?
10) What is the name of Kerry Washington's former White House staffer and now professional fixer character on *Scandal*?

Quiz 39 Answers

1) *Smallville* (2001-2011)
2) *The Mindy Project* (2012-2017)
3) Allen Ludden
4) Larry David - He plays himself.
5) 1939
6) *The Simpsons* - started in 1989
7) Paul Shaffer
8) *Angie* (1979-1980)
9) Employment agency
10) Olivia Pope

U.S. Geography

Quiz 1

1) What state has Lake of the Woods, the 7th largest lake in the U.S.?
2) The Columbia River enters the U.S. in what state?
3) What four states border Texas?
4) What state has Crater Lake National Park?
5) What is the second highest mountain in the contiguous 48 states?
6) What state borders Washington to the east?
7) How many states are doubly landlocked (two states or provinces away from the ocean)?
8) How many time zones does Alaska have?
9) What state's highest mountain is Kings Peak?
10) What state has the nickname "The Equality State"?

Quiz 1 Answers

1) Minnesota
2) Washington
3) New Mexico, Oklahoma, Arkansas, Louisiana
4) Oregon
5) Mount Elbert - 14,440 feet in Colorado
6) Idaho
7) 10 - Colorado, Illinois, Indiana, Iowa, Kansas, Missouri, South Dakota, Utah, Wisconsin, Wyoming
8) Two
9) Utah - 13,534 feet
10) Wyoming

Quiz 2

1) What is the largest desert in the U.S.?
2) What state has one of the largest pyramids in the world featuring a hotel, indoor swamp, aquarium, bowling alley, and the world's tallest freestanding elevator?

3) What state is Mount Shasta in?
4) What southern state capital is on the Mississippi River?
5) What is the deepest river in the U.S.?
6) What state borders Missouri to the south?
7) What is the third longest river in the U.S.?
8) What was the first state to adopt an official sport?
9) What state is Grand Teton in?
10) The Arkansas River flows into what river?

Quiz 2 Answers

1) Great Basin Desert - 200,000 square miles covering most of Nevada and parts of Utah, California, Oregon, and Idaho
2) Tennessee - The Memphis Bass Pro Shops Megastore is 321 feet tall with a 535,000 square foot interior.
3) California - 14,180 feet
4) Baton Rouge, Louisiana
5) St. Lawrence River - maximum depth of 250 feet
6) Arkansas
7) Yukon River - 1,979 miles starting in British Columbia, Canada and flowing through Alaska
8) Maryland - They named jousting as their official sport in 1962.
9) Wyoming - 13,775 feet
10) Mississippi River

Quiz 3

1) If you go north, south, east, or west from Stamford, Connecticut, what is the next state you hit?
2) What state capital is on the Susquehanna River?
3) What is the fourth longest river in the U.S.?
4) The Big Island of Hawaii is getting 42 acres larger each year due to what?
5) What is the fourth longest river entirely in the U.S.?
6) If you define a mountain as an elevation of 2,000 feet or more, how many states don't have any mountains?

7) What state has the largest cave system in the world?
8) By area, what is the largest lake entirely within the U.S.?
9) What state had the first motel in the world?
10) What state borders South Dakota to the south?

Quiz 3 Answers

1) New York
2) Harrisburg, Pennsylvania
3) Rio Grande - 1,759 miles
4) Lava flows from Kīlauea volcano
5) Red River - 1,125 miles
6) 13 - Delaware, Florida, Illinois, Indiana, Iowa, Louisiana, Michigan, Mississippi, Missouri, New Jersey, Ohio, Rhode Island, Wisconsin
7) Kentucky - Mammoth Cave, located near Brownsville, Kentucky, is the longest cave in the world, measuring 405 miles.
8) Lake Michigan - 22,300 square miles
9) California - The first motel in the world was opened in 1925 in San Luis Obispo, California; the original room charge was $1.25 per night.
10) Nebraska

Quiz 4

1) What state's highest mountain is Gannett Peak?
2) What state gets its name from the French for "green mountain"?
3) What is the official state sport of Minnesota?
4) What lake is formed by the Glen Canyon Dam?
5) What is the third most populous state?
6) By area, how many of the five largest lakes in the U.S. are one of the Great Lakes?
7) What state's name is derived from the Ojibwe word for "great or large lake"?
8) What was the last state to be explored by Europeans or Americans (not Native Americans)?
9) What state has the nickname "The Centennial State"?
10) What is the only state that is at least three states or provinces away

from the ocean in every direction?

Quiz 4 Answers

1) Wyoming - 13,809 feet
2) Vermont
3) Ice hockey
4) Lake Powell
5) Florida
6) Five
7) Michigan - from the Ojibwe word "mishigamaa"
8) Idaho - It wasn't explored until Lewis and Clark entered Idaho in 1805 on their expedition across America.
9) Colorado
10) Nebraska

Quiz 5

1) How many states don't have any national parks?
2) What state's highest point is Mount Whitney?
3) What state has the nickname "The Gem State"?
4) By area, what is the third largest lake entirely within the U.S.?
5) What is the name of Hawaii's time zone?
6) What U.S. state has the world's shortest river?
7) What river flows through three state capitals?
8) What state borders Alabama to the west?
9) What state is named in honor of the wife of King Charles I of England?
10) How many oceans does the United States border?

Quiz 5 Answers

1) 23 - Alabama, Connecticut, Delaware, Georgia, Illinois, Indiana, Iowa, Kansas, Louisiana, Maryland, Massachusetts, Mississippi, Missouri, Nebraska, New Hampshire, New Jersey, New York, Oklahoma, Pennsylvania, Rhode Island, Vermont, West Virginia, Wisconsin
2) California - 14,505 feet

3) Idaho
4) Lake Iliamna - 1,012 square miles in Alaska
5) Hawaii-Aleutian Time Zone - It includes Hawaii and Alaska's Aleutian Islands west of 169 degrees 30 minutes west longitude.
6) Montana - The Roe River is recognized as the world's shortest river; it flows for 200 feet between Giant Springs and the Missouri River near Great Falls, Montana.
7) Missouri River - Bismarck, North Dakota; Pierre, South Dakota; Jefferson City, Missouri
8) Mississippi
9) Maryland - in honor of Henrietta Maria
10) Three - Atlantic, Pacific, Arctic (Alaska's northern border in on the Arctic)

Quiz 6

1) What is the least populated permanently inhabited U.S. territory?
2) What states border Lake Huron?
3) What state capital is on the Willamette River?
4) What state has Isle Royale National Park?
5) What state's name is based on the Spanish term for the Easter season meaning "feast of flowers"?
6) What state capital is on the Hudson River?
7) What state had the first McDonald's drive-thru?
8) What state capital is on the Cumberland River?
9) What is the third highest mountain in the U.S.?
10) In what state are you never more than six miles from a body of water?

Quiz 6 Answers

1) American Samoa
2) Michigan
3) Salem, Oregon
4) Michigan
5) Florida - It was discovered on Palm Sunday by Juan Ponce de León, and the Spanish term for the Easter season is Pascua Florida.

6) Albany, New York
7) Arizona - The first McDonald's drive-thru was created in 1975 in Sierra Vista, Arizona near the Fort Huachuca military base. It was designed to serve military personnel who weren't permitted to get out of their cars off base while wearing fatigues.
8) Nashville, Tennessee
9) Mount Foraker - 17,400 feet in Alaska
10) Michigan - It has over 11,000 inland lakes plus four of the five Great Lakes.

Quiz 7

1) What state borders Kansas to the south?
2) What U.S. state experienced the greatest temperature variation ever recorded in a 24-hour period?
3) What are the only two mobile national monuments in the U.S.?
4) What state's largest lake is Lake Pontchartrain?
5) How many states are split into two time zones?
6) What state has the second largest water area?
7) What two states share Lake Champlain?
8) What state has the nickname "The Beehive State"?
9) Of the states that have declared an official state sport, the most popular choice with three states declaring it as their official sport is what?
10) What state gets its name from the Spanish for "ruddy" or "red" in reference to color of one of its primary rivers?

Quiz 7 Answers

1) Oklahoma
2) Montana - On January 23, 1916, Browning, Montana went from a high of 44 degrees to a low of -56 degrees Fahrenheit for a 100-degree change in 24 hours.
3) San Francisco's cable cars and the New Orleans Saint Charles streetcar line
4) Louisiana - 631 square miles, 11th largest lake in the U.S.
5) 14 - Alaska, Florida, Idaho, Indiana, Kansas, Kentucky, Michigan, Nebraska, Nevada, North Dakota, South Dakota, Oregon,

Tennessee, Texas
6) Michigan - 40,175 square miles of water
7) New York and Vermont - 490 square miles
8) Utah
9) Rodeo - South Dakota, Texas, Wyoming
10) Colorado - named for the color of the Colorado River

Quiz 8

1) What state is second to California in wine production?
2) What states border Lake Michigan?
3) By area, what is the sixth largest state?
4) On a per capita basis, what state produces the most serial killers?
5) What state is the source of the Colorado River?
6) What state gets its name from the Oto Indian word meaning "flat water" in reference to one of its primary rivers?
7) What state's highest point is Mount Hood?
8) What is the second most populous state?
9) By area, what is the fourth smallest state?
10) What state has the nickname "The Pine Tree State"?

Quiz 8 Answers

1) Washington
2) Illinois, Indiana, Michigan, Wisconsin
3) Arizona - 113,990 square miles
4) Alaska
5) Colorado
6) Nebraska - The name refers to the Platte River.
7) Oregon - 11,249 feet
8) Texas
9) New Jersey - 8,729 square miles
10) Maine

Quiz 9

1) What state is the source of the Rio Grande River?
2) What state has the nickname "The Peace Garden State"?
3) What state capital is on the Colorado River?
4) What state is the source of the Arkansas River?
5) How many states have more than one national park?
6) What is the third longest river entirely within the U.S.?
7) What state is named after Queen Elizabeth I?
8) What is the longest river that flows entirely within one state?
9) Based on discharge volume, what is the largest river in the U.S.?
10) What state has Guadalupe Mountains National Park?

Quiz 9 Answers

1) Colorado
2) North Dakota
3) Austin, Texas
4) Colorado
5) 13 - Alaska, Arizona, California, Colorado, Florida, Hawaii, Montana, Nevada, South Dakota, Texas, Utah, Washington, Wyoming
6) Arkansas River - The Missouri and Mississippi Rivers are the longest followed by the Arkansas at 1,443 miles.
7) Virginia - Elizabeth I was the Virgin Queen.
8) Colorado River of Texas - It flows for 970 miles entirely within Texas and is the 11th longest river in the U.S.
9) Mississippi River
10) Texas

Quiz 10

1) What are the only two U.S. state capitals with rhyming names?
2) What state has Carlsbad Caverns National Park?
3) By land area, what is the largest state capital city?
4) By area, where would Texas rank as a country?

5) What state has the nickname "Land of Enchantment"?
6) What state is the source of the Red River?
7) Including U.S. territories, what two states or territories have the furthest distance between them?
8) What is the largest canyon in the U.S.?
9) The highest and lowest points in the contiguous United States are in the same county in what state?
10) Which state has more of the 100 largest lakes in the United States than any other?

Quiz 10 Answers

1) Boston and Austin
2) New Mexico
3) Juneau, Alaska - 2,717 square miles
4) 39th - closest in size to Myanmar
5) New Mexico
6) Oklahoma
7) Guam and U.S. Virgin Islands - 9,514 miles from Point Udall, Guam to Point Udall, St. Croix, U.S. Virgin Islands
8) Grand Canyon - 277 miles long, up to 18 miles wide, and a maximum depth of 6,093 feet
9) California - Mount Whitney at 14,494 feet and the Badwater Basin in Death Valley at 282 feet below sea level are separated by 85 miles in Inyo county, California.
10) Minnesota - It has eight lakes in the top 100: Lake Superior, Lake of the Woods, Red Lake, Rainy Lake, Mille Lacs Lake, Leech Lake, Lake Winnibigoshish, Lake Vermilion.

Quiz 11

1) By area, what is the third smallest state?
2) What three states share Yellowstone National Park?
3) The furthest distance between any two states is between which two?
4) What river flows through the most states?
5) What two states share Great Smoky Mountains National Park?

6) What state is the source of the Ohio River?
7) What state gets its name from a Dakota word meaning "sky-tinted water"?
8) What state was named after the future King James II of England?
9) Does Virginia or West Virginia extend further west?
10) What body of water does the Columbia River empty into?

Quiz 11 Answers

1) Connecticut - 5,543 square miles
2) Wyoming (96%), Montana (3%), Idaho (1%)
3) Hawaii and Florida - 5,859 miles from Log Point, Elliot Key, Florida and Kure Island, Hawaii
4) Mississippi River - It flows through or along 10 states: Arkansas, Illinois, Iowa, Kentucky, Louisiana, Minnesota, Mississippi, Missouri, Tennessee, Wisconsin.
5) Tennessee and North Carolina
6) Pennsylvania
7) Minnesota
8) New York - He was the Duke of York.
9) Virginia
10) Pacific Ocean

Quiz 12

1) What states border Lake Superior?
2) What body of water does the Yukon River empty into?
3) What two states border Illinois to the west?
4) What state borders Ohio to the west?
5) What state's highest point is Humphreys Peak?
6) By area, what is the largest lake entirely within one state?
7) What state has the world's longest continuous bridge over water?
8) How many of the 10 highest mountains in the U.S. are in Alaska?
9) What is the most populous state?
10) What state has all five of the largest land area cities in the U.S.?

Quiz 12 Answers

1) Michigan, Minnesota, Wisconsin
2) Bering Sea
3) Iowa and Missouri
4) Indiana
5) Arizona - 12,637 feet
6) Great Salt Lake - 2,117 square miles in Utah
7) Louisiana - The Lake Pontchartrain Causeway is nearly 24 miles in length.
8) 10 – Mount Whitney, the highest mountain in the contiguous U.S., is the 11th highest mountain.
9) California
10) Alaska - Yakutat, Sitka, Juneau, Wrangell, Anchorage.

Quiz 13

1) What state gets its name from a Spanish word meaning "mountain"?
2) What two states share Lake Oahe, the largest man-made lake in the U.S.?
3) By area, what is the largest U.S. territory?
4) What lake is formed by the Hoover Dam?
5) By area, what is the fifth largest state?
6) What state's highest point is Borah Peak?
7) There is a chunk of Africa stuck under the United States from when the supercontinent Pangaea broke apart about 250 million years ago. It is located off the coast nearest to what state?
8) What two states share Lake Tahoe?
9) What is the most visited urban park in the U.S.?
10) What state capital is on the James River?

Quiz 13 Answers

1) Montana
2) North and South Dakota - 685 square miles
3) Puerto Rico - 3,515 square miles

4) Lake Mead
5) New Mexico - 121,590 square miles
6) Idaho - 12,668 feet
7) Alabama
8) California and Nevada
9) Central Park - New York City
10) Richmond, Virginia

Quiz 14

1) What state has Kings Canyon National Park?
2) What state's highest point is Boundary Peak?
3) What state has Acadia National Park?
4) What state has the smallest national park?
5) By area, what is the second largest lake entirely within the U.S.?
6) What states border Lake Erie?
7) What state's highest point is Mount Rainier?
8) What two states border Idaho to the west?
9) By discharge volume, what is the second largest river in the U.S.?
10) On a clear day, how many states can you see from the top of the Empire State Building?

Quiz 14 Answers

1) California
2) Nevada - 13,147 feet
3) Maine
4) Arkansas - Hot Springs National Park at 8.7 square miles.
5) Great Salt Lake - 2,117 square miles
6) Michigan, New York, Ohio, Pennsylvania
7) Washington - 14,417 feet
8) Washington and Oregon
9) Ohio River
10) Five - New York, New Jersey, Connecticut, Massachusetts, Pennsylvania

Quiz 15

1) What state is the source of the Missouri River?
2) What state is named after one of the English Channel Islands?
3) How many states border Canada?
4) What state has the third largest water area?
5) What state has the nickname "The Pelican State"?
6) What is the second highest mountain in the U.S.?
7) What is the official state sport of California?
8) What city got its name in 1845 when Asa Lovejoy from Massachusetts and Francis Pettygrove from Maine flipped a coin with the winner getting to name the new settlement?
9) What state is Mount St. Helens in?
10) What was the first state to enter the Union after the original 13?

Quiz 15 Answers

1) Montana
2) New Jersey - named after Jersey
3) 13 - Alaska, Idaho, Maine, Michigan, Minnesota, Montana, New Hampshire, New York, North Dakota, Ohio, Pennsylvania, Vermont, Washington
4) Florida - 12,133 square miles of water
5) Louisiana
6) Mount Saint Elias - 18,009 feet in Alaska
7) Surfing
8) Portland, Oregon - Lovejoy wanted to name the new settlement Boston; Pettygrove wanted to name the new town Portland.
9) Washington - 8,366 feet
10) Vermont - 1791

Quiz 16

1) What state has the nickname "The Bay State"?
2) What state has the largest number of mountains at least 14,000 feet high?
3) By area, what is the smallest permanently inhabited U.S. territory?

4) What state gets its name from the 1510 book *Las Sergas de Esplandián* by Garci Rodríguez de Montalvo who wrote about a mythical island?
5) What two states share Lake Mead?
6) What two states border Nevada to the north?
7) What state capital is on the Charles River?
8) What two states border Tennessee to the west?
9) What state is Devils Tower National Monument in?
10) What is the only state with no natural lakes?

Quiz 16 Answers

1) Massachusetts
2) Colorado - 53
3) American Samoa - 76 square miles
4) California - The island in the book was named California.
5) Arizona and Nevada - 247 square mile reservoir on the Colorado River
6) Oregon and Idaho
7) Boston, Massachusetts
8) Missouri and Arkansas
9) Wyoming
10) Maryland

Quiz 17

1) By area, what is the fourth largest state?
2) What state has the nickname "The Silver State"?
3) What state's highest point is Wheeler Peak?
4) What is the only state with a floating post office?
5) What state has the nickname "The Granite State"?
6) What state has the nickname "The Evergreen State"?
7) After Washington, what is the second most common town or city name in the U.S.?
8) What is the largest national park in the U.S.?
9) What state has North Cascades National Park?

10) What state capital is on the Chattahoochee River?

Quiz 17 Answers

1) Montana - 147,040 square miles
2) Nevada
3) New Mexico - 13,167 feet
4) Michigan – It delivers to ships in Detroit.
5) New Hampshire
6) Washington
7) Springfield
8) Wrangell-St. Elias National Park and Preserve - 20,587 square miles in Alaska
9) Washington
10) Atlanta, Georgia

Quiz 18

1) By area, where would Alaska rank as a country?
2) How many mountains of at least 14,000 feet are there in the U.S.?
3) What state has Great Basin National Park?
4) What state has Shenandoah National Park?
5) What state has the largest water area?
6) What northern state capital is on the Mississippi River?
7) Wisconsin isn't known as the Badger State because of the animal. Miners in the 1830s lived in temporary caves cut into the hillsides which became known as badger dens, and the miners who lived in them were known as badgers; what were they mining?
8) What is the most populous U.S. territory?
9) What states border Lake Ontario?
10) What is the only state without a straight line in its border?

Quiz 18 Answers

1) 16th - closest in size to Libya
2) 96
3) Nevada

4) Virginia
5) Alaska - 94,743 square miles of water
6) St. Paul, Minnesota
7) Lead
8) Puerto Rico
9) New York
10) Hawaii - Its borders are entirely defined by natural features.

Quiz 19

1) Which state consumes the most alcohol per capita?
2) By area, what is the second smallest state?
3) What state is named after an English county?
4) What state has Voyageurs National Park?
5) What state produces about 95% of the bourbon in the world?
6) What river has the largest drainage basin in the U.S.?
7) The Ohio River flows into what river?
8) What state's highest point is Black Elk Peak (formerly Harney Peak)?
9) What state has the most colleges?
10) What state has the nickname "The First State"?

Quiz 19 Answers

1) New Hampshire - Its consumption is 103% higher than the national average and more than one gallon per capita higher than the second highest state, Delaware.
2) Delaware - 2,489 square miles
3) New Hampshire
4) Minnesota
5) Kentucky
6) Mississippi River - It has a drainage basin of 1,245,000 square miles including all or parts of 31 states.
7) Mississippi River
8) South Dakota - 7,242 feet
9) Texas

10) Delaware

Quiz 20

1) What state is the source of the Snake River?
2) What state is the source of the Canadian River, the longest tributary of the Arkansas River?
3) What state borders Colorado to the west?
4) By area, what is the second largest lake entirely within one state?
5) What is the highest mountain east of the Rockies?
6) The Snake River flows into what river?
7) By area, where would the U.S. territory of Puerto Rico rank as a state?
8) What is the deepest canyon in the U.S.?
9) What state capital is built next to the second largest lake entirely in the U.S.?
10) What state's highest point is Granite Peak?

Quiz 20 Answers

1) Wyoming
2) Colorado – The Canadian River is 906 miles long.
3) Utah
4) Lake Iliamna - 1,012 square miles in Alaska
5) Black Elk Peak (formerly Harney Peak) - 7,242 feet in South Dakota
6) Columbia River
7) 49th
8) Kings Canyon - maximum depth of 8,200 feet in California
9) Salt Lake City, Utah
10) Montana - 12,807 feet

Quiz 21

1) What state borders New Mexico to the north?
2) What state has Theodore Roosevelt National Park?
3) How many states are singly landlocked (one state or province away from the ocean)?

4) By area, where would California rank as a country?
5) What state has Lake Okeechobee, the 10th largest lake in the U.S.?
6) What is the official state sport of Alaska?
7) Lake Powell is shared by what two states?
8) What state has the lowest alcohol consumption per capita?
9) What state gets its name from the Spanish word for "snowy" or "snow-capped" in reference to its mountain peaks?
10) What state has the second most national parks with eight?

Quiz 21 Answers

1) Colorado
2) North Dakota
3) 16 - Arizona, Arkansas, Idaho, Kentucky, Michigan, Minnesota, Montana, Nevada, New Mexico, North Dakota, Ohio, Oklahoma, Pennsylvania, Tennessee, Vermont, West Virginia.
4) 58th - closest in size to Iraq
5) Florida - 662 square miles
6) Dog mushing
7) Arizona and Utah - 251 square mile reservoir on the Colorado River
8) Idaho
9) Nevada
10) Alaska – behind California's nine national parks

U.S. Presidents

Quiz 1

1) Who was the first president to win a Grammy Award?
2) What president helped to make the word OK popular?
3) Who was the only president to serve in the Confederate Congress?
4) What president signed the Civil Rights Act that extended the rights of emancipated slaves?
5) Who is the only president who received a Nobel Peace Prize after leaving office?
6) Who was the first president to appoint a secretary of energy?
7) Who was the first president to live at least 35 years after leaving office?
8) What president played in the first two College World Series baseball tournaments?
9) Who was the first president to send an email?
10) Who was the only president to serve in WWI and WWII?

Quiz 1 Answers

1) Bill Clinton
2) Martin Van Buren - One of his nicknames was "Old Kinderhook" based on the town he was from in New York; during his presidential campaign, people held up signs and chanted OK.
3) John Tyler - He served in the Confederate Congress representing Virginia from 1861 until just before his death in 1862; his term as president was 1841-1845.
4) Ulysses S. Grant - 1875
5) Jimmy Carter - 2002
6) Jimmy Carter
7) Jimmy Carter
8) George H.W. Bush
9) Bill Clinton
10) Dwight D. Eisenhower

Quiz 2

1) Who was the first president to appear on U.S. coinage while he was still alive?
2) Who was the first president under the age of 50?
3) Who was president when the National Forest Service was established?
4) Which president established the Secret Service?
5) What president was arrested and taken into custody for speeding with a horse and buggy in Washington D.C. while he was in office?
6) Who was the first president to live at least 30 years after leaving office?
7) Who was the first president who was a lawyer?
8) What president was the first American to own a Siamese cat?
9) Who was president when the 18th Amendment establishing prohibition was passed?
10) Who is regarded as the most fashionable president and owned 80 pair of pants which he liked to change several times a day?

Quiz 2 Answers

1) Calvin Coolidge
2) James K. Polk
3) Theodore Roosevelt - 1905
4) Abraham Lincoln - He established the Secret Service on the day he was assassinated, but it was originally only focused on counterfeiting and didn't protect the president until 1902 after McKinley's assassination.
5) Ulysses S. Grant - The police seized his horse and buggy; he paid a fine and walked back to the White House.
6) Herbert Hoover - He left office in 1933 and died in 1964.
7) John Adams
8) Rutherford B. Hayes - The cat was a gift to the president and first lady from the American consul in Bangkok.
9) Woodrow Wilson - ratified on January 29, 1919
10) Chester A. Arthur

Quiz 3

1) How many presidents didn't have a vice president for all or part of their term?
2) Who was the first president to have served in the U.S. House of Representatives?
3) Who was the first president to have a State of the Union broadcast live on the internet?
4) Who was the first president to be elected after losing as vice president on a major party ticket?
5) Who was the first president inaugurated in Washington, D.C.?
6) What two presidents appeared five times on a national ticket for either president or vice president?
7) Who was the first president to be sworn in by another president?
8) Who was the first president to have been widowed?
9) Who was president when Hawaii was annexed?
10) Who was the first president to have two vice presidents?

Quiz 3 Answers

1) 17 - James Madison, Andrew Jackson, John Tyler, Millard Fillmore, Franklin Pierce, Andrew Johnson, Ulysses S. Grant, Chester A. Arthur, Grover Cleveland, William McKinley, Theodore Roosevelt, William H. Taft, Calvin Coolidge, Harry S. Truman, Lyndon B. Johnson, Richard Nixon, Gerald Ford
2) James Madison
3) George W. Bush
4) Franklin D. Roosevelt - He lost as vice president in the 1920 election running along with James M. Cox.
5) Thomas Jefferson - 1801
6) Franklin D. Roosevelt (1920, 1932, 1936, 1940, 1944) and Richard Nixon (1952, 1956, 1960, 1968, 1972)
7) Calvin Coolidge - He was sworn in by William Howard Taft who was U.S. Supreme Court Chief Justice at the time of Coolidge's second inauguration in 1925.
8) John Adams
9) William McKinley - 1898
10) Thomas Jefferson

Quiz 4

1) What president was credited with saving 77 people from drowning?
2) What president had a wife who was technically a bigamist since she was still married to her former husband?
3) Who was the first president to be sworn in by a woman?
4) Which first lady was the first who wasn't born a citizen of the United States?
5) Who was the first president to spend part of his time in office without a vice president?
6) Who was the first president to be impeached by the House of Representatives?
7) Who was the first president of the U.S. under the Articles of Confederation?
8) Which first lady was the first to own and drive a car?
9) Who was the first president to turn 70 while in office?
10) Who was the first president born after the Declaration of Independence?

Quiz 4 Answers

1) Ronald Reagan - In seven years as a lifeguard at Lowell Park in Dixon, Illinois, Reagan was credited with saving 77 people from drowning in the waters of the Rock River. He started his lifeguard position at the age of 15.
2) Andrew Jackson - His wife Rachel had separated from her first husband, Captain Lewis Robards, in 1790 but never finalized the divorce before marrying Jackson. She remarried Jackson once the divorce was finalized in 1794.
3) Lyndon B. Johnson - Federal Judge Sarah T. Hughes administered the oath of office after John F. Kennedy's assassination on November 22, 1963.
4) Melania Trump - Louisa Adams was also born outside the U.S., but her father was American, so she was still a citizen by birthright.
5) James Madison - Both his vice president choices for his first and second terms died part way through their terms, so he finished his terms without a vice president.
6) Andrew Johnson
7) John Hanson - He was chosen by Congress and was in office from

1781-1782. Under the Articles of Confederation, the president was limited to a one-year term during any three-year period.

8) Helen Taft
9) Dwight D. Eisenhower - in 1960
10) Martin Van Buren

Quiz 5

1) Due to the U.S. Electoral College, what is theoretically the smallest percentage of the popular vote you could get and still win the election?
2) Who was the first president to be defeated for a second term in office?
3) What president had a sport invented by his physician to help keep him fit?
4) Who was the first president to be named *Time* magazine's Man of the Year?
5) Who was the first president who attended an Ivy League college?
6) Who was the first president with a beard?
7) What president hated public speaking and only made two speeches which were both inaugural speeches and hardly audible during his entire eight-year presidency?
8) Who was the only president who was a licensed bartender?
9) Who was the first president whose first language wasn't English?
10) Who was the first president with a Medicare card?

Quiz 5 Answers

1) 23% - This requires winning the required 270 electoral votes in the smallest electoral vote states by one vote in each state and not getting any votes in the largest electoral vote states.
2) John Adams
3) Herbert Hoover - His physician invented a sport known as Hooverball to help keep the president fit. It is a combination of volleyball and tennis and is played with a six-pound medicine ball.
4) Franklin D. Roosevelt
5) John Adams - Harvard
6) Abraham Lincoln

7) Thomas Jefferson
8) Abraham Lincoln
9) Martin Van Buren - He spoke Dutch as his first language and learned English in school.
10) Harry S. Truman - He received the first Medicare card ever from President Lyndon B. Johnson in 1965 in honor of his work for government healthcare.

Quiz 6

1) Who was president when the 14th Amendment was ratified granting citizenship to all persons born or naturalized in the United States including former slaves?
2) Richard Nixon was an accomplished musician and regularly played how many different instruments?
3) Who was the first president to show a motion picture in the White House?
4) Who was the first president to attend a World Series baseball game?
5) Who was the first president widowed in office?
6) Who was the first president to have a secretary of homeland security?
7) What president believed the Earth's core was hollow and signed off on an expedition to explore it?
8) What president kept a pair of grizzly bear cubs in a cage on the White House front lawn for a few months?
9) Who was the first president to wear long pants?
10) Who was the first president to live at least 25 years after his presidency?

Quiz 6 Answers

1) Andrew Johnson - 1868
2) Five - piano, saxophone, clarinet, accordion, violin
3) Woodrow Wilson - *Birth of a Nation* in 1915
4) Woodrow Wilson - 1915
5) John Tyler
6) George W. Bush
7) John Quincy Adams - The expedition never took place.

8) Thomas Jefferson - They were a gift; he decided they were too dangerous to keep and bequeathed them to a museum.
9) James Madison - Previous presidents wore knee breeches.
10) John Adams

Quiz 7

1) Who was the first president to receive the Purple Heart?
2) Which first lady was the first to enter a combat zone?
3) Who was the first president to die before the age of 50?
4) What president grew hemp on his farm?
5) Who was president when the Civil Rights Act was passed?
6) Who was the first divorcee to be first lady of the United States?
7) Who was the first president inaugurated with a living grandparent?
8) Which first lady was the first to give birth to a child in the White House?
9) Which first lady was the first to vote?
10) Who was the first president to have a White House chief of staff?

Quiz 7 Answers

1) John F. Kennedy
2) Pat Nixon
3) James A. Garfield
4) George Washington - He grew hemp at Mount Vernon for rope and canvas making.
5) Lyndon B. Johnson - 1964
6) Florence Harding
7) John F. Kennedy
8) Frances Cleveland
9) Florence Harding
10) Harry S. Truman

Quiz 8

1) What president was reportedly involved in over 100 duels?
2) Who was the first president to visit the Soviet Union?

3) What president survived four plane crashes during WWII?
4) How many people have served as president, vice president, U.S. senator, and U.S. representative?
5) How was Theodore Roosevelt related to Eleanor Roosevelt?
6) Who was president when the U.S. declared war on Germany in WWI?
7) What president holds the record with over 1,000 rounds of golf played while he was in office?
8) What president could simultaneously write in Greek with one hand and Latin with the other?
9) What president worked as a sports announcer?
10) Who was president when the 1830 Indian Removal Act was passed authorizing the president to grant unsettled lands west of the Mississippi in exchange for Indian lands within existing state borders?

Quiz 8 Answers

1) Andrew Jackson
2) Franklin D. Roosevelt
3) George H.W. Bush
4) Four - John Tyler, Andrew Johnson, Lyndon B. Johnson, Richard Nixon
5) Uncle - He was also Franklin D. Roosevelt's fifth cousin.
6) Woodrow Wilson - 1917
7) Woodrow Wilson
8) James A. Garfield - He was ambidextrous and taught both languages while attending college.
9) Ronald Reagan
10) Andrew Jackson

Quiz 9

1) How many presidents were never inaugurated (didn't have a public inauguration and address)?
2) Which first lady was the first to live to see her son become president?
3) Who was president when the first U.S. Census was completed?

4) What president often swam in the Potomac River in the buff?
5) Who was the first president to appear on color television?
6) Who was the first Whig party president?
7) What president banished liquor and wine from the White House?
8) Who was the first president over the age of 65 on taking office?
9) Which president ordered the integration of the U.S. armed forces?
10) What is the only year in which three future presidents were born?

Quiz 9 Answers

1) Five - John Tyler, Millard Fillmore, Andrew Johnson, Chester A. Arthur, Gerald Ford - All five ascended to the presidency after the death or resignation of a president; they weren't elected president.
2) Barbara Bush
3) George Washington - 1790
4) John Quincy Adams - He wrote of waking at 4 a.m. and taking a nude morning dip.
5) Dwight D. Eisenhower
6) William Henry Harrison
7) Rutherford B. Hayes
8) William Henry Harrison
9) Harry S. Truman - 1948
10) 1946 - Bill Clinton, George W. Bush, Donald Trump

Quiz 10

1) Who was president when the Iran Hostage Crisis began?
2) Who was the first president to serve in Congress after his presidency?
3) How many of Abraham Lincoln's children survived him?
4) Who was the first president who went his entire term without a vice president?
5) Who was the first president to name a woman to their cabinet?
6) Who was president when the 19th Amendment giving women the right to vote was ratified?
7) What 20th century president was known as Tommy growing up?

8) Who was the first president who signed the Declaration of Independence?
9) What president kept a journal from the age of 12 until just before his death totaling 51 volumes and 14,000 pages?
10) Who was the first president with a telephone on his desk?

Quiz 10 Answers

1) Jimmy Carter - 1979
2) John Quincy Adams
3) Two - Robert and Thomas (Tad) - He had two other sons who died as children.
4) John Tyler - He became president on the death of William Henry Harrison and never chose a vice president.
5) Franklin D. Roosevelt - In 1933, he named Frances Perkins as secretary of labor.
6) Woodrow Wilson
7) Woodrow Wilson - He was born Thomas Woodrow Wilson but dropped his first name when he was 24.
8) John Adams
9) John Quincy Adams
10) Herbert Hoover

Quiz 11

1) What president was born with the last name Blythe?
2) Who was president when the 22nd Amendment limiting the president to two terms was ratified?
3) Who was president when Florida was acquired from Spain?
4) Who was the first president to have served as director of Central Intelligence?
5) How many vice presidents did Franklin D. Roosevelt have?
6) Who was the only president wounded in the Civil War?
7) What two Mexican American War generals became president?
8) Who was the first president whose inauguration was streamed on the internet?
9) Who was the first president to live to the age of 90?

10) Who was the first president to leave office on January 20 as the normal ending date for a term?

Quiz 11 Answers

1) Bill Clinton - His biological father died shortly before he was born, and he took the last name of his stepfather, Roger Clinton Sr., when he was 15.
2) Harry S. Truman - 1951
3) James Monroe - 1819
4) George H.W. Bush
5) Three - John Nance Garner, Henry A. Wallace, Harry S. Truman
6) Rutherford B. Hayes
7) Zachary Taylor and Franklin Pierce
8) Bill Clinton
9) John Adams
10) Harry S. Truman - March 4 had been the prior ending date.

Quiz 12

1) Who was the first Democratic president to die in office?
2) Who was the first president who didn't have any recognized biological children?
3) Which first lady was the first to live in the White House?
4) Who was president when North Dakota, South Dakota, Montana, Washington, Idaho and Wyoming joined the Union?
5) Who was the first president known to have died of cancer?
6) Who was the first president to complete at least one full term in office and not make a nomination to the U.S. Supreme Court?
7) Who was the first president paid a salary of $200,000?
8) Who was the first president to have previously been a governor?
9) How many Civil War generals became president?
10) Who was the first president to have their photo taken while in office?

Quiz 12 Answers

1) Franklin D. Roosevelt

2) George Washington
3) Abigail Adams
4) Benjamin Harrison - The states were added from 1889-1890.
5) Ulysses S. Grant - He died of throat cancer after smoking 20 cigars a day for much of his adult life.
6) Jimmy Carter
7) Richard Nixon - 1969
8) Thomas Jefferson - governor of Virginia
9) Six - Andrew Johnson, Ulysses S. Grant, Rutherford B. Hayes, James A. Garfield, Chester A. Arthur, Benjamin Harrison
10) William Henry Harrison

Quiz 13

1) Who was the first president to be term limited by the 22nd Amendment?
2) What president wrote his own translation of the Bible?
3) What future president was the only southern senator to keep his seat in Congress at the outbreak of the Civil War?
4) What year did the U.S. have three presidents?
5) What president was the target of an assassination plot that involved taking over a jet and crashing it into the White House?
6) Who was the first president born in the 19th century?
7) Who was the first president to win the electoral vote but lose the popular vote?
8) Who was the first president born on the west coast?
9) What president was on dollar coins issued from 1971-1978?
10) What president was married the longest?

Quiz 13 Answers

1) Dwight D. Eisenhower
2) Thomas Jefferson - He didn't agree with some of the supernatural elements of the Bible and wrote his own version eliminating what he didn't agree with.
3) Andrew Johnson - He was pro-slavery but disagreed with secession and stayed loyal to the Union.

4) 1881 - Rutherford B. Hayes started the year as president and was succeeded by James A. Garfield in March after his election and then Chester A. Arthur, Garfield's vice president, became president in September after Garfield's assassination.
5) Richard Nixon - Samuel Byck successfully managed to take over a Delta Airlines plane but didn't get it off the ground; his plan was to have the pilots fly close to the White House where he would take over and crash the plane.
6) Franklin Pierce
7) Rutherford B. Hayes
8) Richard Nixon
9) Dwight D. Eisenhower
10) George H.W. Bush - 73 years to Barbara Bush

Quiz 14

1) Who was the first president to serve in the U.S. Senate after being president?
2) Who was president when the 16th Amendment allowing the federal government to collect an income tax from all Americans was ratified?
3) Who was the last president who didn't have a vice president for all or part of their term?
4) Which president had a pet hyena named Bill?
5) Which first lady was the first to also be the mother of a president?
6) Who was president when the Interstate Highway System was created?
7) Who is the only president buried in Washington, D.C.?
8) Who was the first president to receive a British monarch during a visit to the U.S.?
9) What future president delivered an 84-minute campaign speech after being shot just before the event?
10) Who was the first president to be inaugurated on an airplane?

Quiz 14 Answers

1) Andrew Johnson
2) William Howard Taft - 1913

3) Gerald Ford - He was without a vice president from August 9 to December 19, 1974.
4) Theodore Roosevelt - It was a present from the Emperor of Ethiopia.
5) Abigail Adams
6) Dwight D. Eisenhower - 1956
7) Woodrow Wilson
8) Franklin D. Roosevelt - George VI in 1939
9) Theodore Roosevelt - He was shot as he stood up in the open-air automobile and waved his hat to the crowd; fortunately, the bullet was slowed by his dense overcoat, steel-reinforced eyeglass case, and 50-page speech squeezed into his jacket pocket. X-rays taken after the speech showed the bullet lodged against Roosevelt's fourth right rib on an upward path toward his heart.
10) Lyndon B. Johnson - aboard Air Force One in 1963

Quiz 15

1) Before getting married in the White House, which president had his sister perform the duties normally done by the president's wife?
2) Which first lady was the first to earn a college degree?
3) Who was the first president to travel by jet aircraft and helicopter?
4) Which president said, "The ballot is stronger than the bullet"?
5) Who was vice president when the atomic bomb was dropped on Hiroshima?
6) Who is the only president to be grandson of another president?
7) Who was the first president to have a television installed in the White House?
8) The tradition in the White House Roosevelt Room has been to hang Franklin Delano Roosevelt's portrait over the mantel during Democratic administrations and hang whose portrait over the mantel during Republican administrations?
9) What president was the target of the first known attempted assassination of a U.S. president?
10) What president had a bowling alley installed in the White House?

Quiz 15 Answers

1) Grover Cleveland

2) Lucy Webb Hayes - 1850
3) Dwight D. Eisenhower
4) Abraham Lincoln
5) No one - Harry S. Truman did not have a vice president for the remainder of his first term (1945-1949) after taking over as president on April 12, 1945 after Franklin D. Roosevelt's death.
6) Benjamin Harrison - grandson of William Henry Harrison
7) Harry S. Truman
8) Theodore Roosevelt - Whichever painting is not over the mantel is hung on the south wall of the room.
9) Andrew Jackson - In 1835, he was attending the funeral of South Carolina congressman Warren R. Davis when Richard Lawrence fired two pistols at point-blank range. Both misfired.
10) Harry S. Truman

Quiz 16

1) Who was the first president to be married twice?
2) What president served as a Yellowstone Park Ranger?
3) Who was the last president who didn't have any recognized biological children?
4) Who was the first president to have his voice recorded?
5) Which first lady was the first to have no children?
6) Which first lady was the first born in the 20th century?
7) Which first lady was the first to die in the White House?
8) Who was the first president who was a Quaker?
9) Who had the shortest time in office of any president who didn't die in office?
10) Who was the first president to marry a divorced woman?

Quiz 16 Answers

1) John Tyler
2) Gerald Ford
3) Warren G. Harding
4) Benjamin Harrison
5) Sarah Polk

6) Jacqueline Kennedy
7) Letitia Tyler
8) Herbert Hoover
9) Gerald Ford - 895 days
10) Andrew Jackson

Quiz 17

1) Who was the first president to attend the U.S. Naval Academy?
2) Which first lady was the first to attend an Ivy League college for her undergraduate degree?
3) Who was president when the 15th Amendment was ratified guaranteeing the right of citizens to vote regardless of race, color, or previous condition of servitude?
4) Who was the first president to have both major political parties recruit him for the presidential nomination?
5) How many U.S. presidents got married while in office?
6) Which first lady was the first to earn a postgraduate degree?
7) What president had a nervous breakdown at the age of 24 and spent several weeks in a sanitarium?
8) Who was the first president to appear on U.S. paper currency while in office?
9) Who is the only person in history known to have witnessed the assassination of three U.S. presidents?
10) Who was the first president to have a national security advisor?

Quiz 17 Answers

1) Jimmy Carter
2) Michelle Obama - Princeton University
3) Ulysses S. Grant - 1870
4) Dwight D. Eisenhower - He ran as a Republican.
5) Three - John Tyler and Woodrow Wilson remarried after losing their wives; Grover Cleveland got married for the first time in the White House.
6) Hillary Clinton
7) Warren Harding

8) Abraham Lincoln
9) Robert Lincoln - He was Abraham Lincoln's son and witnessed the assassinations of his father, James A. Garfield, and William McKinley.
10) Dwight D. Eisenhower

Quiz 18

1) Which first lady was the first who was not a native speaker of English?
2) What president was the youngest naval aviator in U.S. history at the age of 18?
3) Who was the first president who didn't have any full siblings?
4) Which first lady was the first to hold seances in the White House?
5) Who was president when the Berlin Wall fell?
6) What two War of 1812 generals became presidents?
7) Who was the first president born a citizen of the United States?
8) Who was the first president to live in the White House?
9) Who was the first president who did not immediately succeed the president he served as vice president?
10) Who was the first president to remarry in office?

Quiz 18 Answers

1) Melania Trump
2) George H.W. Bush
3) Franklin D. Roosevelt - He had a half-brother.
4) Mary Todd Lincoln
5) Ronald Reagan - 1989
6) Andrew Jackson and William Henry Harrison
7) Martin Van Buren
8) John Adams
9) Richard Nixon - He served from 1953-1961 as Eisenhower's vice president but did not become president until 1969.
10) John Tyler

Quiz 19

1) What president lost the nuclear launch codes for months and nobody found out?
2) What president played football at West Point and was injured trying to tackle Olympic and NFL star Jim Thorpe?
3) Who was president when the Statue of Liberty was presented to the U.S. by France?
4) Who was president when the 26th Amendment giving 18-year-olds the right to vote was ratified?
5) Who was the first president to own a radio?
6) What president lived for 80 days after being shot?
7) Who was the first president to have served in the U.S. Senate?
8) Who was the first president with a defense secretary?
9) When Thomas Jefferson sent Lewis and Clark on their expedition, what extinct animal did he ask them to look for?
10) Who was the first president to die before the age of 60?

Quiz 19 Answers

1) Bill Clinton - The president must keep the launch codes nearby; every 30 days, a Pentagon staffer is required to check the codes to ensure they're correct, and the codes are replaced every four months. During one of these periods, the Pentagon staffer was told each time they came to check the codes that the president was too busy, and the staffer would leave. At the end of the fourth month, it became clear that Clinton had lost the codes. The procedure has since been changed, and the Pentagon official must physically wait for as long as it takes to verify the codes.
2) Dwight D. Eisenhower
3) Chester A. Arthur - 1884
4) Richard Nixon - 1971
5) Warren G. Harding
6) James A. Garfield
7) James Monroe
8) Harry S. Truman
9) Wooly mammoth - Jefferson believed that there might be wooly mammoths still living in the west.

10) James K. Polk

Quiz 20

1) Who was president when the 21st Amendment repealing prohibition was ratified?
2) Who was the first president to complete a marathon?
3) Who was the last U.S. president without a college degree?
4) Who was the first president to learn to drive a car?
5) Who was the first president to be filmed?
6) Who was the first president to be physically attacked while in office?
7) Who was the first president to be inaugurated on January 20?
8) Who was president when the Louisiana Purchase was completed?
9) Who was the first president to hold the White House Easter Egg Roll?
10) Who was the first president with facial hair?

Quiz 20 Answers

1) Franklin D. Roosevelt - 1933
2) George W. Bush
3) Harry S. Truman
4) Warren G. Harding
5) Grover Cleveland
6) Andrew Jackson - A man punched him and ran away.
7) Franklin D. Roosevelt
8) Thomas Jefferson - 1803
9) Rutherford B. Hayes
10) John Quincy Adams

Quiz 21

1) What president was the first American to earn a brown belt in judo?
2) What president installed a putting green at the White House and played more than 800 rounds of golf while in office?
3) What president was known for his gambling and once lost a set of

priceless White House china on a bet?

4) What president was arrested for running over a woman with his horse while he was in office?
5) Which first lady was the first to give birth to twins?
6) What president's wife was the first to be referred to as the first lady?
7) Who was the first president elected in the 20th century?
8) What president wasn't fond of formal events and often greeted foreign dignitaries in his pajamas?
9) Who was the first president born in Texas?
10) Who is the only president who did not represent a political party when he was elected?

Quiz 21 Answers

1) Theodore Roosevelt
2) Dwight D. Eisenhower
3) Warren G. Harding
4) Franklin Pierce - The charges were dropped due to lack of evidence.
5) Laura Bush
6) Rutherford B. Hayes - Lucy Hayes was referred to as the first lady in 1877.
7) Theodore Roosevelt
8) Thomas Jefferson
9) Dwight D. Eisenhower
10) George Washington

Quiz 22

1) Of the first five U.S. presidents, three died on the same day of the year; what day?
2) Which first lady was the first to die the same year as her husband?
3) Who was the first president to speak over the radio?
4) What president married his teacher?
5) What U.S. Constitution amendment moved the beginning and ending of the president's term to January 20?
6) Who was the first vice president to become president after the

death of the president?

7) How many presidents served their entire term without a vice president?
8) Which first lady was the first to win an Emmy Award?
9) Who was the first Democratic president?
10) Who was the first president to have both parents alive during their presidency?

Quiz 22 Answers

1) July 4 - John Adams and Thomas Jefferson both died on July 4, 1826; James Monroe died five years later on July 4, 1831.
2) Barbara Bush
3) Warren G. Harding - 1922
4) Millard Fillmore - Fillmore's first wife, Abigail Powers, was his teacher when he was 19 years old.
5) 20th Amendment
6) John Tyler
7) Four - John Tyler, Millard Fillmore, Andrew Johnson, Chester A. Arthur
8) Jacqueline Kennedy - She won a Trustees Award for a 1962 televised tour of the White House.
9) Andrew Jackson
10) Ulysses S. Grant

Quiz 23

1) Which first lady was the first to outlive her husband?
2) Who was the first president to win election after previously being defeated?
3) Who was the first president to have served as U.S. senate majority whip?
4) Who was the first elected president to have served as acting president?
5) Woolsey Hall auditorium at Yale University still has an extra wide seat built specifically for what U.S. president?
6) Who was president when the Soviet Union broke up into independent republics?

7) George Washington was taphephobic; what is it?
8) Who was the first president to serve in the U.S. Army Air Force?
9) What president and first lady were so afraid of being electrocuted when electricity was first installed in the White House that they never touched the light switches and always had staff turn the lights on and off?
10) Who was the first president to be survived by both his parents?

Quiz 23 Answers

1) Martha Washington
2) Thomas Jefferson
3) Lyndon B. Johnson
4) George H.W. Bush - He served as acting president for eight hours when Ronald Reagan was sedated for colon surgery.
5) William Howard Taft - After his presidency, Taft went on to teach at Yale which installed several special chairs with extra-wide seats to accommodate Taft who was well over 300 pounds. One of the chairs is still in use in Woolsey Hall today; it is balcony seat E-9.
6) George H.W. Bush - 1991
7) Fear of being buried alive
8) Ronald Reagan
9) Benjamin Harrison and his wife
10) John F. Kennedy

Quiz 24

1) What president lost his wife to kidney failure after giving birth to their daughter only 11 hours after losing his mother to typhoid fever in the same house?
2) Who is the only president who served as an ordained minister?
3) Who was the first president elected after women gained the right to vote?
4) Under the Articles of Confederation, how many presidents were there prior to George Washington?
5) What president had an adopted niece who took over many of the responsibilities that would normally go to the president's wife?
6) What presidential nominee considered Clint Eastwood as his

running mate?

7) Who was the first Republican vice president of the U.S. and Abraham Lincoln's first vice president?
8) Who was the first president to attend and open an Olympics while in office?
9) What president gave the White House its name?
10) What president received a pet alligator as a surprise gift and kept it in the White House East Room bathroom for two months before returning it?

Quiz 24 Answers

1) Theodore Roosevelt
2) James A. Garfield
3) Warren G. Harding
4) Eight - Each served a one-year term.
5) James Buchanan - He is the only president to never marry.
6) George W. Bush
7) Hannibal Hamlin
8) Ronald Reagan - 1984 Los Angeles Olympics
9) Theodore Roosevelt - 1901
10) John Quincy Adams

Quiz 25

1) Franklin D. Roosevelt was put on the dime largely for his work for what organization?
2) Who was the first president not of Irish or British descent?
3) What president has an African national capital city named after him?
4) At the time of his death, George Washington was one of the largest U.S. producers of what alcoholic beverage?
5) Who was the first president born after WWII?
6) Who was the first president over the age of 60 when entering office?
7) Which U.S. President was shot by Charles J. Guiteau on July 2, 1881?
8) What president was the first graduate student ever at Princeton

University?

9) Which first lady was the first to have a U.S. stamp honoring her?
10) Who was the first president to receive an Emmy Award?

Quiz 25 Answers

1) March of Dimes - originally called National Foundation for Infantile Paralysis
2) Martin Van Buren - Dutch
3) James Monroe - Monrovia, Liberia
4) Whiskey - His distillery produced nearly 11,000 gallons in 1799 making it one of the largest whiskey distilleries in America at the time.
5) Bill Clinton
6) John Adams
7) James A. Garfield - He died two months later from infections related to the injury.
8) James Madison
9) Martha Washington
10) Dwight D. Eisenhower - 1956 Governor's Award for his use and encouragement of television

Quiz 26

1) What president said, "Not making the baseball team at West Point was one of the greatest disappointments of my life, maybe my greatest"?
2) Who was the first president to die in office?
3) Who was the first president to serve in the Air National Guard?
4) What president was an indentured servant in his early life?
5) Who was the only vice president to serve under two different presidents?
6) What political party has had the most presidents?
7) Who was president when the Peace Corps was created?
8) Who was the first president to leave office with both parents still alive?
9) Which first lady was the first to win a Grammy Award?

10) How many times was Franklin D. Roosevelt elected president?

Quiz 26 Answers

1) Dwight D. Eisenhower
2) William Henry Harrison - 1841
3) George W. Bush
4) Andrew Johnson - He was three years old when his father died, and he and his brother became indentured servants to a tailor.
5) John C. Calhoun - vice president to both John Quincy Adams and Andrew Jackson
6) Republican
7) John F. Kennedy - 1961
8) George W. Bush
9) Hillary Clinton - for best spoken word album for her audio recording of her book *It Takes a Village*
10) Four - He won the 1932, 1936, 1940, and 1944 elections.

Quiz 27

1) Who was the first president to have a secretary of health, education, and welfare?
2) Who was the first president with a mustache?
3) Who was the first president to be orphaned?
4) What is the most common prior occupation for presidents?
5) How many presidents haven't had any recognized biological children?
6) Who was the first president to pardon a Thanksgiving turkey?
7) Who was the only president to live in subsidized housing for the poor?
8) Who was the first president to have a pilot's license?
9) Who was the first president to pay off the entire national debt?
10) Who was the first president photographed at his inauguration?

Quiz 27 Answers

1) Dwight D. Eisenhower
2) Ulysses S. Grant

3) Andrew Jackson - His mother, father, and two older brothers all died by the time he was 14.
4) Lawyer
5) Five - Washington, Buchanan, Polk, Jackson, Harding
6) Harry S. Truman
7) Jimmy Carter - His father was relatively wealthy, but he canceled debts and spread his remaining wealth around widely after his death leaving Carter with little.
8) Dwight D. Eisenhower
9) Andrew Jackson
10) Abraham Lincoln

World Geography

Quiz 1

1) What river flows through Baghdad, Iraq?
2) What is the easternmost national capital city in South America?
3) What is the main river that flows through Shanghai, China?
4) In 1937, Liechtenstein added a crown to their flag after discovering at the 1936 Summer Olympics that their flag was identical to what country?
5) What is the deepest lake in Asia?
6) What country has the northernmost permanent settlement in the world?
7) What island nation was once one of the wealthiest countries on a GDP per capita basis due to phosphate mining but became one of the poorest after strip mining 80% of the country and depleting the phosphate deposits?
8) What is the capital of the Canadian province of Quebec?
9) What is the smallest landlocked country in the world?
10) What is the largest city in the Southern Hemisphere?

Quiz 1 Answers

1) Tigris
2) Brasilia, Brazil - 47.9 degrees west longitude
3) Huangpu River
4) Haiti
5) Lake Baikal - 5,387 feet in Russia
6) Canada - Alert, Nunavut, Canada is at 82.5 degrees north latitude, about 508 miles from the North pole
7) Nauru - 8 square miles in the South Pacific. The phosphate deposits were based on the decay of marine microorganisms and thousands of years of seabird droppings.
8) Quebec City
9) Vatican City - 0.17 square miles
10) Sao Paulo, Brazil

Quiz 2

1) The island of Hispaniola is divided into what two countries?
2) What country is bordered by Mexico and Guatemala?
3) What country has the northernmost 18-hole golf course in the world?
4) What is the most populous national capital city in South America?
5) By population, what is the largest country in the European Union?
6) What is the largest desert in Asia?
7) What country has the southernmost point in North America?
8) What is Australia's largest island?
9) What is the major river that flows through Delhi, India?
10) What is the southernmost urban area in the world with a population over 20 million?

Quiz 2 Answers

1) Haiti and Dominican Republic
2) Belize
3) Norway - Tromsø Golfpark at Breivikeidet near Tromsø, Norway at 69.7 degrees north latitude
4) Lima, Peru
5) Germany
6) Arabian Desert - 900,000 square miles
7) Costa Rica - Cocos Island at 5.5 degrees north latitude
8) Tasmania - 25,105 square miles
9) Yamuna River
10) Sao Paulo, Brazil at 23.9 degrees south latitude

Quiz 3

1) What river flows through Rome, Italy?
2) What country has the easternmost point in Asia?
3) What is the deepest sea in the world?
4) What is the most densely populated European country?
5) What is the second highest mountain in North America?

6) What country consists of more than 17,500 islands with about 6,000 of them inhabited?
7) What national capital city is closest to the equator?
8) What river flows through Lisbon, Portugal?
9) What country has the most bicycles per capita?
10) What is the capital of the Canadian province of New Brunswick?

Quiz 3 Answers

1) Tiber River
2) Russia - Big Diomede at 169.1 degrees west longitude
3) Caribbean Sea - 25,217 feet maximum depth
4) Monaco
5) Mount Logan - 19,551 feet in Yukon province of Canada
6) Indonesia
7) Quito, Ecuador - 15.9 miles south of the equator
8) Tagus River
9) Netherlands - almost one per person
10) Fredericton

Quiz 4

1) What is the most popular letter for country names to begin with?
2) What is the westernmost national capital city in Africa?
3) By area, what is the largest lake in Antarctica?
4) What country is Mount Kilimanjaro in?
5) What is the largest volume lake in North America?
6) What new country was established in 2011?
7) What African country has the most lakes?
8) What is the largest volume lake in South America?
9) Based on number of members, what country has the largest legislature in the world?
10) What is the largest island in the Pacific Ocean?

Quiz 4 Answers

1) A - 11 countries - Afghanistan, Albania, Algeria, Andorra, Angola,

Antigua and Barbuda, Argentina, Armenia, Australia, Austria, Azerbaijan

2) Praia, Cape Verde - 23.5 degrees west longitude
3) Lake Vostok - 6,058 square miles
4) Tanzania
5) Lake Superior - U.S. and Canada
6) South Sudan
7) Uganda
8) Lake Titicaca - Peru and Bolivia
9) China - The National People's Congress is a single house made up of 2,980 members.
10) New Guinea - 303,476 square miles

Quiz 5

1) What is the deepest river in South America?
2) What country has the second highest average elevation?
3) What mountain range is Mount Kilimanjaro part of?
4) What country is bordered by Russia, Azerbaijan, Armenia, and Turkey?
5) The southern end of the Suez Canal is at Port Tewfik at the city of Suez, Egypt; what port city is at the northern end?
6) What is the longest mountain range in Asia?
7) What country is bordered by Chile, Uruguay, Brazil, Paraguay, and Bolivia?
8) By area, what is the largest island nation in the world?
9) How many European countries share a name with their capital city?
10) By area, what is the third largest island in the world?

Quiz 5 Answers

1) Amazon - 328 feet maximum depth
2) Nepal - 10,715 feet average elevation
3) None – At 19,340 feet, it is the highest mountain in the world that isn't part of a range.
4) Georgia

5) Port Said, Egypt
6) Kunlun Mountains - 1,900 miles in China
7) Argentina
8) Indonesia - 735,400 square miles
9) Five - Vatican City, Monaco, Luxembourg, Andorra, San Marino
10) Borneo - 287,000 square miles

Quiz 6

1) What is the largest volume lake in Africa?
2) What country has the southernmost point in mainland North America?
3) How many federated states does Mexico have?
4) What country's flag has the most stars?
5) How many countries does the Arctic Circle pass through?
6) By population, what is the second largest city in Australia?
7) What are the only two countries in the world with square flags?
8) How many countries don't have any airports within their boundaries?
9) How many North American countries have a land border with only one other country?
10) What is the second smallest landlocked country in the world?

Quiz 6 Answers

1) Lake Tanganyika - Tanzania, DRC, Burundi, and Zambia
2) Panama - Punta Mariato at 7.2 degrees north latitude
3) 31 - plus the Federal District of Mexico City
4) United States
5) Eight - Norway, Sweden, Finland, Russia, United States, Canada, Denmark (Greenland), Iceland
6) Melbourne
7) Switzerland and Vatican City
8) Five - Vatican City, San Marino, Liechtenstein, Andorra, Monaco
9) Three - Canada, Haiti, Dominican Republic
10) San Marino - 23.6 square miles

Quiz 7

1) What river has the largest drainage basin area in the world?
2) What country has the highest minimum elevation?
3) What mountain range passes through the most countries?
4) What is the smallest population national capital city in the world?
5) What is the only Central American country that doesn't border the Pacific Ocean?
6) By area, what is the largest country in Central America?
7) What is the highest mountain in China?
8) How many countries border the Gulf of Mexico?
9) What country has the highest average elevation?
10) What continent has the largest number of individual deserts?

Quiz 7 Answers

1) Amazon - 2.7 million square miles drainage basin
2) Lesotho - 4,593 feet minimum elevation
3) Andes - seven countries - Venezuela, Colombia, Ecuador, Peru, Bolivia, Chile, Argentina
4) Ngerulmud, Palau - It has less than 400 residents; Palau is an island nation in the Pacific Ocean.
5) Belize
6) Nicaragua - 50,337 square miles
7) Mount Everest - 29,020 feet
8) Three - Mexico, United States, Cuba
9) Bhutan - 10,760 feet average
10) Asia

Quiz 8

1) What country has the easternmost point in North America?
2) What country has the world's largest rock?
3) What river flows through Prague, Czech Republic?
4) What is the least densely populated Canadian province?
5) What country has the largest area devoted to national parks?

6) What country has the world's highest elevation airport?
7) If you wanted to dig a hole straight through the center of the Earth and end up in China, what country would you have to start in?
8) What mountain range is Canada's highest peak a part of?
9) What country is bordered by Germany, Austria, Slovakia, and Poland?
10) What province or territory has the southernmost point in Canada?

Quiz 8 Answers

1) Denmark (Greenland) - Nordostrundingen at 11.5 degrees west longitude
2) Australia - Mount Augustus in the Australian Outback is 2,350 feet high and 5 miles long occupying an area of about 18.5 square miles. It is about 2.5 times larger than Ayers Rock.
3) Vltava River
4) Newfoundland and Labrador
5) Canada – It has over 145,000 square miles of national parks, an area larger than Norway.
6) China - Daocheng Yading Airport at 14,472 feet
7) Argentina
8) Saint Elias Mountains – They run through southeastern Alaska, southwestern Yukon, and the very far northwestern part of British Columbia, Canada.
9) Czech Republic
10) Ontario

Quiz 9

1) What country has the southernmost national park in the world?
2) What country has the oldest city in Europe?
3) What country has the longest coastline in Asia?
4) What country is bordered by Honduras and Guatemala?
5) What is the oldest national capital city in South America?
6) How many provinces are there in China?
7) What is the northernmost national capital city in Africa?
8) How many European countries have a land border with only one

other country?

9) The largest uninhabited island in the world is part of what country?
10) What national capital city is built on 14 islands?

Quiz 9 Answers

1) Chile - Cabo de Hornos National Park, Tierra Del Fuego, Chile at 55.8 degrees south latitude
2) Bulgaria - The city of Plovdiv was founded about 6000 BC.
3) Indonesia - 33,939 miles
4) El Salvador
5) Quito, Ecuador - founded in 980 AD
6) 23
7) Tunis, Tunisia - 36.8 degrees north latitude
8) Seven - Portugal, Ireland, United Kingdom, Denmark, San Marino, Monaco, Vatican City
9) Canada - Devon Island in Nunavut Territory is 21,331 square miles at an elevation of 6,300 feet. It is at 75.2 degrees north latitude and is the 27th largest island in the world.
10) Stockholm, Sweden

Quiz 10

1) What is the least populous country in Asia?
2) The five smallest landlocked countries in the world are all in what continent?
3) What is the most densely populated North American country?
4) What is the northernmost city in the world with a population over 1 million?
5) What tiny country of just over 20,000 people is divided into 16 states each with an elected legislature and a tribal chiefdom?
6) What are the names of the two main islands that make up over 98% of New Zealand's area?
7) What province or territory has the westernmost point in Canada?
8) French Sudan is the former name of what country?
9) How many Asian countries does the equator pass through?
10) What river flows through Dublin, Ireland?

Quiz 10 Answers

1) Maldives
2) Europe - Vatican City, San Marino, Liechtenstein, Andorra, Luxembourg
3) Bermuda
4) St. Petersburg, Russia - 59.9 degrees north latitude
5) Palau - It is an archipelago of over 500 islands in the western Pacific Ocean occupying 177 square miles in total.
6) North Island is the 14th largest island in the world at 43,082 square miles, and South Island is the 12th largest in the world at 56,308 square miles.
7) Yukon
8) Mali
9) Two - Maldives and Indonesia
10) River Liffey

Quiz 11

1) What river flows through Bangkok, Thailand?
2) What four national capital cities does the Danube River flow through?
3) If you exclude the Vatican as a national capital, what pair of national capital cities are closest together?
4) What country has the easternmost point in mainland South America?
5) What is the capital of the Canadian province of Newfoundland and Labrador?
6) What country is closest to 0 degrees latitude and 0 degrees longitude (the intersection of the equator and the prime meridian)?
7) What is the least populous country in Europe?
8) Based on average depth, what is the deepest of the Great Lakes?
9) The most national capital cities start with what letter?
10) Among countries that share a land border, what pair of national capital cities are the greatest distance apart?

Quiz 11 Answers

1) Chao Phraya River
2) Vienna, Austria; Bratislava, Slovakia; Budapest, Hungary; Belgrade, Serbia
3) Brazzaville, Republic of the Congo and Kinshasa, Democratic Republic of the Congo - two miles apart
4) Brazil - Ponta do Seixas at 34.8 degrees west longitude
5) St. John's
6) Ghana - The equator and prime meridian intersect 380 miles south of Ghana in the Gulf of Guinea.
7) Vatican City - less than 1,000 people
8) Superior - 483 feet average depth
9) B - Baghdad, Baku, Bamako, Bandar Seri Begawan, Bangkok, Bangui, Banjul, Basseterre, Beijing, Beirut, Belgrade, Belmopan, Berlin, Bern, Bishkek, Bissau, Bogota, Brasilia, Bratislava, Brazzaville, Bridgetown, Brussels, Bucharest, Budapest, Buenos Aires
10) Brasilia, Brazil and Paris, France - 5,427 miles - French Guiana which borders Brazil is a part of France just as Alaska or Hawaii are part of the U.S.

Quiz 12

1) What is the northernmost national capital city in Asia?
2) What country has the southernmost international airport in the world?
3) How many country's official currency is the dollar (either U.S. dollar or other dollar)?
4) By population, what is the second largest city in Africa?
5) What country is bordered by Mexico, Belize, Honduras, and El Salvador?
6) What is the largest desert in Australia?
7) What is the westernmost national capital city in Asia?
8) What is the longest mountain range in Antarctica?
9) By population, what is the second largest city in Canada?
10) What country has the longest coastline in mainland Africa?

Quiz 12 Answers

1) Astana, Kazakhstan - 51.2 degrees north latitude
2) Argentina - Malvinas Argentinas International Airport, Ushuaia, Argentina at 54.8 degrees south latitude
3) 32 - Australia, Bahamas, Barbados, Belize, Brunei, Canada, Dominica, East Timor, Ecuador, El Salvador, Fiji, Grenada, Guyana, Jamaica, Kiribati, Liberia, Marshall Islands, Micronesia, Namibia, Nauru, New Zealand, Palau, Saint Kitts and Nevis, Saint Lucia, Saint Vincent and the Grenadines, Singapore, Solomon Islands, Suriname, Taiwan, Tuvalu, United States, Zimbabwe
4) Cairo, Egypt
5) Guatemala
6) Great Victoria Desert - 220,000 square miles
7) Ankara, Turkey - 32.9 degrees east longitude
8) Transantarctic Mountains - 2,200 miles
9) Montreal
10) Somalia - 2,071 miles

Quiz 13

1) What is the most populous national capital city in Europe?
2) What is the second deepest lake in the world?
3) What country has the longest coastline in North America?
4) What country has the easternmost point in Africa?
5) What country has the largest number of paid newspapers?
6) Besides its canals, what river flows through Amsterdam, Netherlands?
7) What is the deepest river in the world?
8) What is the highest mountain in the United Kingdom?
9) What is the warmest ocean?
10) What was the capital of West Germany before Germany was reunited?

Quiz 13 Answers

1) Moscow, Russia

2) Lake Tanganyika - 4,820 feet deep in southeastern Africa
3) Canada - 125,567 miles
4) Mauritius - Rodrigues, Mauritius at 63.5 degrees east longitude
5) India
6) Amstel
7) Congo - up to 750 feet deep
8) Ben Nevis - 4,409 feet in Scotland
9) Indian Ocean
10) Bonn

Quiz 14

1) Until It gained its independence in 1825, what country was known as Upper Peru?
2) What country is the leading producer of uranium in the world?
3) What is the largest island in the Philippines?
4) What is the most densely populated Canadian province?
5) What country has the world's highest unclimbed mountain?
6) What are the three city-states in the world?
7) What is the highest coastal mountain in the world?
8) Unimak is the largest island in what chain?
9) What country is bordered by Colombia, Brazil, and Guyana?
10) What is the only carbon negative (produces less carbon dioxide than it absorbs) country in the world?

Quiz 14 Answers

1) Bolivia
2) Kazakhstan
3) Luzon - 42,458 square miles
4) Prince Edward Island
5) Bhutan - Gangkhar Puensum at 24,840 feet is the tallest unclimbed mountain in the world. It has been off limits to climbers since 1994 when Bhutan prohibited all mountaineering above 6,000 meters due to spiritual and religious beliefs.
6) Vatican City, Monaco, Singapore

7) Mount Logan - 19,551 feet in the Saint Elias range in the Yukon province of Canada
8) Aleutian Islands – It is 1,571 square miles.
9) Venezuela
10) Bhutan – About 72% of the country is still forested.

Quiz 15

1) How many stars are on the flag of China?
2) What point on Earth is farthest from the center of the Earth?
3) What is the capital of the Canadian province of Alberta?
4) What is the capital of the Canadian province of Nova Scotia?
5) What is the largest island in the Atlantic Ocean?
6) Based on annual average temperature, what is the coldest national capital city in the world?
7) Based on volume, what continent has the largest man-made lake in the world?
8) What is the deepest river in Asia?
9) What is the largest island in the Indian Ocean?
10) What is the easternmost national capital city in Asia?

Quiz 15 Answers

1) Five - One large gold star representing communism and four smaller stars representing the people
2) Mount Chimborazo in Ecuador at 20,700 feet elevation - Due to the bulge of the Earth at the equator, Mount Chimborazo is farthest from the center of the Earth even though it isn't the highest mountain in the world.
3) Edmonton
4) Halifax
5) Greenland - 836,300 square miles
6) Ulaanbaatar, Mongolia - 29.7 degrees Fahrenheit average annual temperature
7) Africa - Lake Kariba on the Zambezi River in Zambia and Zimbabwe contains 43.3 cubic miles of water.
8) Yangtze - 656 feet maximum depth, 2nd deepest in the world

9) Madagascar - 226,658 square miles
10) Tokyo, Japan - 139.7 degrees east longitude

Quiz 16

1) How many national anthems have no official words?
2) What are the only two countries with coastlines on the Aegean Sea?
3) What is the longest river in the European Union countries?
4) What country has the southernmost point in Europe?
5) On the Amazon River, what is the Pororoca?
6) What country has the highest percentage of its energy consumption from renewable resources?
7) What country has the northernmost point in South America?
8) By area, what is the largest Australian state or territory?
9) Canada has a strategic reserve of 2.4 million gallons of what food item?
10) What country has the northernmost point in mainland Europe?

Quiz 16 Answers

1) Four - Spain, Bosnia and Herzegovina, Kosovo, San Marino
2) Turkey and Greece
3) Danube - 1,771 miles
4) Greece - Gavdos Island at 34.8 degrees north latitude
5) Tidal bore wave - It is up to 13 feet high and travels up to 500 miles inland upstream on the Amazon river. The wave occurs during new and full moons when the ocean tide is the highest and water flows in from the Atlantic Ocean. The phenomenon is most pronounced during the spring equinox in March when the Moon and Sun are in direct alignment with the Earth, and their gravitational pull is combined. The wave can be quite destructive as it moves upriver, and the water is filled with debris. It has also become popular with surfers who have surfed the wave for 8 miles and over 30 minutes continuously.
6) Iceland
7) Colombia - Santa Catalina Island at 13.4 degrees north latitude
8) Western Australia - 975,598 square miles
9) Maple syrup - It is kept to ensure the global supply in the case of

emergency; Quebec province produces about 75% of the global supply of maple syrup.

10) Norway - Cape Nordkinn at 71.1 degrees north latitude

Quiz 17

1) What country is bordered by Belgium, France, and Germany?
2) What is the southernmost national capital city in South America?
3) By population, what is the second largest city in Asia?
4) What country is bordered by Peru, Brazil, Paraguay, Argentina, and Chile?
5) What country has the southernmost point in mainland Asia?
6) What country or territory has the northernmost national park in the world?
7) What is believed to be the oldest continuously inhabited city in South America?
8) What is the oldest lake in the world?
9) English is the official language of more countries than any other language; what is the second most popular official language?
10) What is the second highest elevation national capital city in the world?

Quiz 17 Answers

1) Luxembourg
2) Montevideo, Uruguay - 34.9 degrees south latitude
3) Delhi, India
4) Bolivia
5) Malaysia - Tanjung Piai at 1.3 degrees north latitude
6) Greenland - Northeast Greenland National Park at 76 degrees north latitude is also the largest national park in the world at 375,291 square miles which is larger than all but 29 countries in the world.
7) Quito, Ecuador - founded in 980 AD
8) Lake Zaysan - about 65 million years old in eastern Kazakhstan
9) French - 29 countries
10) Quito, Ecuador - 9,350 feet

Quiz 18

1) What country has the westernmost point in North America?
2) In what country or territory is the northernmost island in the world?
3) What is the highest active volcano in Europe?
4) What country is bordered by Brazil, French Guiana, and Guyana?
5) What is the capital of the Canadian province of Prince Edward Island?
6) What country has the northernmost point in Africa?
7) What country has the oldest operating zoo in the world?
8) By population, what is the largest city entirely in Europe?
9) What very small country generates as much as 10% of its entire national revenue from the sale of its postage stamps to foreign collectors?
10) What is the westernmost national capital city in North America?

Quiz 18 Answers

1) United States - Amatignak Island, Alaska at 179.2 degrees west longitude
2) Greenland - Kaffeklubben Island (Coffee Club Island) is a small island off the northern tip of Greenland at 83.7 degrees north latitude.
3) Mount Etna - 10,810 feet in Sicily, Italy
4) Suriname
5) Charlottetown
6) Tunisia - Iles des Chiens at 37.5 degrees north latitude
7) Austria - The Vienna Zoo has been open to the public since 1779.
8) Moscow, Russia
9) San Marino
10) Mexico City, Mexico - 99.1 degrees west longitude

Quiz 19

1) What is the highest mountain in Antarctica?
2) In what country can you swim between the European and North

American tectonic plates?

3) What is the northernmost national capital city in Europe?
4) What country contains the geographic center of South America?
5) What is the southernmost city in the world with a population over 1 million?
6) What is the only country outside of Europe where Dutch is spoken by most of its population?
7) What country has the most cities with a population over 1 million?
8) What two islands in the Mediterranean Sea are independent nations?
9) In what ocean are the Seychelles located?
10) What is the highest mountain in Turkey?

Quiz 19 Answers

1) Mount Vinson - 16,050 feet
2) Iceland - The Silfra fissure in Thingvellir National Park is a crack between the two continental plates and is the only spot in the world where you can swim directly between the North American and European continents. The crack is filled with extremely clear cold water which remains about 35-39 degrees Fahrenheit all year.
3) Reykjavik, Iceland - 64.1 degrees north latitude
4) Paraguay
5) Melbourne, Australia - 37.8 degrees south latitude
6) Suriname - former Dutch colony in South America
7) China - over 100 cities
8) Cyprus and Malta
9) Indian Ocean - off the east coast of Africa
10) Mount Ararat - 16,854 feet

Quiz 20

1) What country has the world's heaviest building?
2) What country has the largest percent of its area devoted to national parks?
3) What is the most populous national capital city in the world?
4) What is the only African country that borders the Mediterranean

Sea and the Red Sea?

5) What country is bordered by Nicaragua and Panama?
6) What is the most populous island in the Mediterranean Sea?
7) The most remote inhabited island in the world is part of what country?
8) What country has the oldest mountain range in the world?
9) What is the deepest lake in Africa?
10) What is the highest mountain in Pakistan?

Quiz 20 Answers

1) Romania - The Palace of Parliament in Bucharest is 275.6 feet high and covers an area of 1.41 square miles with a volume of 2.55 million cubic meters and weighs about 9 billion pounds. It is the second largest building in the world by surface area.
2) Zambia - National parks make up 32% of its area.
3) Beijing, China
4) Egypt
5) Costa Rica
6) Sicily
7) United Kingdom - Tristan da Cunha Island in the South Atlantic is a British overseas territory and is 1,511 miles off the coast of Cape Town, South Africa. It is 38 square miles and is only accessible via boat, a six-day trip from South Africa.
8) South Africa - The Barberton Greenstone Belt is 3.5 billion years old with a maximum elevation of 5,900 feet.
9) Lake Tanganyika - 4,820 feet deep in southeastern Africa
10) K2 - 28,251 feet

Quiz 21

1) By area, what is the second largest freshwater lake in the world?
2) Since the 1940s, Canada has had a policy of naming thousands of its unnamed lakes after whom?
3) What is the second largest desert in Asia?
4) What country has the most United States emigrants?
5) What is the deepest canyon in the world?

6) What is the most densely populated Asian country?
7) What is the southernmost national capital city in Africa?
8) What was the first European country to create national parks?
9) How many states does Brazil have?
10) What country is bordered by Latvia, Lithuania, Poland, Ukraine, and Russia?

Quiz 21 Answers

1) Lake Victoria - 26,950 square miles
2) Fallen soldiers from all three branches of its armed forces
3) Gobi Desert - 500,000 square miles in China and Mongolia
4) Mexico
5) Yarlung Tsangpo Canyon (Tibet) - 19,714 feet maximum depth
6) Singapore
7) Cape Town, South Africa - 33.9 degrees south latitude
8) Sweden - 1909
9) 26 - plus the Federal District for the national capital
10) Belarus

Quiz 22

1) What is the largest island in Canada?
2) What country is bordered by Ecuador, Peru, Brazil, Venezuela, and Panama?
3) What is the least densely populated African country?
4) What is the highest active volcano in Asia?
5) What desert contains the largest continuous body of sand in the world?
6) What island has the longest river?
7) What is the capital of the Canadian province of Saskatchewan?
8) What is the oldest city in Canada?
9) What is the second largest desert in Africa?
10) What is the lowest elevation national capital city in the world?

Quiz 22 Answers

1) Baffin - 195,928 square miles
2) Colombia
3) Namibia
4) Mount Damavand – 18,406 feet in Iran
5) Arabian Desert - The contiguous sand body within it is known as the Rub 'al-Khali or the "Empty Quarter" and is about 250,966 square miles.
6) Borneo - The Kapuas River is 710 miles long.
7) Regina
8) St. John's, Newfoundland – founded in 1497
9) Kalahari Desert - 360,000 square miles in Namibia, Botswana, and South Africa
10) Baku, Azerbaijan - 92 feet below sea level

Quiz 23

1) What is the third longest river in the world?
2) What is the only country that borders the Black Sea and the Mediterranean Sea?
3) What is the largest volume lake in Europe?
4) By area, what is the second largest island nation in the world?
5) What country has the largest number of rivers at least 600 miles long?
6) What country is bordered by Turkey, Iran, Syria, Jordan, Saudi Arabia, and Kuwait?
7) What is the most populous national capital city in North America?
8) How many letters are in the shortest country name in the world?
9) In what country or territory is the northernmost point of land in the world?
10) By area, what is the largest country in the world without any mountains (points greater than 2,000 feet elevation)?

Quiz 23 Answers

1) Yangtze - 3,915 miles

2) Turkey
3) Lake Ladoga - Russia
4) Madagascar - 226,658 square miles
5) Russia - 36
6) Iraq
7) Mexico City, Mexico
8) Four letters - Chad, Togo, Mali, Iraq, Iran, Oman, Laos, Niue, Fiji, Cuba, Peru
9) Greenland - Kaffeklubben Island (Coffee Club Island) is a small island off the northern tip of Greenland at 83.7 degrees north latitude.
10) Belarus - 80,155 square miles with a maximum elevation of 1,130 feet

Quiz 24

1) How many countries are in Central America?
2) What country changed its name to Myanmar in 1989?
3) Where are the Thousand Islands located?
4) What country has the longest national anthem?
5) What country has the northernmost skyscraper (at least 150 meters tall) in the world?
6) What is the oldest national capital city in Europe?
7) What is the most populous national capital city in Africa?
8) The Pacific Ocean is so large that at some points it is antipodal to itself; what does antipodal mean?
9) What is the westernmost national capital city in South America?
10) What are the only three countries with coastlines on both the Atlantic and Indian Oceans?

Quiz 24 Answers

1) Seven - Belize, Costa Rica, El Salvador, Guatemala, Honduras, Nicaragua, Panama
2) Burma
3) Saint Lawrence River - They are an archipelago of 1,864 islands between the United States and Canada.

4) Greece - Its national anthem, "Hymn to Liberty", has 158 verses. The anthem is a poem written in 1823 by Dionysios Solomos and set to music by Nikolaos Mantzaros.
5) Russia - Vysotsky Business Center in Yekaterinburg, Russia at 60.0 degrees north latitude
6) Athens, Greece - founded in about 3000 BC
7) Cairo, Egypt
8) Two points are antipodal if they are on diametrically opposite sides of the Earth, so in some points of the Pacific Ocean you could go straight through the center of the Earth and come out the other side and still be in the Pacific Ocean.
9) Quito, Ecuador - 78.5 degrees west longitude
10) Egypt, Israel, South Africa

Quiz 25

1) By population, what is the second largest island nation in the world?
2) What country has the most beaches?
3) What is the southernmost city in the world with a population over 10 million?
4) By area, what is the largest country in the European Union?
5) What is the main river that flows through Tokyo, Japan?
6) What country has the highest percentage of its population in the military (active, reserves, and paramilitary)?
7) What island is nicknamed "The Spice Isle" for its production of nutmeg and mace?
8) What is the deepest river in Europe?
9) What two countries share the island of New Guinea?
10) What is the highest mountain in Russia?

Quiz 25 Answers

1) Japan
2) Australia - Its coastline is over 16,000 miles long and has over 10,000 beaches.
3) Buenos Aires, Argentina - 34.6 degrees south latitude
4) France

5) Sumida River
6) North Korea - over 30%
7) Grenada
8) Danube - 584 feet maximum depth, 3rd deepest in the world
9) Indonesia and Papua New Guinea
10) Mount Elbrus - 18,510 feet

Quiz 26

1) What country is the largest mango producer in the world?
2) Portuguese West Africa is the former name of what country?
3) What is the deepest lake in Europe?
4) What country has the highest percentage of its area that is desert?
5) By population, what is the largest city in Canada?
6) Which country has the longest official name?
7) What is the highest active volcano in North America?
8) What is the oldest national capital city in the world?
9) What is the highest mountain range in North America?
10) What is the least populous country in the world?

Quiz 26 Answers

1) India
2) Angola
3) Hornindalsvatnet - 1,686 feet in Norway
4) Libya - about 99%
5) Toronto
6) United Kingdom - Its official name is United Kingdom of Great Britain and Northern Ireland.
7) Popocatépetl - 17,802 feet in Mexico
8) Damascus, Syria - inhabited for about 11,000 years
9) Alaska Range - 20,343 feet maximum elevation
10) Vatican City - less than 1,000 people

Quiz 27

1) What country has the westernmost point in mainland South America?
2) By population, what is the second largest city in North America?
3) What is the longest mountain range in Africa?
4) What is the longest river in the world that flows entirely within one country?
5) What country is bordered by Ecuador, Colombia, Brazil, Bolivia, and Chile?
6) Zanzibar is part of what country?
7) What province or territory has the northernmost point in Canada?
8) What is the highest mountain in Argentina?
9) What is the longest mountain range in Europe?
10) What country has the most desert area in the world?

Quiz 27 Answers

1) Peru - Punta Pariñas at 81.3 degrees west longitude
2) New York City
3) Atlas Mountains - 1,600 miles through Morocco, Algeria, and Tunisia
4) Yangtze - 3,964 miles entirely in China
5) Peru
6) Tanzania
7) Nunavut
8) Aconcagua - 22,835 feet
9) Scandinavian Mountains (Scandes) - 1,095 miles through the Scandinavian Peninsula
10) Australia - 965,000 square miles of desert

Quiz 28

1) What river flows through more countries than any other in the world?
2) What is the deepest lake in North America?
3) By population, what is the largest island nation in the world?

4) What country has the longest coastline in Europe?
5) What country is bordered by Yemen, Saudi Arabia, and United Arab Emirates?
6) Not including the U.S., how many countries use the U.S. dollar as their official currency?
7) What country consumes the most milk per capita?
8) By area, what is the largest country with no natural rivers?
9) What country is bordered by France, Italy, Austria, and Germany?
10) What is the highest mountain in India?

Quiz 28 Answers

1) Danube - 10 countries - Germany, Austria, Slovakia, Hungary, Croatia, Serbia and Montenegro, Romania, Bulgaria, Moldova, Ukraine
2) Great Slave - 2,015 feet in Canada
3) Indonesia
4) Norway - 36,122 miles
5) Oman
6) Seven - Ecuador, El Salvador, Zimbabwe, Timor-Leste, Micronesia, Palau, Marshall Islands
7) Finland
8) Saudi Arabia - 12th largest country
9) Switzerland
10) Kangchenjunga - 28,169 feet

Quiz 29

1) What is Australia's most significant mountain range and the third longest range in the world?
2) What is the southernmost national capital city in North America?
3) What country has the southernmost point in mainland South America?
4) What is the only country that borders the Persian Gulf and the Red Sea?
5) What is the highest mountain in Japan?
6) What country has the southernmost university in the world?

7) What is the highest mountain in Nepal?
8) What country is bordered by Angola, Zambia, Botswana, and South Africa?
9) What is the southernmost national capital city in Asia?
10) What city of 1 million or more is closest to the equator?

Quiz 29 Answers

1) Great Dividing Range - 2,300 miles
2) Panama City, Panama - 9 degrees north latitude
3) Chile - Cape Froward at 53.9 degrees south latitude
4) Saudi Arabia
5) Mount Fuji - 12,388 feet
6) Argentina - National University of Tierra del Fuego in Ushuaia, Argentina at 54.8 degrees south latitude
7) Mount Everest - 29,020 feet
8) Namibia
9) Dili, East Timor - 8.6 degrees south latitude
10) Quito, Ecuador - 15.9 miles south of the equator

Quiz 30

1) By population, what is the largest city at least partly in Europe?
2) What country has the westernmost point in Asia?
3) What are the two main tributaries of the Nile River?
4) In what city do the two main tributaries of the Nile River come together?
5) What national capital city's full official name is Krung Thep Mahanakhon Amon Rattanakosin Mahinthara Yuthaya Mahadilok Phop Noppharat Ratchathani Burirom Udomratchaniwet Mahasathan Amon Piman Awatan Sathit Sakkathattiya Witsanukam Prasit?
6) What country is bordered by India, Afghanistan, Iran, and China?
7) What is the largest peninsula in the world?
8) In what country or territory is the northernmost active volcano in the world?
9) What is the oldest national capital city in North America?

10) What is the highest mountain located on an island?

Quiz 30 Answers

1) Istanbul, Turkey
2) Turkey - Cape Baba at 26.1 degrees east longitude
3) White Nile and Blue Nile
4) Khartoum, Sudan
5) Bangkok, Thailand
6) Pakistan
7) Arabian Peninsula - 1,250,006 square miles
8) Norway - Beerenberg volcano on the Norwegian island of Jan Mayen in the Arctic Ocean at 71.1 degrees north latitude
9) Mexico City, Mexico - founded in 1325
10) Jaya Peak - 16,503 feet in New Guinea

Quiz 31

1) What country is Sulawesi island part of?
2) By area, what is the largest bay in the world?
3) What is the only Central American country that doesn't border the Caribbean Sea?
4) What country has the longest coastline in mainland Asia?
5) What river flows through the city center of Berlin, Germany?
6) China has the largest Buddhist population of any country; what country has the second largest?
7) What is the least populous country in South America?
8) Going west from Ecuador, what is the next country the equator passes through?
9) By population, what is the second largest city in South America?
10) What is the most densely populated South American country?

Quiz 31 Answers

1) Indonesia - 11th largest island in the world at 69,761 square miles
2) Bay of Bengal - 839,000 square miles
3) El Salvador

4) Russia - 23,396 miles
5) Spree River
6) Thailand
7) Suriname
8) Kiribati
9) Buenos Aires, Argentina
10) Ecuador

Quiz 32

1) What country has the world's oldest working library?
2) What is the largest volume lake in Australia?
3) What two countries are connected by the Karakoram Pass?
4) What island country has the Bahamas to the north and Jamaica to the south?
5) What is the highest active volcano in South America?
6) What country has the southernmost point in mainland Europe?
7) By area, what is the largest of the Canary Islands?
8) The island of Borneo is shared by what three countries?
9) What is the least densely populated Asian country?
10) What is the least visited country in the world?

Quiz 32 Answers

1) Morocco - The al-Qarawiyyin library in Fez is the world's oldest working library operating since 859 AD.
2) Lake Eyre
3) China and India - The pass is a gap between two mountains in the Karakoram Range and is about 148 feet wide at an elevation of 18,176 feet.
4) Cuba
5) Ojos del Salado - 22,615 feet on the Chile and Argentina border
6) Spain - Punta de Tarifa at 36.0 degrees north latitude
7) Tenerife - 785 square miles
8) Malaysia, Indonesia, Brunei
9) Mongolia

10) Tuvalu - It is the 4th smallest country in the world with 10 square miles across nine islands in the Pacific midway between Hawaii and Australia and has about 2,000 visitors annually.

Quiz 33

1) What is the northernmost city in the world with a population over 10 million?
2) How many states does India have?
3) By area, what is the third largest freshwater lake in the world?
4) What is the southernmost national capital city in Europe?
5) What tiny country is the world's biggest exporter of false teeth?
6) What country is bordered by Eritrea, Djibouti, Somalia, Sudan, South Sudan, and Kenya?
7) With the dissolution of the Soviet Union, how many independent republics were created?
8) What is the only South American country with English as an official language?
9) What country has the shortest national anthem?
10) By area, what is the largest lake in Central America?

Quiz 33 Answers

1) Moscow, Russia - 55.8 degrees north latitude
2) 29
3) Huron - 23,000 square miles
4) Valletta, Malta - 35.9 degrees north latitude
5) Liechtenstein - Vivadent AG in the city of Schaan is the largest manufacturer of false teeth in the world.
6) Ethiopia
7) 15 - Russia, Ukraine, Georgia, Belarus, Uzbekistan, Armenia, Azerbaijan, Kazakhstan, Kyrgyzstan, Moldova, Turkmenistan, Tajikistan, Latvia, Lithuania, Estonia.
8) Guyana
9) Japan - “Kimigayo” is the title of Japan’s four-line national anthem; it is one of the oldest anthems in the world and has a total of 32 characters and runs a length of eleven measures.
10) Lake Nicaragua - 3,191 square miles

Quiz 34

1) By area, what is the largest plateau in the world?
2) How many countries lie on the prime meridian (0 degrees longitude)?
3) What is the easternmost national capital city in Africa?
4) In what ocean are the Solomon Islands located?
5) What is the highest elevation city in the world with a population over 5 million?
6) What country has the easternmost point in Europe?
7) By population, what is the second largest city entirely in Europe?
8) What is the easternmost national capital city in Europe?
9) The Kremlin is on the bank of what river that flows through Moscow, Russia?
10) What city has the highest number of American emigrants?

Quiz 34 Answers

1) Tibetan Plateau - 970,000 square miles in China and Pakistan
2) Eight - Algeria, Burkina Faso, France, Ghana, Mali, Spain, Togo, United Kingdom
3) Port Louis, Mauritius - 57.5 degrees east longitude
4) Pacific - northeast of Australia
5) Bogota, Colombia - 8,596 feet
6) Russia - Cape Flissingsky at 69 degrees east longitude
7) Paris, France
8) Moscow, Russia - 37.5 degrees east longitude
9) Moskva River
10) Mexico City

Quiz 35

1) Outside of Asia, what is the highest mountain range in the world?
2) What country is bordered by Botswana, Mozambique, South Africa, and Zambia?
3) What country has the oldest restaurant in the world?
4) How many countries don't have any natural rivers?

5) By population, what is the largest city in Australia?
6) What is the most populated island in the world?
7) What is the northernmost national capital city in South America?
8) What is believed to be the oldest continuously inhabited city in North America?
9) What is the least densely populated North American country?
10) What country has the most tornadoes per square mile?

Quiz 35 Answers

1) Andes - maximum elevation of 22,841 feet
2) Zimbabwe
3) Austria - St. Peter Stiftskulinarium restaurant in Salzburg, Austria is the oldest restaurant in the world and has been in operation since 803 AD.
4) 18 - Bahamas, Bahrain, Comoros, Kiribati, Kuwait, Maldives, Malta, Marshall Islands, Monaco, Nauru, Oman, Qatar, Saudi Arabia, Tonga, Tuvalu, United Arab Emirates, Vatican City, Yemen
5) Sydney
6) Java - Indonesia
7) Caracas, Venezuela - 10.5 degrees north latitude
8) Cholula, Mexico - founded in 2000 BC
9) Canada
10) United Kingdom

Quiz 36

1) What South American country has a higher percentage of its land covered in forest than any other country in the world?
2) What is the largest desert at least partially in North America?
3) Measured from base to summit, what is the tallest mountain in the world?
4) What country has the longest coastline in South America?
5) What is the deepest river in North America?
6) What country is completed surrounded by Russia and China?
7) What country has the longest coastline in Africa?
8) What is the northernmost city in the world with a population over 5

million?

9) What country has the northernmost permanent airport with flights, but none scheduled?

10) After the Andes, what is the second longest mountain range in the world?

Quiz 36 Answers

1) Suriname

2) Arctic Desert - 5.4 million square miles in Canada, Greenland, Norway, Russia, Sweden, U.S.

3) Mauna Kea in Hawaii - Measured from the seafloor where it starts, Mauna Kea is about 33,500 feet tall, almost 4,500 feet taller than Mount Everest; it only reaches 13,796 feet above sea level.

4) Brazil - 4,934 miles

5) St. Lawrence - 250 feet maximum depth, 8th deepest in the world

6) Mongolia

7) Madagascar - 3,000 miles

8) St. Petersburg, Russia - 59.9 degrees north latitude

9) Canada - Alert Airport in Alert, Nunavut, Canada is about 520 miles south of the North Pole at 82.5 degrees north latitude.

10) Rocky Mountains - 3,000 miles through Canada and U.S.

Quiz 37

1) After the Himalayas, what is the second highest mountain range in the world?

2) What is the largest island in Norway?

3) At the population density of New York City, the entire population of the world would fit in an area closest to what U.S. state?

4) Based on average depth, what is the shallowest of the Great Lakes?

5) How many African countries does the equator pass through?

6) What is the second most populated island in the world?

7) What famous city is built on 118 small islands?

8) What is the highest mountain in Kenya?

9) Does the Northern Hemisphere or the Southern Hemisphere contain more of the world's land area?

10) What is the least densely populated South American country?

Quiz 37 Answers

1) Karakoram Range - Pakistan, China, India
2) Spitsbergen - 14,546 square miles
3) Texas - about 4% larger
4) Huron - 195 feet average depth
5) Seven - Sao Tome & Principe, Gabon, Republic of the Congo, Democratic Republic of the Congo, Uganda, Kenya, Somalia
6) Honshu - Japan
7) Venice, Italy
8) Mount Kenya - 17,057
9) Northern Hemisphere - 68% of the total land
10) Falkland Islands

Quiz 38

1) What country has the most visitors annually?
2) What is the largest desert in South America?
3) In what country was the first mile of concrete highway in the world built?
4) Based on number of islands, what is the largest archipelago in the world?
5) What is the highest mountain in Ecuador?
6) What country has the westernmost point in Africa?
7) What mountain has the largest base circumference of any non-volcanic mountain in the world?
8) What country does China share its longest land border with?
9) What country has the southernmost point in Asia?
10) What is the only African country that borders the Mediterranean Sea and the Atlantic Ocean?

Quiz 38 Answers

1) France
2) Patagonian Desert - 200,000 square miles in Argentina and Chile

3) United States - In 1909, Wayne County (Detroit, Michigan) built the first mile of concrete highway in the world.
4) Norwegian Archipelago - at least 240,000 islands, coral reefs, cays, and islets
5) Chimborazo - 20,561 feet
6) Cape Verde - Santo Antão at 25.4 degrees west longitude
7) Mount Logan - 19,551 feet in the Saint Elias range in the Yukon province of Canada; it has 11 peaks over 5,000 meters (16,400 feet).
8) Mongolia - 2,906 miles
9) Indonesia - Pamana Island at 11 degrees south latitude
10) Morocco

Quiz 39

1) What is Japan's second largest island?
2) What is the least densely populated European country?
3) What is the capital of the Canadian province of British Columbia?
4) What country is bordered by Ethiopia, Somalia, South Sudan, Tanzania, and Uganda?
5) What country is Ellesmere Island part of?
6) What country has the northernmost university in the world?
7) What city of 5 million or more is closest to the equator?
8) What is the only South American country that borders the Caribbean Sea and the Pacific Ocean?
9) How many South American countries does the equator pass through?
10) Going by land, what is the minimum number of countries you would have to cross going from Norway to North Korea?

Quiz 39 Answers

1) Hokkaido - 32,210 square miles
2) Iceland
3) Victoria
4) Kenya
5) Canada - 10th largest island in the world at 75,767 square miles
6) Norway - University of Tromsø in Tromsø, Norway at 69.7 degrees

north latitude

7) Singapore - 85 miles north of the equator
8) Colombia
9) Three- Ecuador, Colombia, Brazil
10) One - Russia

Quiz 40

1) What country has the northernmost airport with scheduled flights?
2) What river flows through Madrid, Spain?
3) What is the smallest island country?
4) What is the largest non-polar desert in the world?
5) What is the official language of Greenland?
6) Based on cargo volume, what is the busiest port in the world?
7) What is the highest mountain in Tanzania?
8) What is the only country in the world that doesn't have either a rectangular or square flag?
9) What is the deepest lake in South America?
10) What is the easternmost national capital city in North America?

Quiz 40 Answers

1) Norway - Svalbard Airport, Longyear in Svalbard, Norway at 78.2 degrees north latitude
2) Manzanares River
3) Nauru - 8 square miles in the South Pacific
4) Sahara - 3.3 million square miles
5) Greenlandic - It is an Eskimo-Aleut language closely related to the Inuit languages in Canada.
6) Shanghai, China
7) Kilimanjaro - 19,331 feet
8) Nepal - It has a combination of two triangular pennants.
9) O'Higgins/San Martin Lake - 2,743 feet deep on the Chile-Argentina border
10) Bridgetown, Barbados - 59.6 degrees west longitude

Made in the USA
Monee, IL
09 November 2019

16578111R00178